The COLUMBO PHILE

The COLUMBO PHILE:

A CASEBOOK

Mark Dawidziak

THE MYSTERIOUS PRESS

New York • London • Tokyo

For my mother and father,
no mystery why

 The Mysterious Press, 129 West 56th Street, New York, N.Y. 10019

Printed in the United States of America
First Trade Printing: May 1989
10 9 8 7 6 5 4 3 2 1

DESIGNED BY GIORGETTA BELL McREE

Library of Congress Cataloging in Publication Data

Dawidziak, Mark, 1956-
  The Columbo phile.

  Biography: p. 344
  Summary: Discusses the origins, plots, and personnel
of the innovative television mystery show which starred
Peter Falk as the scruffy Columbo.
    1. Columbo (Television program)   [1. Columbo (Tele-
vision program) 2. Mystery and detective television
programs. 3. Television programs] I. Title.
PN1992.77.C583D38   1989   791.45 '72   88-43479
ISBN 0-89296-984-9 (pbk.) (U.S.A.)
      0-89296-985-7 (pbk.) (Can.)

Author's Note

This book was completed in the fall of 1987 and accepted for publication in March 1988. In May 1988, ABC announced that it was reviving *Columbo* as part of a new *Mystery Movie* package. Although plans for the revival are detailed in the ninth section of this study (see the chapter titled "More Columbos"), the focus of *The Columbo Phile* is the character's ten-year stint at NBC (1968–78)—two TV movies and 43 episodes.

Contents

Selected Quotes

"Columbo, you're magnificent. You really are. . . . You're the most persistent creature I ever met, but likable. The astonishing thing is you're likable. . . . You're a sly little elf."

—DR. RAY FLEMING (GENE BARRY)
Prescription: Murder (1968)

"Columbo is so obsessive. He is so curious. I think he's unaware of just how good he is. These little problems are so interesting and bothersome to him, he doesn't know he forgot to shave that morning. He's a genuine eccentric."

—PETER FALK

"It was one of those once-in-a-lifetime weddings of character and actor. They come along very rarely."

—RICHARD LEVINSON
Co-creator of *Columbo*

Columbo: "The most influential, probably the best, and certainly the most endearing cop series on TV."

—*Time* magazine

"Mystery is solving a problem, not gunplay and fights and car chases."

—VINCENT PRICE

"Peter fought every inch of the way for quality."

—PATRICK McGOOHAN

"You sure don't look like a policeman."

—MRS. WALTERS (KATE REID)
"Dead Weight" (1971)

Mysteries: "They're tricky, I'll tell you that. I could never figure those things out."

—LIEUTENANT COLUMBO
"Murder by the Book" (1971)

"I can look like a mess. That part is me. I can be stubborn. That part is me, too. But I have no great detective powers like Columbo. I'm not good at solving mysteries or puzzles. I mean, Columbo . . . what a mind! Who has a mind that sharp? Maybe Sherlock Holmes is that clever. It's a photo finish."

—PETER FALK

"This is a murder now, and I kind of figure that's my department."

—LIEUTENANT COLUMBO

Ransom for a Dead Man (1971)

Acknowledgments

This book has its origins in a 1984 interview with Richard Levinson. I asked him what he thought about my idea for a study of *Columbo*, the series he and William Link created. He said, "Go to it. I'd love to have a book like that so my grandchildren can see what I did."

Nobody helped my research more than Dick Levinson. Nobody opened more doors. He unselfishly gave his time and advice. I interviewed him three times, more than anyone else for this book, and his is a constant voice throughout these pages.

A week after I actually started writing, Dick Levinson died of a heart attack.

He wanted to see this book happen. The day after his death, Bill Link said, "You have to finish it."

So, in addition to containing the most important acknowledgments, the following lines are meant to be something of a second dedication:

To Dick Levinson for saying, "Go to it."

To Bill Link for saying, "Keep going."

And to Peter Falk for saying, "It will happen."

My deep gratitude also goes to Peter S. Fischer, a genial contributor with valuable insights and an infectious enthusiasm.

For graciously summoning memories and providing bits of information, my sincere thanks to Steven Bochco, Dean Hargrove, Richard Irving, Stephen J. Cannell, Ben Gazzara, Norman Lloyd, Vincent Price, Lee Grant, Howard Berk, Leonard Nimoy, Martin Sheen, Roddy McDowall, Richard Kiley, George Hamilton, Susan Clark, Robert Conrad, Hector Elizondo, Mariette Hartley, Ricardo Montalban, Theodore Bikel and Nicol Williamson.

Special thanks to Patrick McGoohan, who agreed to be interviewed under especially trying circumstances—the closing of his Broadway show *Pack of Lies*. He started out by saying, "I don't know what I can tell you." At a difficult time, the colorful actor/director warmed to the subject and spent thirty minutes he really didn't have to spare.

For his thoughtful observations about Columbo's past and future, my gratitude goes to Richard Alan Simmons.

I am indebted to MCA TV/Universal City Studios for making

certain materials available and for allowing passages of copyrighted scripts to be quoted in this work.

And thanks to Sara for remaining patient and supportive, for reading what was written, for copying credits and making corrections, for understanding and for reminding me to get back to work.

Foreword

Now I know what it feels like to be one of the murder victims on *Columbo*—stretched out on an autopsy table with an expert going over you piece by piece.

Mark Dawidziak has done a first-rate job dissecting the whole *Columbo* series, not only the lieutenant himself but every character, clue, guest star, you name it. After reading his book I really think he knows more about the damn show than I do.

And one more thing—there isn't one more thing you need to know about *Columbo* after you have read Mark's fascinating book. I really hope you like it as much as I do.

—PETER FALK

Introduction

Take a few seconds and think about the great detective characters. Got some in mind? Okay, now where did they start their careers? No, not the cities and countries. Name the medium, my friend, the medium.

Whoever came to mind, chances are that he or she began sniffing out clues between the covers of a clothbound volume. This is really no contest at all. Even Nigel Bruce's bumbling Dr. Watson could figure it out. Literature has been the primary breeding ground for inquiring minds and private eyes. Books have given us the longest and most distinguished list of brilliant investigators—from Edgar Allan Poe's C. Auguste Dupin to P.D. James' Adam Dalgleish, from Sir Arthur Conan Doyle's Sherlock Holmes to Ross Macdonald's Lew Archer, from Agatha Christie's Miss Jane Marple to Raymond Chandler's Philip Marlowe, from G.K. Chesterton's Father Brown to Dashiell Hammett's Continental Op, from Dorothy L. Sayers' Lord Peter Wimsey to Erle Stanley Gardner's Perry Mason, from . . . well, you get the idea. Most of these super-sleuths jumped from the printed page to enjoy great successes in films and television.

They are the snooping elite, and each's enduring popularity is a matter of chemistry. It's a brilliant by-product manufactured by the explosive reaction that occurs when a fascinating character is mixed with an ingenious mystery.

Commercial television has spawned only one character worthy of raising a magnifying glass in this celebrated company of clever cops and clue-chasers. Hercule Poirot might turn up his nose at the very suggestion. Sherlock Holmes would think him a bourgeois clod. But go ahead and underestimate Lieutenant Columbo. That little mistake tripped up forty-eight murderers in ten years.

The brainchild of writers Richard Levinson and William Link, *Columbo* was both innovative television and classic mystery. Like most of the notable fictional detectives already mentioned, the good lieutenant is a bit eccentric and intriguingly elusive. Almost anyone can tell you the surface characteristics. It seems as if we all know the sloppy little guy. Try to get past the outward appearance, though, and you discover that he's a marvelous example of less being more.

We immediately recognize the familiar trademarks: the wrinkled suit, the cigar, the rumpled raincoat, the three-day stubble, the asthmatic car, the humble demeanor. The voice and the mannerisms have become part of our pop-culture consciousness. Impressions of Columbo—usually bad ones—crop up at parties and in nightclub acts. It's almost as easy as Stan Laurel or Groucho Marx. Try it. Slouch a little. That's right. Pick up the nearest pencil or pen and brandish it like a cigar. Good, good. Now say, "There's just one thing bothering me about this."

The cigar and the raincoat are Columbo's equivalent of a pipe and deerstalker. His one more question is a signature as well-kenned as, "Elementary, my dear Watson" (or, for you purists, "The game is afoot"). We instantly latch on to these identifiable items. Yet how much do we really know about Columbo? We never see his wife. We never see him at home. We rarely see him at the office. We get only tantalizing hints about his personal life.

From the start, Levinson and Link decreed that Columbo himself would remain a somewhat mysterious figure. And that is one of the reasons he is so fascinating.

"By being smaller than life, Columbo becomes larger than life," said Peter S. Fischer, a *Columbo* writer and story editor. "He has a wife, a car and a dog and a lot of relatives. You hurt the mystique if you tell them much more than that. You have to remember that television is not a character-oriented medium. That's what makes a Columbo so special."

Fans can argue about Columbo's background and never-revealed first name with the same relish that members of the Baker Street Irregulars debate Sherlock's childhood and the number of times Dr. Watson was married.

Of course, you can't overlook Peter Falk's devotion to the role. The actor played Columbo enveloped in a raincoat and great ambiguity (something commercial television dreads). Was he really all that humble? Or was it all an act to trick the supremely confident criminals into a false sense of security? Did he actually have a relative to fit every conversation? Or was he making them up to suit the occasion? You never knew.

As novelist/literary critic Anthony Burgess pointed out in an article for *TV Guide*, you sense enormous complexity behind the simple exterior. Falk's consistent portrayal enhanced that curious contradiction between shabby looks and a sharp mind.

"At the same time that there was great simplicity, there was great complexity," said Vincent Price, the host of public television's *Mystery!* series. "And he was so charming. Most series don't give that

*Sherlock Holmes had his pipe
and Lieutenant Columbo
had his beloved cigar.*

much thought to the character. *Columbo* is one of television's few genuine contributions to the mystery field."

You wonder about the Lieutenant Columbo we don't see.

Can you say that about other TV detectives? Do we truly want to know more about Cannon or Kojak? McMillan or McCloud? Baretta or Barnaby Jones? Ironside or Joe Friday? We know too much about them already.

Only James Garner's Jim Rockford comes anywhere close, and, interestingly enough, he is more in the two-fisted Hammett/Chandler/Macdonald American tradition while Columbo belongs in the British drawing-room school of Doyle/Christie/Sayers. Rockford raced through the alleys and streets of Los Angeles. Columbo matched wits with suave, intellectual, sophisticated murderers.

If Levinson and Link's format owed much to English mystery literature, however, their character was distinctly American—middle-class, hard-working, unpretentious. Indeed, Columbo is the American work ethic in practice. He gets to the conclusion through fierce dedication and Yankee ingenuity. I'm not sure even Levinson and Link realized this aspect of the character's appeal, perhaps because Falk's interpretation had so much to do with it. When I compared Columbo with Hammett's bulldoggish, stocky, keep-your-head-down Continental Op, Dick Levinson seemed completely surprised. He cited other obvious influences, but he had never thought of the Op as a Columbo ancestor.

There's a rarefied air about Holmes, Poirot and Wimsey, you see. Each is somewhat untouchable by mere mortals such as you and I. There's a macho dynamism about Archer, Marlowe and Sam Spade. There's a foreign mysticism to Charlie Chan and Mr. Moto. Columbo is Mr. Everyday American. He could be the fellow sitting at the next desk. He could be the guy next door.

Certainly part of Columbo's appeal stemmed from his pursuit of wealthy adversaries. Here was this scruffy cop—the son of immigrants, obviously raised on the streets of New York City—outmaneuvering the condescending snobs who looked down on him. Let's hear it for the uncommon common man.

"By design," said *Hill Street Blues* and *L. A. Law* co-creator/producer Steven Bochco, the author of several *Columbo* scripts, "the show exploited people's basic mistrust of the rich. The villain was always enormously rich, successful and arrogant. The cat-and-mouse game that ensued was incredibly satisfying for the audience."

Some villains think they see through his technique.

"You know, Columbo, you're almost likable in a shabby sort of way," says lawyer Leslie Williams (Lee Grant) in *Ransom for a Dead Man*. "Maybe it's the way you come slouching in here with your shopworn bag of tricks. . . . The humility, the seeming absentmindedness, the homey anecdotes about the family, the wife. Yeah, Lieutenant Columbo fumbling and stumbling along, but it's always the jugular he's after. And I imagine that more often than not, he's successful."

But not this time, right, Leslie? They think they're too smart for him. Their arrogance proves their undoing.

That seems simple enough. Still, even here, Falk searched for the kind of depth television typically scorns.

"People like to see the powerful brought down," the actor conceded, "but Columbo had no argument against the rich. He's regretful when he arrests the murderer. He would think, 'Gee, here's this guy with a wonderful home and wonderful clothes. He talks well. He has a good education. It's a terrible thing he should have to do this.' Once in a while, he actually disliked a murderer. Usually, I think, it made him sad."

Our reaction can be summed up by Fischer: "You look at those mansions on the hill and you think, 'Those bastards think they're above the law. Those bastards think they're better than we are. Those bastards think they can get away with anything.' It was the little guy who came in and pulled them down."

Columbo never reacted that way. There was no class hatred in the police lieutenant. To him, a murderer was a murderer. It was his job to catch the murderer. His job sometimes made him sad.

Yet the character, no matter how winning, is only half of the chemical equation. He requires the challenges of seemingly unsolvable murders.

Please keep in mind that a good murder is not so easily planned. Most require time, a luxury television can rarely afford.

The genre is deceptively difficult. It takes more than just a mind capable of weaving intricate plots, taut pacing and memorable characters. The top-drawer mystery writer draws us in, stimulates a few of what Poirot called "little grey cells" and, before letting us go, satisfies our desire for light and resolution. In a century when life supposedly is more and more bewildering, the mystery—P.D. James says—offers a complete plot with answers.

Along with science fiction, humor and horror, mystery too often is dumped in literature's slums. Sure, there's a lot of bad detective fiction. In lesser hands, the mystery is little more than a cheap parlor trick—gimmicks for the sake of gimmicks. But the best mystery writers are not mere craftsmen. They are artists.

Under the intense (often panicky) pressures of commercial television, *Columbo* managed to emerge as quality mystery and quality programming. The mystery enthusiast could admire it. Any viewer could delight in it. From a purely cerebral standpoint (*Columbo* never trafficked in the type of massage-parlor detection that became prevalent with *Charlie's Angels*), the series seduced, stimulated and satisfied.

Oh, there's just one more thing . . . one more splendid motive behind this celebration of *Columbo*. Yes, it was more than fiendishly clever mystery, wonderful characterization and an oasis in Newton Minow's "vast wasteland." It was a rule-breaker.

Television executives—the commercial network variety, I mean—love to tell producers what they can't do. "You can't do a Western anymore. Westerns are dead." "You can't have a minority playing that lead character. Sponsors won't like it." "You can't show that." "You can't say that." "You can't use that character." "You can't use that actor." "You can't use that word."

The medium lives and dies by these arbitrary rules. *I Dream of Jeannie* couldn't show Barbara Eden's navel. *The Ed Sullivan Show* wouldn't show the Elvis pelvis. *The Odd Couple* had to fight to show a toilet. *Laugh-In* had to battle to show a pregnant woman.

Commandments like these caused Rod Serling to call television an absurdity of our times.

Prime-time television's unlikeliest hero—Peter Falk as Lieutenant Columbo.

By the rules that television holds sacred, *Columbo* shouldn't have been a hit:

- It had very little action, less sex and almost no violence.
- The central character often didn't enter until fifteen to twenty minutes after the opening credits.
- The plots were complex, demanding the viewer's strict attention.
- Entire episodes could be nothing more than stretches of point-counterpoint dialogue.
- When he did finally show up, the leading man wasn't a six-foot, granite-jawed, two-fisted hunk of mail-order macho man. He was a short, badly groomed, ill-attired career officer who couldn't shoot and was easily winded.

According to the prevailing network intelligence (which Fischer says is a contradiction in terms), *Columbo* should have been a failure. At the most, it should have had a limited but intellectual following. Instead, Lieutenant Columbo regularly found his way to the top of the A.C. Nielsen Company's weekly network ratings.

What follows is a history of the series and a casebook that charts the wily lieutenant's career. It is, I hope, a lighthearted overview of one of commercial television's shining moments.

As a television critic, I see a good many books about series esteemed for one reason or another. There have been tomes on most of the quality shows and some lesser efforts. Don't take my word for it. Go into any mall bookstore and you'll discover several volumes dedicated to M*A*S*H, Star Trek and The Honeymooners. There are at least two each on I Love Lucy and The Andy Griffith Show. Search a little further and you might find studies of The Twilight Zone, Leave It to Beaver, The Prisoner, Dallas, The Dick Van Dyke Show, Gilligan's Island, The Odd Couple, Batman, Dynasty, Get Smart, Alfred Hitchcock Presents and The Outer Limits. Scan the bookcases of your local library and you might see tracts about Masterpiece Theatre, 60 Minutes, The Today Show, The Ed Sullivan Show, The Monkees, The Avengers, The Jack Benny Show, Monday Night Football, Burns and Allen and Wide World of Sports. My own humble collection includes works on Your Show of Shows, Groucho Marx's You Bet Your Life, Superman, The Tonight Show and Laugh-In. Amazing, isn't it? The medium has developed its own pop literature. Soon, no doubt, we'll see a book about the books about series.

You'll notice that there is no examination of Columbo's exploits. Perhaps the lieutenant is once again being underestimated. Observing the gap on the shelf labeled television, I rush to fill it.

—MARK DAWIDZIAK

PART I

THE PLOT THICKENS OR HOW COLUMBO FOUND NBC

"We didn't realize how effective the cop character would be."

—RICHARD LEVINSON

The Good Lieutenant

The coroner is on the scene, trying to reach preliminary conclusions about the murder. Chaos surrounds him. Police detectives are asking questions. Objects are being removed in clear plastic bags. One officer is shouting on the telephone. Neighbors and friends are being told to wait. One man is dusting for fingerprints.

Looking for something, a little man makes his way through this bustle of activity. He's lost his pencil. His wife gives him one every morning, but he just can't seem to keep track of the darn thing.

Important matters are happening in this opulently furnished room. A murder has been committed. The little man, though, has other things on his mind. He's looking for a match to light the soggy stump of his cigar. He's moving from person to person. "Excuse me. Gotta match?"

The sun is shining, yet he wears a raincoat badly in need of laundering. He could use a shave and, from the looks of him, a cup of coffee. Nobody pays Lieutenant Columbo much heed.

Before the corpse is taken to the morgue, however, Lieutenant Columbo will have noticed the one bothersome detail that all the other trained eyes have missed.

This is typical of the way Columbo would make his entrance into prime time. TV's unlikeliest hero, Peter Falk's blue-collar police detective started his network career on the night of February 20, 1968. That was the Tuesday NBC aired a TV movie titled *Prescription: Murder*. About ten years and several Emmys later, the network told producing company MCA/Universal that, well, they had seen enough of the still-popular L.A.P.D. lieutenant.

Because *Columbo* lasted seven seasons, many viewers think that there are hundreds of episodes floating around in the television rerun heaven known as syndication. Not quite. For most of its existence, *Columbo* was part of *The NBC Mystery Movie*. It generally was seen once every four weeks, alternating with *McCloud*, *McMillan and Wife* and a fourth slot that was difficult to keep occupied (*Hec Ramsey*, *Amy Prentiss*, *McCoy*).

The typical network series order is about twenty-two shows each season. Put them all together and you'll only get forty-five *Columbo*

mysteries. Most are gems. A few are merely ordinary. There are one or two stinkers. That's an incredible batting average for any medium—stage, literature, film, radio. It's particularly impressive for television.

This is the story of those forty-five episodes. But it doesn't start on February 20, 1968. We'll get to that shortly. This investigation starts two decades before the premiere of *Prescription: Murder*.

As with most *Columbo* adventures, we have to wait for the entrance of our hero. First, we get the setup. And this setup begins on the day that young Richard Levinson met young William Link.

Levinson & Link (or Is It Link & Levinson?): The Men Behind the Raincoat

It was the first day of classes at Elkins Park Junior High School in suburban Philadelphia. Friends had told tall Dick Levinson to look for a short guy who loved magic and mysteries. Short Bill Link had been told to look for a tall guy who loved magic and mysteries.

They met. They compared notes. They discovered that their childhoods were remarkably similar.

Each had grown up on a diet of pop culture served at the local movie houses, through the radio airwaves, between the covers of pulp magazines and in the panels of brightly inked comic books.

Each's tastes were formed by cherished sessions with Captain Marvel, Superman, Saturday afternoon serials, Walt Disney, Abbott & Costello, Dashiell Hammett, Raymond Chandler, Ellery Queen, Erle Stanley Gardner and such radio shows as *Jack Armstrong, Inner Sanctum, Lights Out* and *Suspense*.

Each performed magic. Each devoured mysteries at a voracious rate. Each liked to write.

"We became best friends immediately," Bill Link would recall about forty years later. "You could say that our sensibilities coincided and collided. We were both products of upper-middle-class families. We read the same books and were interested in the same things. I think we were both expected to go into our fathers' businesses. Dick's father was in automotive products. Mine was in textiles. But we started writing together in junior high school, and we never stopped."

Significantly enough, the partnership was formed just as television was poised to start its invasion of America's living rooms. Levinson and Link would become one of the medium's most distinguished and successful writing teams.

During their junior high school days, Bill and Dick convinced their parents to buy them the type of wire recorders popular after World War II. Putting together a jury-rigged repertory company, the teen collaborators started writing their own radio scripts.

At Cheltenham High School, the duo penned "gloomy" short stories influenced by Poe and O. Henry. An original musical comedy was staged in their senior year.

Enamored of the mystery form, the high school classmates mailed off one detective story after another to such major magazines as *The New Yorker* and the *Saturday Evening Post*. Not surprisingly, rejection slips poured in at a steady rate.

While not abandoning the pop culture of their youth, Levinson and Link dug deeper and deeper into literature. Ellery Queen and Ross Macdonald remained constants, but there were the more sophisticated influences of Sartre, Camus, Shakespeare, Salinger, Hemingway and Faulkner.

The partnership continued when both were accepted at the University of Pennsylvania. Any lingering chance of careers in textiles and automotive hardware was doomed when *Ellery Queen's Mystery Magazine* became the first publication to buy a Levinson and Link short story. Although it would take four years to sell another story, the joint direction of their lives had been established.

They contributed to Penn's humor and literary magazines. They wrote film criticism for the *Daily Pennsylvanian*. They founded the university's *Highball* humor magazine. They scripted "Mask and Wig" musicals. They even were allowed to collaborate on a senior thesis, which turned out to be four television scripts.

After graduation, Link was drafted for a two-year hitch. Levinson enlisted in a six-month reserve program and worked at a Philadelphia television station. The partnership continued by mail.

When Link returned as a civilian, the boyhood chums headed for New York and found that the heyday of the live anthology drama was over. They supported themselves by selling short stories to *Alfred Hitchcock's Mystery Magazine, Playboy* and other publications. Two scripts were produced by *General Motors Presents*, an anthology series aired by the Canadian Broadcasting Company.

Their American TV debut was auspicious. "Chain of Command," an Army drama set in the South, was produced by *Desilu Playhouse*. *TV Guide* called it one of the best shows of the 1958–59 season. Levinson and Link were both twenty-four years old.

Encouraged, they traveled to California in the summer of 1959. Signing a two-year contract with Four Star Television, the team wrote scripts for the series *Michael Shayne, The June Allyson Show* and *Richard Diamond, Private Eye*.

The work wasn't fulfilling, though, so Levinson and Link decided to split their time between the theater world of New York and the television world of Los Angeles. Before giving up on this arrangement and settling permanently in California, they would write a play titled *Prescription: Murder*. It would introduce a character named Lieutenant Columbo. More about that in the next chapter (I promise).

Their television credits started to mount. There were Levinson and Link scripts represented on such series as *The Rogues*, *Dr. Kildare*, *The Fugitive*, *Burke's Law* and *The Man from U.N.C.L.E.* In 1961, they began a fruitful association with director-turned-TV-host Alfred Hitchcock. The duo contributed two scripts to the half-hour *Alfred Hitchcock Presents* and five to *The Alfred Hitchcock Hour*. "Dear Uncle George," a 1963 episode, featured Gene Barry as a man who kills his wife. Five years later, the actor would play a similar role in the TV movie version of *Prescription: Murder*.

The first L&L *Hitchcock* script, "Services Rendered," included a character named Mannix (they had a high school chum named William Mannix). They liked the name well enough to use it for a detective series. Starring Mike Connors as a two-fisted private eye, *Mannix* lasted eight seasons (CBS, 1967–75).

Hoping to do more serious work for television, Levinson and Link turned their attentions to the unrealized possibilities of the TV movie. This is where they would do their finest work.

At a time when the networks wanted the safe entertainment of *Gomer Pyle*, *The Lucy Show* and *The Beverly Hillbillies*, Levinson and Link decided that television could and should have a social conscience. They became known for breaking new ground for the medium.

The Whole World Is Watching (1969) dealt with student unrest. *My Sweet Charlie* (1970) told of the relationship between a Southern teenage girl and a black New York lawyer. *That Certain Summer* (1972) starred Hal Holbrook as a divorced man coming to terms with his homosexuality. *The Execution of Private Slovik* (1974) was a fact-based TV movie about the only American soldier since the Civil War to be executed for desertion. *The Gun* (1974) raised questions about handguns in our society. *The Storyteller* (1977) examined the effects of TV violence on children. *Crisis at Central High* (1981) recreated the 1957 integration of Central High School in Little Rock, Arkansas. *Prototype* (1984) was a thoughtful science-fiction drama about a Nobel Prize–winning scientist (Christopher Plummer) concerned about the government's plans for the humanoid he created. *The Guardian* (1984), a drama aired by pay-cable service Home Box Office, raised troublesome issues about safety in big cities.

With the advent of *Columbo* as a series, Levinson and Link became the executive producers of most of their TV projects. They launched the much-admired but short-lived *Adventures of Ellery Queen* (NBC,

Martin Sheen (center) and Ned Beatty (right) starred in The Execution of Private Slovik, *one of several acclaimed TV movies written by Richard Levinson and William Link.*

1975–76). They helped to create such series as *Murder, She Wrote* (CBS, 1984–present), *Blacke's Magic* (NBC, 1986) and *Hard Copy* (CBS, 1987).

Levinson and Link never did abandon the mystery. In addition to the series about sleuthing heroes, they wrote several TV movies in the genre: *Murder by Natural Causes* (1979), *Rehearsal for Murder* (1982), *Guilty Conscience* (1985) and *Vanishing Act* (1986). The team finally made it to Broadway with *Merlin*, a musical about one of the mutual interests that first brought them together—magic.

The partnership came to a premature end on March 12, 1987. Dick Levinson died of a heart attack at his Brentwood, California, home. He was fifty-two.

"We weren't collaborators," Bill Link said the day afterward. "We were brothers. He was a classic coronary candidate. He smoked constantly. He was an obsessive worker. He was the one always at the typewriter. He ignored all the warning signs."

Their nearly four decades of joint efforts had resulted in two Emmys, two Golden Globe awards, a Peabody Award, a Writers Guild of America award and four Edgar Allan Poe Awards from the Mystery Writers of America.

When television "Golden Age" writers—Paddy Chayefsky, Rod Serling, Reginald Rose, Gore Vidal—were driven away from the medium or frustrated by it, Richard Levinson and William Link helped bring horizons back to the wasteland. But three years before his death, Dick Levinson may have made the most prophetic comment about their legacy: "If we're remembered for anything, it may say *Columbo* on our gravestones."

Filling the Raincoat

Peter Falk is so completely identified with Lieutenant Columbo that people are shocked to discover that other actors played the character before him.

The earliest trace of Columbo can be found in a short story Levinson and Link called "May I Come In." *Alfred Hitchcock's Mystery Magazine* changed the title to "Dear Corpus Delecti."

"It contained the alibi for the crime," Levinson said. "The story ended with a knock on the door, right before the entrance of a police officer."

Had the officer made an entrance, it would have been Lieutenant Columbo. Levinson and Link adapted "May I Come In" for a one-hour installment of NBC's *The Chevy Mystery Show*. This time out, the story was called "Enough Rope," and veteran character actor Bert Freed, later a regular on ABC's brief series version of *Shane* (1966), had the distinction of becoming the first actor to play Columbo.

The partners would give different origins for the name Columbo.

"Neither of us really remember where it came from," Levinson said in 1986. "To this day, we don't know if it was one of three possibilities. We've told different stories in interviews. It may have just popped into mind. It may have come from a restaurant in Philadelphia called Palumbo's. Or it came from Columbus."

"Enough Rope" was a live television production and, in Bill Link's estimation, not a very good one.

"It was a very sloppy show," he said. "It just wasn't particularly well done, but it's interesting from an archaeological standpoint. I met Bert Freed at a party a few years ago and told him he was the first actor to play Columbo. He didn't remember playing it. It was just another cop role to him."

But an intriguing thing happened during rehearsals for "Enough Rope." Although the murderer was written as the central character, the policeman refused to remain a subordinate role.

"The lead actor of that show got angry with what he perceived as the cop stealing the show," Levinson recalled. "Bert Freed was told to tone it down. The character was flattened out by the director, so none of the comedy and none of the subtle values were played."

When Levinson and Link embarked on their bicoastal plan, the first project was to turn "Enough Rope" into a full-length stage play called *Prescription: Murder*. They found a producer. The producer found a cast—an excellent one.

The play opened in San Francisco with Joseph Cotton as Dr. Ray Fleming, the suave psychiatrist who cooks up the ideal way to kill his wife. Agnes Moorehead, who co-starred with Cotton in Orson Welles' *Citizen Kane* and *The Magnificent Ambersons*, played his ill-fated spouse. Academy Award–winning actor Thomas Mitchell was chosen to portray Lieutenant Columbo.

Mitchell, who was nearing his seventieth birthday, had been one of Hollywood's busiest supporting players. In 1939 alone, he had memorable roles in *Gone With the Wind*, *Mr. Smith Goes to Washington*, *Stagecoach*, *The Hunchback of Notre Dame*, and *Only Angels Have Wings*. The stocky, Irish-faced actor's long list of film credits also included *Lost Horizon*, *The Hurricane*, *Our Town*, *It's a Wonderful Life* and *High Noon*.

"Mitchell was terrific, but we didn't get good reviews," Link said. "It needed work. But it went on tour for twenty-five weeks in the United States and Canada, and it made a fortune."

The third act was weak. Levinson and Link suggested rewrites. Their suggestions were ignored by the management. The play was making money, wasn't it? Why fool with it?

Meanwhile, history was repeating itself on stages all across the country. In Detroit and Fargo, it was the same darn thing. That impish cop was stealing the show.

"The cast would take their bows and the applause would be enthusiastic," Levinson remembered. "When Thomas Mitchell took his curtain call, the applause would go through the roof. Then Cotton would come out to take his bow as the lead, and the applause would drop off a bit. Cotton was the lead, but Mitchell was getting the big ovation. We didn't realize how effective the cop character would be."

"They loved the Columbo character," Link said. "We thought he was a character of secondary importance."

Still, the young writers were frustrated because they couldn't hone a good thing.

"The producer wanted to take it to New York," Link stated. "We were actually upset by the idea. We threatened to slap an injunction on it because he wouldn't let us make changes. It wasn't right. Later, we rewrote it the way we wanted it, and that's the version that was published by Samuel French."

Columbo's career was cut short just at a time when his creators were recognizing his potential. Levinson and Link returned to television.

"Joe Cotton used to refer to (the youthful, brilliant and murder-minded) Levinson and Link as Loeb and Leopold (the brilliant Chicago youths convicted of a 1924 thrill slaying)," said another Orson Welles graduate, Norman Lloyd, who worked as a director, producer and actor on *Alfred Hitchcock Presents*. In the eighties, he became best known as Dr. Daniel Auschlander on NBC's *St. Elsewhere*. "They submitted the Columbo idea to me, and I kept turning them down. That shows you how bright I am. My secretary once said to me, 'Mr. Wevinson is here to see you.' I said, 'Ask him if Mr. Wink is with him.'"

Hearing that Universal Studios was looking for TV movie projects, Levinson and Link dusted off their rewritten version of *Prescription: Murder* and told their agent to submit it. Director Don Siegel (*Invasion of the Body Snatchers*) was excited by the script and called the writers in for a meeting.

Siegel was assigned a feature film, so seasoned director, producer, studio executive Richard Irving was brought in to replace him. Fortunately, he worked well with Levinson and Link. Professional and gentlemanly, Irving was not about to exclude the duo. He sought out their advice on changes in the script. Would it be all right to change the setting from New York to Los Angeles? It would cut down on production costs. Yes, that was acceptable.

Writers are supposed to be the doormats of Hollywood. Irving made it a welcome mat for Levinson and Link. It was only logical to him that they help in transforming *Prescription: Murder* from a play into a TV movie.

"It was proven material as a play," Irving said. "The challenge was to open it up for film. But it came to me so well developed that it was an easy movie to direct. There were no big holes, no big questions. You only hope that you get something that well written."

But who should play Columbo? Thomas Mitchell had passed away in December of 1962.

Peter Falk, an actor Levinson and Link knew socially, had seen the script and was interested. His résumé was impressive. Many critics compared him to John Garfield.

The New York City native had won an Academy Award nomination for his portrayal of vicious mobster Abe Reles in *Murder, Inc.* (1960). He had proven his worth as a comic performer in such films as *Pocketful of Miracles*, *Robin and the Seven Hoods*, *The Great Race* and *Luv*. And he had starred as sloppy but brilliant lawyer Daniel J. O'Brien in producer Richard Alan Simmons' highly praised and low-rated *The Trials of O'Brien* (CBS, 1965–66). O'Brien, like the police lieutenant Falk portrayed in the 1966 film *Penelope*, contained elements of his eventual Columbo characterization.

Levinson and Link, however, thought the forty-year-old actor was far too young for the role. They wanted Lee J. Cobb. Remembering the sly leprechaun charm of Thomas Mitchell, they added Bing Crosby's name to their list of suggestions.

"Don't ask me why," Bill Link said. "We were hung up on the idea of an older actor."

The notion of Cobb or Crosby in that raincoat seems improbable today. When one considers the context, though, the team's suggestions are perfectly understandable.

But Cobb couldn't do it. Crosby turned it down (it was reported that a series commitment would have interfered with his golf game). Falk's name came up again. It was Irving who believed that Falk was right for the part. He convinced Levinson and Link that the actor could do a "passable" job as Lieutenant Columbo. On the night of February 20, 1968, they watched to see if the director was right.

CASE # 1: PRESCRIPTION: MURDER

(originally aired February 20, 1968)

Written by RICHARD LEVINSON & WILLIAM LINK (based on their play)
Directed and produced by RICHARD IRVING
Music by DAVE GRUSIN
Director of photography: RAY RENNAHAN, A.S.C.
Art director: RUSSELL KIMBELL
Film editor: RICHARD G. WRAY, A.C.E.
Unit manager: EDWARD K. DODDS
Assistant director: GEORGE BISK
Set decorators: JOHN McCARTHY and JAMES S. REDD
Sound: JAMES T. PORTER
Color coordinator: ROBERT BROWER
Associate producer: JERROLD FREEDMAN
Editorial supervision: RICHARD BELDING
Musical supervision: STANLEY WILSON
Costumes by BURTON MILLER
Makeup by BUD WESTMORE
Hair stylist: LARRY GERMAIN
Running time: 99 minutes

CAST

LT. COLUMBO .... PETER FALK

DR. RAY FLEMING .... GENE BARRY

JOAN HUDSON .... KATHERINE JUSTICE

CAROL FLEMING .... NINA FOCH

BURT GORDON .... WILLIAM WINDOM

With VIRGINIA GREGG, ANDREA KING, SUSANNE BENTON, ENA HARTMAN, SHERRY BOUCHER and ANTHONY JAMES.

Synopsis—High-priced psychiatrist Dr. Ray Fleming has guests completely baffled. The game is Botticelli (a variation of "Who-Am-I?") and, as usual, he revels in the chance to show off his intelligence. Everyone concedes defeat. The historical personality Ray is pretending to be is exceedingly obscure. He is Joseph Brewer, Freud's collaborator on *Studies in Hysteria*.

The party is in honor of Ray and Carol Fleming's wedding anniversary. The phone rings. It is Ray's mistress, aspiring actress Joan Hudson. She has to see him.

Ray tells his enraged wife that he must see a patient. Carol suspects the truth. Six months ago, she warned him to end his extramarital affairs or face divorce and drastically reduced finances. Since that ultimatum was issued, Ray has been plotting his wealthy wife's murder.

He's talked Joan into helping him stage the perfect alibi. The Flemings are going on an anniversary trip to Acapulco. Ray plans to strangle Carol before leaving their apartment, arranging things to look like the work of robbers. He'll put jewelry and other items in his suitcases, disposing of them while on a fishing trip in Mexico. Joan will arrive after the murder. Posing as Carol, she'll accompany Ray to Los Angeles International Airport. They will stage a fight on the airplane, and Joan—dressed in Carol's dress, hat and sunglasses—will storm off the plane and return to the apartment. She'll leave Carol's dress in a bag left for the dry cleaner.

So Ray will be in Mexico when the murder is supposed to have happened.

Everything goes according to plan until Ray returns home. Casually sauntering about the apartment, he notices a police outline on the floor and boards on the broken window. Carrying a raincoat and smoking a cigar, Lieutenant Columbo emerges from the bedroom.

"Dr. Fleming?" (The first words spoken by Columbo on television.)

"Who are you?"

"Lieutenant Columbo—police."

Columbo is immediately suspicious of the psychiatrist. When Ray walked into the apartment, he made no effort to call out to his wife. Wouldn't he at least want to know if she was home? Worse, Ray showed no signs of panic when he saw evidence of a break-in and attack.

Columbo observes Ray's reaction when he tells him that someone tried to kill Carol. Tried? Yes, she's barely alive. She's in a coma and doctors don't hold out much hope. If she could only regain consciousness long enough to identify her assailant.

Ray and Columbo head for the hospital, where they're told that Carol has died.

"If it's any consolation," the doctor tells Ray, "the one thing she said was your name."

Little things bother Columbo: Ray not calling to his wife; the fact that Ray's luggage weighed nine pounds less on his return flight from Mexico; interference from Ray's influential friends.

Columbo sees Joan leaving Ray's office and is suspicious when casual questions upset her.

In Prescription: Murder, *psychiatrist Ray Fleming (Gene Barry) be-comes the first murderer to underestimate the seemingly inept Lieutenant Columbo.*

The fateful game begins in earnest, but Ray is sure that Columbo, no matter what his suspicions are, can't prove anything.

"Eventually, he'll lose interest and start hounding someone else," Ray tells Joan.

Confronting the actress on a movie studio set, a seemingly angry Columbo tells Joan that she's the weak link. He'll get to Ray through her.

The next day, Ray sees a body being pulled from Joan's pool. Columbo tells him that, rather than betraying their guilty secret, Joan took her own life.

"We both killed that girl," Columbo says. He asks Ray to confess. After all, Joan is dead, and she was the reason he murdered Carol.

Ray laughs at him. The girl was nothing, he says. If there was a motive, it was his wife's money. And now Columbo can never touch him. The weak link is gone.

Is that right? It's a voice from the door. It's Joan, alive and ready to tell all she knows. Columbo has staged this suicide scene to show Joan what Ray is really like. With awareness of the situation dawning on his face, Ray looks at Columbo and realizes that his only mistake was in underestimating the sloppy lieutenant.

In their 1981 book, *Stay Tuned*, Levinson and Link recount their sitting down to watch *Prescription: Murder* to see if they had fixed the play's mistakes. The details were soon forgotten. Instead, they found themselves enchanted by Peter Falk's wonderfully quirky performance. The mystery plot worked fine, yet it was the actor's portrayal that made their TV movie something special.

Twenty years later, *Prescription: Murder* still holds up very well. Barry makes a smooth villain, but it's Falk's Columbo that demands our constant attention. Richard Irving's sure direction and Dave Grusin's jazzy score give the TV movie a feel that's part Ellery Queen and part Conan Doyle.

"Dick Irving is a very nice man," Dick Levinson said. "Creatively, all the components were there in the play, and he worked at enhancing them. Peter didn't tumble to the character at first. He was playing a straight cop. When he realized the possibilities and started playing them, he went way past our expectations. It's a very stylish film."

Prescription: Murder, like the second Columbo TV movie, *Ransom for a Dead Man*, is not syndicated with the forty-three *Mystery Movie* episodes, but it does show up regularly on independent TV stations. MCA also issued a home video version in 1987. Columbo is billed as "TV's favorite detective," and, for once, an advertising puff contains a measure of accuracy.

Levinson was basically correct in saying that all the components were in place. There's no car. There's no dog. But *Prescription: Murder*

Falk makes his first appearance as Lieutenant Columbo. The costume would stay the same, but the look would get shaggier.

established a formula that would be duplicated again and again, with only slight variations.

You start with the concept that *Columbo* is an inverted or open mystery. In other words, instead of the traditional whodunit, we get to see the murder committed. We know who dun it. *Columbo* is a howzhegonnacatchhim.

It was a daring idea for television, yet mystery fans can tell you that the literary device was being used long before *Columbo* showed up. R. Austin Freeman, author of such books as *John Thorndyke's Cases* (1909), *The Eye of Osiris* (1911) and *The Singing Bone* (1912), is credited with inventing the inverted mystery. Anthony Berkeley Cox, writing under the pseudonym of Francis Iles, used the open mystery in the 1931 novel *Malice Aforethought.*

The character of Lieutenant Columbo also had definite literary ancestors.

"There were two major influences that we're aware of," Levinson said. "The humbleness we got from Father Brown. The fawning manner we got from Petrovich in Dostoyevsky's *Crime and Punishment.* He's always saying, 'You're so much brighter than I am. I'm just a humble civil servant.'"

Most of the other familiar aspects of the *Columbo* series can be found in *Prescription: Murder*: references to his wife, the delayed entrance, talk about his many relatives, the cigar, the seminal Columbo lines.

"There's one detail that bothers me . . ."

"I seem to be making a pest of myself."

"Gee, you don't have a pencil, do you? Thanks. You know, my wife, she gives me one every morning, and I just can't seem to hold on to it."

"My sister, she has a living room that's very, very modern."

"Oh, listen, there's one more thing . . ."

"Do you know where the one more thing came from?" Levinson asked with a grin. "When Bill and I were writing the play, we had a scene that was too short, and we had already had Columbo make his exit. We were too lazy to retype the scene, so we had him come back and say, 'Oh, just one more thing . . .' It was never planned."

Twenty years after *Prescription: Murder* aired, Falk still would have nothing but praise for Levinson and Link's script. "That was absolutely flawless," he said. "I don't remember changing a comma. That was a terrific script."

The major change from the play, of course, was the switch from New York to Los Angeles. "And several reviewers pointed out that Columbo, especially Falk's Columbo, was obviously a New York cop," Levinson said. "But we had switched coasts, so why not Columbo?"

There was another change that seemed minor at the time. Levinson and Link had clothed Columbo in an overcoat. "We had put Mitchell in a shabby overcoat that he got cigar ashes all over," Levinson pointed out.

Falk read the script and thought it said raincoat. He brought in a beat-up favorite from his own wardrobe. "The raincoat was his idea," Levinson said. "It used to drive people crazy because it made a lot of noise and Peter is a natural actor who doesn't like to loop [dub in obscured dialogue or rewritten lines]. And he's very good at looping. But in the middle of a scene, there'd be this great ruffling noise. It was that raincoat. The sound guys would go nuts."

In fact, Columbo was about the cheapest character Universal ever had to costume. The clothes all belonged to Falk, and he wore the same suit, shoes and raincoat for all forty-five *Columbo* outings.

"Yeah, it was my raincoat, my brown leather shoes, my suit," Falk chuckled. "The suit was one of those cool, baggy summer suits. But they only had them in blue and white. I asked them if they could dye one of them, and it became that brownish tan. I wore the same suit for the whole series."

Prescription: Murder slipped onto the air with relatively little fanfare. Jack Gould, then TV critic for *The New York Times*, devoted his February 20 column to a German-made documentary about Hitler, which PBS aired. Still, the ratings were good enough to put *Prescrip-*

tion: *Murder* among the ten highest-rated TV movies made to that date. Universal, one of Hollywood's busiest studios, offered Levinson and Link a contract that they turned down and then accepted.

The real surprise, though, was Falk's performance.

"We put in a servile quality, but Peter added the enormous politeness," Levinson said. "He stuck in sirs and ma'ams all over the place. We had a humble guy, but Peter stressed that. Mitchell was a bit more brusque."

"Peter had definite ideas," Link said, "and, in a large measure, he's responsible for the success of *Columbo*. There's a great similarity to Peter and the character: the energy, the perfectionist, the charm, the forgetfulness. Peter is a forgetful person. He was always forgetting his car keys. In a large way, it's him."

Everything clicked—the disheveled appearance, the voice, the squint caused by his false right eye. It was all used to magnificent advantage in Falk's characterization.

"Maybe somebody else could have played Columbo," said Steven Bochco, story editor for the first season of *Columbo*. "It's possible. My feeling is that it just wouldn't have been the enormous hit it became. Without him, it wouldn't have been the same. You can't discount how wonderful Peter was in that role. It was one of those fortuitous accidents of chemistry."

Universal recognized that and approached Falk about turning the Columbo character into a series. He wasn't interested. The actor was pursuing feature projects, and he still had a bad taste in his mouth from the cancellation of *The Trials of O'Brien*.

"I thought the scripts on *Trials of O'Brien* were high-quality scripts," Falk said. "Richard Simmons, who was the producer, is a writer of fantastic fertility and invention and speed. In hindsight, maybe the concept wasn't as good. Maybe I was on screen too much. I certainly didn't say that at the time."

"At that point, he wasn't ready for series television," Irving said.

As pleased as they were with Falk's interpretation, Levinson and Link didn't have any desire to see Columbo go to series.

"It was a one-shot to us," Link related. "We didn't see it as a series. It was a world premiere movie, and we were content to leave it at that."

Three years after *Prescription: Murder*, Universal and NBC tried again. Network executives had a plan that might make a *Columbo* series more palatable to Falk. Would he do *Columbo* if it rotated with two other series as part of a *Mystery Movie* package? Instead of doing twenty-four one-hour episodes, he'd be looking at six ninety-minute shows. The umbrella rotation, later known as the wheel, worked fairly well on the Peacock Network's *The Name of the Game*, which each week featured one of three stars (Tony Franciosa, Robert Stack and good ol' Doc Fleming himself, Gene Barry).

The concept appealed to Falk. Levinson and Link, however, were still not sure it could work as a series. Besides, Universal television boss Sid Sheinberg had them working on a rewrite of the pilot episode for a series loosely based on the Clint Eastwood film *Coogan's Bluff* (which, ironically, was directed by the man originally interested in *Prescription: Murder*, Don Siegel). It would be called *McCloud*. They also were developing their own series, *The Psychiatrist*.

Then NBC made a request that stunned Levinson and Link. They asked for a *Columbo* pilot. But there's already a pilot, right? *Prescription: Murder*, right? That proved how successful the character and the formula could be, right? The network didn't see it that way.

Although baffled, the team agreed to concoct a story for a second two-hour *Columbo* movie. Because of other commitments, writing a full script was out of the question. They suggested the task be given to a talented young Universal contract writer named Dean Hargrove. Sheinberg took their recommendation.

"I declined because there would be no royalties involved," said

Hargrove, who has written scripts for such series as *The Man from U.N.C.L.E.* and *The Name of the Game.* "Universal owned the rights to the character, so it would have been just a one-time assignment."

Sheinberg took the project to a second contract writer, who also turned it down. That sent him back to Hargrove, who was looking at ways to establish himself as a producer.

"Sid Sheinberg offered me a bonus if I'd write the script," Hargrove recalled. "That was fine, but I had something else in mind. I only had a couple of producing credits at that time, and I asked him if I could be the producer for the pilot. I had a two- or three-page story notion by Levinson and Link. I liked the story, so I was very happy."

With Irving again called upon to direct, Falk climbed into the raincoat for a second time.

FOOTNOTE #1: *The Raincoat*

The Lone Ranger's mask, the mighty Sherlock's deerstalker, Superman's cape, Batman's cowl and Columbo's raincoat. The most familiar part of Lieutenant Columbo's "uniform" was purchased by Peter Falk on 57th Street during a rainy New York day in 1967. To this day, Falk swears that the television script for *Prescription: Murder* specified a raincoat—not an overcoat—for the unkempt lieutenant. Although the switch to a raincoat would seem natural enough for the change in locations from New York to Los Angeles, Levinson and Link always maintained that their star was mistaken.

Falk wore the same raincoat throughout the NBC run of *Columbo*, but there were two or three stand-in coats. In March 1974, one of these was auctioned off for $1,000 at an Easter Seal dinner in Bridgeport, Connecticut (the actor was the Easter Seal national chairman in 1975).

When *Columbo* ended its NBC run in 1978, Falk lovingly stored the famous garment in a closet of his Beverly Hills home.

"I have a great deal of affection for it," Falk said in 1988. "I take great care of it. I've been known to say I put out a saucer of milk for it every night."

CASE # 2: RANSOM FOR A DEAD MAN

(originally aired March 1, 1971)

Written by DEAN HARGROVE (from a story by Levinson and Link)
Directed by RICHARD IRVING
Produced by DEAN HARGROVE
Executive producer: RICHARD IRVING
Music by BILLY GOLDENBERG
Director of photography: LIONEL LINDON, A.S.C.
Art director: JOHN J. LLOYD
Film editor: EDWARD M. ABROMS
Set decorations: BERT F. ALLAN
Unit manager: DON GOLD
Assistant director: GEORGE BISK
Sound: ROBERT BERTRAND
Editorial supervision: RICHARD BELDING
Costumes by BURTON MILLER
Aerial sequences by TALLMANTZ AVIATION, INC.

CAST

LT. COLUMBO	PETER FALK
LESLIE WILLIAMS	LEE GRANT
CARLSON	HAROLD GOULD
MARGARET WILLIAMS	PATRICIA MATTICK
MICHAEL	JOHN FINK
HAMMOND	PAUL CARR
PHIL	JED ALLAN
RICHARD	CHARLES MACAULAY
ATTORNEY	HENRY BRANDT
PAT	JEANE BYRON
PERKINS	RICHARD ROAT
CELIA	NORMA CONNOLLY
PAUL WILLIAMS	HARLAN WARDE
CROWELL	BILL WALKER
BERT	TIMOTHY CAREY
JUDGE	JUDSON MORGAN
PRIEST	RICHARD O'BRIEN
GLORIA	CELESTE YARNALL
NANCY	LISA MOORE

WAITRESS .... LOIS BATTLE
MECHANIC .... REGINALD FENDERSON

Synopsis—Brilliant lawyer Leslie Williams shoots her older husband, also an attorney, in the living room of their ornate home. The body is pushed into the ocean, and Leslie makes it look like a kidnapping. She's fashioned a ransom note from letters cut out of the newspaper. She's also taken a tape recording of her husband, Paul, talking about a business deal and clipped out one key phrase: "They got me." Using that as proof that her husband is still alive, she fakes a call from the "kidnappers." The FBI is called in. So is a representative of the Los Angeles police force.

Leslie opens the door to find Lieutenant Columbo looking for a pen he just dropped. FBI agent Carlson will only barely recognize Columbo's presence.

A computerized tape recorder in Leslie's office makes the call from the phantom kidnappers. They want $300,000. Columbo notices that she doesn't ask her husband if he's all right. That bothers him.

Leslie, a licensed pilot, is to drop the ransom money from a plane. Going through with the phony arrangement, she removes the money from her bag and throws the empty pouch from the plane. The FBI finds the bag, of course, but no kidnappers. Something else bothers Columbo. Why would criminals making a fast pickup take ransom money out of a bag and leave the bag behind? It doesn't make any sense.

When Paul Williams' body is discovered, Columbo takes over what is now a murder investigation. The ever-watchful lieutenant closely observes Leslie's reactions. After being completely cool and composed during the kidnapping, she breaks down in front of friends and strangers. That bothers him. She never asks where the body was found or how Paul was killed. That bothers him.

At the funeral Columbo sees Margaret Williams—Paul's teenage daughter from his first marriage—slap her stepmother, whom she despises.

Columbo is not done with bothersome details. The driver's seat in Paul's car was pulled way up, as if someone much shorter drove it last. The bullet entered Paul's body at a 45-degree angle and was fired at close range, which probably means that Paul was standing and the killer was sitting. And the gun used was a .22 caliber pistol. Why a .22? Most criminals use a .32 or a .38. Maybe the killer didn't want the bullet to travel through the body. Maybe it was done somewhere, like a living room, where no traces could show.

Comparing notes with Margaret, Columbo discovers that Leslie had a motive for murder. She could always make Paul do what she wanted. She had convinced him to end his distinguished career as a judge so they could start a law firm together. His reputation built her practice. After getting that, Leslie told Paul that she thought he was a dull, tiresome old man. She wanted to be partners in name and business only. He stood up to her.

Margaret suspects the truth. Columbo tells her there's no real evidence, just several inconsistencies.

Leslie is hounded by Columbo and Margaret. The teenager promises to go away and leave her stepmother alone—for a rather substantial price. Leslie is only too glad to agree. She'll give Margaret the $300,000 "ransom" money and send all her troubles to Europe. With Margaret will go the only real piece of incriminating evidence.

Columbo is waiting at the airport. Margaret had made the deal at his request. He reasoned that the only way to catch Leslie was to force her to use the ransom money. Her lack of conscience, he tells the shrewd lawyer, is her only weakness. She couldn't conceive of anyone not taking that much cash to forget a murder.

It has been suggested that the unique nature of *Columbo* may have been the reason NBC wanted a second pilot. Network executives may have just wanted to have been convinced that the success of *Prescription: Murder* wasn't a fluke.

Whatever the rationale, programming history repeated itself. *Ransom for a Dead Man*, like *Prescription: Murder*, was a success in the ratings and the reviews. In many ways, it's a better TV movie than *Prescription: Murder*.

Irving had to look for ways to translate *Prescription: Murder* from a stage play into a TV drama. While that transition was smooth, *Ransom for a Dead Man* had the advantage of being designed as a movie. Using Levinson and Link's established formula and cunning story idea, Dean Hargrove concocted scenes that took fuller benefit of the medium.

Levinson particularly liked the scene in which Leslie Williams takes Columbo for an airplane ride. The detective, obviously airsick, tries to continue his interrogation.

"*Columbo* is a very talky concept," he said. "It's a lot of people talking in rooms. Now, if you're going to have people talking in rooms a lot, you'd better change the rooms. They put Falk in a private plane.

Lawyer Leslie Williams (Lee Grant) finds an antagonistic message from her stepdaughter in the second Columbo TV movie, Ransom for a Dead Man.

Well, that's a great innovation. He could play the airsickness and the questions."

If *Prescription: Murder* was a stylish TV movie, *Ransom for a Dead Man* was even more stylish. If *Prescription: Murder* set the mold, *Ransom for a Dead Man*—thanks to Irving's direction, Edward M. Abroms' editing and Billy Goldenberg's thrilling musical score—refined it.

"The format was locked in," Levinson said. "So was the character. But in both movies, Irving helped shape Peter's performance."

The strangling of Carol Fleming was gruesomely played out before the camera in *Prescription: Murder*. The shooting of Paul Williams was shown through a stylized sequence of cuts in *Ransom for a Dead Man*. It was an important step for *Columbo*. Future episodes either wouldn't show the murder or would depict it in a highly sanitized way.

Falk was fond of the entrance Hargrove conceived for Columbo.

"I'm not a mystery fan, but as a kid I read Sherlock Holmes," the actor said. "I remember being very impressed by Sherlock Holmes. He'd show up and everybody would turn to him for the answer. I thought it was important in the opening of *Ransom for a Dead Man* that no one turn to me for anything. I was just a local. All these FBI agents had their job to do. I couldn't know anything except maybe the name of a certain street. I wanted to be ignored.

"That gives me a problem. You can't interrupt. There are important people doing things. The more celebrated approach is to have the great detective arrive and everyone turns to him for the answer. Nobody wanted to know this guy's opinion. There's a lack of pretension. You expect something quite different from a great detective. The great detective arrives and, instead of people turning to him, their attention is on this major kidnapping. What's he doing? He's looking for this engraved pen that he's dropped. That's a nice quality. It's amusing, but it's also a very humanizing thing. It's not humor just for its own sake. It says something about the character. There's a contrast between his position and the reality. It made him very likable. Nobody is going to take him seriously."

Columbo again was matched against a worthy adversary, which meant that Falk again was blessed with a wonderful co-star. Lee Grant's portrayal of Leslie Williams earned her an Emmy nomination.

"It came along at a time when I was making a string of good TV movies," recalled Grant, who would later also receive acclaim as a director. "It was a great experience, but I had no idea that it was being thought of as a series. It was another good script. I just thought of the idea of working with Peter Falk. I had worked with Peter a lot, so it was an easy and fun collaboration.

"I love the mystery format, so it was great fun for me. I loved the opening. What a way to start! There was no mystery. Bang! Right away, you knew what she was all about. The mystery wasn't did she do it. The mystery was is she catchable."

Within a year of *Ransom for a Dead Man*, Falk and Grant would be co-starring on Broadway in Neil Simon's *The Prisoner of Second Avenue*.

Ransom for a Dead Man aired March 1, 1971. In April, Sid Sheinberg asked Levinson and Link if they would produce a series version of *Columbo*. There was one little proviso. Falk would open in *The Prisoner of Second Avenue* on September 12. They needed to complete six ninety-minute episodes by then.

"To this day," Bill Link said, "I don't know why we said yes."

PART II

THE FIRST SEASON (1971–72)

"*Columbo* was the hardest work we've ever done. I'd come home and almost faint."

—RICHARD LEVINSON

Getting the Wrinkles in

Even when pilot TV movies are successful, a network will rush to change things. *Columbo* was no exception.

Although both *Prescription: Murder* and *Ransom for a Dead Man* had been ratings winners, NBC was still uneasy with the format. The inevitable list of suggestions was submitted.

- What's all this about the audience always knowing who the murderer is? There's no suspense. That novelty will wear off.
- A main character should have a "family" of regulars. Columbo should have at least a young sidekick.
- Get the main character on earlier. Viewers won't stick around that long. Don't you know that Falk's the star? Where the hell is he, guys?
- Get more action (i.e. violence) into the show.
- There's too much talk. There's no tempo, no tension.
- An unseen wife? Dumb idea, fellows. Let's get rid of the wife. Viewers like it when the leading man is free to have occasional romantic encounters.

It was, to say the least, the moment of truth for *Columbo* and two writers trying to become producers. Faced with such overwhelming "conceptual concerns" from NBC, Levinson and Link decided to tough it out. They threatened to quit. The gamble paid off. The shooting schedule was too tight to risk alienating the production team. The network had no choice.

NBC backed down. For better or worse, *Columbo* would fly by Levinson and Link's design.

Having had to swallow their objections, NBC executives must have been convinced that *Columbo* would be the weak link in the *Mystery Movie* package, which they gave the 8:30–10:00 P.M. Wednesday time slot. The surer bets would be Dennis Weaver in *McCloud* and Rock Hudson and Susan Saint James in *McMillan and Wife*.

Bill Link and Richard Irving agree that if the concept of the wheel hadn't been developed, *Columbo* would have never existed as a series.

"I don't think Falk would have done a weekly series," Link said.

Lieutenant Columbo (Peter Falk) and the two detectives who stayed with him during the entire run of NBC's Mystery Movie wheel: Deputy Marshal Sam McCloud (Dennis Weaver) and San Francisco Police Commissioner Stewart McMillan (Rock Hudson).

"But, beyond that, *Columbo* was too rich a brew for audiences to swallow every week. Every three weeks was good. It gave viewers time to anticipate and savor the next one."

The first order of business for Levinson and Link was the selection of a creative staff. They looked around the Universal lot to scout strong prospects. The writers were tenderfoots as producers, so a knowledgeable and experienced associate producer was a must. They found one in Robert F. O'Neill. Since *Columbo* would be a complex, talk-oriented, formula show, a talented and energetic story editor also was needed. Irving suggested a promising young writer named Steven Bochco.

"I was sort of bullied into getting involved by Dick Irving," Bochco remembered. "After directing the two *Columbo* movies, he became the executive at Universal in charge of the *Mystery Movie*. I told him that the mystery really isn't my kind of stuff, but Dick Irving encouraged me to give it a try. He thought it would be good for me."

And they needed writers. Because the concept was so definite, Levinson and Link arranged a screening of *Ransom for a Dead Man*. About sixty freelance writers showed up. Two displayed an interest. One of them was mystery veteran Jackson Gillis, who had contributed several scripts to CBS's *Perry Mason* series.

There would end up being seven, not six, *Columbo* episodes that first season. Gillis would do one by himself and co-author another. Bochco would write three, relying on his producers for plotting suggestions. Levinson and Link would find time to complete one script.

You think mysteries are easy to knock off? Just try plotting one sometime. The *Columbo* formula was intimidating enough to scare off the vast majority of Hollywood writers. As a result, there was no talent pool to draw on. There was no B-team.

"Deceptively difficult? There was nothing deceptive about it," Dick Levinson said. "The problem with *Columbo* was that you had no other characters, and the leading man didn't enter until the second act, which is unheard of in television. You had to create a perfect crime that had a loophole, then provide a perfect clue. After the crime, since Bill and I refused to put any violence into the show, we had to have a conversation between two individuals for ninety minutes. The cat-and-mouse dialogue would create the tension. Well, there aren't many writers who can do all that, which we found out."

In fact, there never would be all that many writers contributing scripts for *Columbo*. Of the lieutenant's forty-five escapades, Levinson and Link wrote two scripts and provided the stories for at least five others, Bochco wrote or co-wrote six teleplays, Gillis worked on seven scripts and helped fashion the plots of others, and Peter S. Fischer authored five episodes while concocting the story of another. In other words, one of these five men had a hand in more than half of the forty-five cases.

During that first season, a *Columbo* gestalt emerged from the writers in the production office. Levinson and Link would sketch out a plot idea. Bochco would hammer out a rough draft. The team would polish it up. Gillis would contribute a vital clue. Writer/director Larry Cohen would drop by and suggest solutions and storylines.

Adding to Levinson and Link's headaches were frequent clashes with Falk. The actor's demanding nature has become the stuff of Hollywood legend. Just how difficult was he during *Columbo*? It depends on whom you ask.

A studio executive will paint a dark picture.

"He was difficult in terms of being a perfectionist," Irving said. "He never wanted to make the compromises that are necessary in television. You had to worry about budgets and the reality of working in television. He didn't seem to care about those things. He was a perfectionist, so we went way over budget and way behind schedule. Peter happened to be just great for that role, but getting there was too expensive. His domain should be movies. He's a liability in television."

The same perfectionism that drove studio executives to their budget sheets, however, endeared Falk to his fellow actors. The people who guest-starred on *Columbo* have nothing but praise for Falk and his demands for quality.

"He was wonderful to work with," said George Hamilton, a guest murderer during the fourth season. "He worked at everything to make the series good. And if you had a problem as another actor, he would work with you and say, 'Let's work this out.' I don't know many actors who take that time and effort."

"Peter is a consummate actor," Ricardo Montalban said. "He's very professional. He's an actor's dream—very generous and caring."

"Peter worked very hard to maintain the series' standards," said Patrick McGoohan, a guest star on two *Columbo* episodes and the director of another. "When the scripts didn't come up to his standards, he'd go crazy. Peter fought every inch of the way for quality."

"He's a passionate man," Hector Elizondo said. "He cares. People in television tend to be embarrassed by passion. It's very refreshing to find someone with a genuine passion for quality. He's the hardest-working actor I've ever worked with. He works constantly on his character. In between, you laugh a lot."

"Peter was marvelous," Richard Kiley said. "He set the mood for the whole set. He's a wonderful actor to work with."

"His technique of working was quite extraordinary," Vincent Price commented. "And it was entirely legitimate. He could not set his lines until he had seen and worked with the other people in the scene, which makes perfectly good sense. It doesn't make any sense to do a scene without thoroughly rehearsing first. You would never do it in the theater. You'd never do it in a movie. But in television, with the whip on you, it happens all the time."

This could go on and on. Admiring dedication and quality, the actors say Falk was a saint. Craving efficiency and economy, studio executives say he was a monster (albeit a likable monster).

Levinson and Link, though, were caught in the middle. As writers, they saw reason in Falk's fiery accusations about Universal being a sausage factory. As producers, they wanted sanity and cooperation.

Stay Tuned, Levinson and Link's witty book about laboring in television's vineyards, describes a love/hate relationship. There were power struggles. There were arguments. And there was enormous mutual respect.

Levinson and Link believe that Falk came to *Columbo* mistrustful of a series, the studio and NBC. He wasn't even too sure about the producers.

"We had enormous affection for him," Levinson said. "For one thing, he's a very likable, very charming man. For another, he's very bright. And he had a lot to do with the success of a huge hit. So even when we were fighting with him, we liked him tremendously. The problem was that we were too damn busy to do that kind of star massage that is sometimes required. It was just too difficult a show, and we were doing most of it ourselves.

"Then he started getting rough drafts of *Columbo* scripts from a friend. He hated them and he wasn't sophisticated enough in the television business to know that a rough draft is not something you show the star of a series. You get a rough draft and you work on it."

A game of high intrigue started to be played out behind the Universal Studio gates. Levinson and Link ordered the editors to lock Falk out. Scenes were written to keep him away from the dailies. Hoping to occupy the actor, the producers asked him to write a script.

"We did that for two reasons," Levinson said. "We did it to keep him from pestering us. You know, in many ways, he's just like Columbo. And we did it to show him how tough those scripts are to write. So he went home and wrote a couple of acts, which were excellent. He said, 'I got this far. How do I do the ending?' Bill and I smiled and said together, 'Ahhhhh!'"

Levinson and Link never doubted that Falk was dedicated to the Columbo character. They never took anything personally.

"And there were some tremendous fights," Levinson recalled. "In 'Death Lends a Hand,' we wanted to introduce Columbo as a guy whose license had run out and he had been pulled over for having a broken headlight. That was a huge fight with Falk. He said, 'Nobody drives around with a broken headlight.' The three of us fought about it on the way to have lunch. On our way to the commissary, we passed his old Jaguar. One of the headlights was broken. He looked at it and said, 'I withdraw my argument.'

"When he wasn't arguing, he was extraordinarily charming. You liked him so much that you wanted to do what he wanted."

Being in the middle of a demanding studio and a demanding star, the producers discovered another bright side to Falk's battling nature. It could be used to buy precious time.

Most network series are shot within a week. While *Columbo* didn't have to produce twenty-two shows in a season, Levinson and Link were expected to finish six ninety-minute movies in less than five months. Look at it as just six episodes, and it seems terrific. Look at it as six movies, it seems horrible.

Each *Columbo* was supposed to take twelve days to shoot. It started to take longer and longer. When it started taking fourteen days, the studio decided that *Columbo* must be a problem show. Falk's reaction was predictable. Levinson and Link were sure that the explosions were the shrewd, calculated responses of a street fighter who knew how to rattle studio cages. Whether this was true or not, the outbursts caused executives to scurry for cover and provided the producers with a chance to make better episodes.

"Peter, Bill and I often were in collusion," Levinson admitted. "We knowingly made use of his intransigence to get more time and better quality. If we were up against a deadline gun, we'd say to Peter, 'If you want to unleash yourself and be difficult, that's fine with us.'

"The studio had titanic battles with Peter and us over money. Dick Irving didn't think we knew what we were doing, and he was right. He and Peter would just scream and yell and battle, and, for some reason, Peter won, even though the show wasn't yet on the air. It wasn't a hit.

"There was a lot of barbed humor in those days. You know what Bill and I gave Peter for Christmas that first year? A half-bottle of Murine. He loved it. People would say, 'Which is the glass eye?' We'd say, 'The one with a gleam of intelligence.'"

Somehow, despite all the intrigue and wrangling, the team completed the six shows. Now it was NBC's turn to ask for "one more thing." Could they do a seventh? Fighting the calendar and exhaustion, they finished a seventh in time for Falk to leave to do *The*

Prisoner of Second Avenue. Looking back at his *Columbo* tenure, does the actor think he was overly demanding and difficult to work with?

"I suppose I have the reputation," Falk said with a playful grin. "I'm not shy. I was not bashful. I don't think anyone would accuse me of that."

More than twenty series premiered in the fall of 1971. They included one or two notable efforts (*Nichols* and *Owen Marshall, Counselor at Law*) and the usual flock of forgettable flops: *The Partners, The Chicago Teddy Bears, Cade's County, The Persuaders, The Funny Side, Shirley's World, The Good Life* and *Getting Together.* It was the year that network television said goodbye to such venerable prime-time favorites as *The Ed Sullivan Show, Lassie, Lawrence Welk, The Beverly Hillbillies* and the last incarnation of *The Andy Griffith Show,* the Griffith-less *Mayberry, R.F.D.* A September 12 *New York Times* overview by John J. O'Connor was titled "Will It Pay to Be Different?" Oddly enough, he makes no mention of a completely different type of cop who was preparing to make his NBC bow.

Three days after O'Connor's article appeared, *Columbo* made its regular series debut. NBC selected the shabby snooper to start the *Mystery Movie* wheel rolling.

The first episode filmed was "Death Lends a Hand," a Levinson and Link script featuring former *I Spy* star Robert Culp as the murderer. Looking over the seven episodes, the producers decided that the second show filmed, "Murder by the Book," was the strongest. They led with it.

CASE # 3: MURDER BY THE BOOK

(originally aired September 15, 1971)

Written by STEVEN BOCHCO
Directed by STEVEN SPIELBERG
Produced by RICHARD LEVINSON AND WILLIAM LINK
Associate producer: ROBERT F. O'NEILL
Story editor: STEVEN BOCHCO
Music Score: BILLY GOLDENBERG
Sunday Mystery Movie Theme: HENRY MANCINI
Director of photography: RUSSELL L. METTY, A.S.C.
Art director: ARCH BACON
Film editor: JOHN KAUFMAN, JR.
Set decorations: RICHARD FRIEDMAN
Assistant director: RALPH FERRIN
Sound: DAVID H. MORIARTY
Unit manager: HENRY KLINE
Editorial supervision: RICHARD BELDING
Costumes by BURTON MILLER
Main title design: ATTILA DE LADO
Titles and optical effects by UNIVERSAL TITLE

CAST

LT. COLUMBO .... PETER FALK

KEN FRANKLIN .... JACK CASSIDY

JAMES FERRIS .... MARTIN MILNER

JOANNA FERRIS .... ROSEMARY FORSYTH

LILY LA SANKA .... BARBARA COLBY

GLORIA JR. .... LYNNETTE METTEY

MIKE TUCKER .... BERNIE KUBY

SERGEANT .... HOKE HOWELL

WOMAN .... MARCIA WALLACE

SECOND REPORTER .... HAVEN EARLE HALEY

Synopsis—America loves the Mrs. Melville mystery novels penned by the bestselling team of Franklin and Ferris. What America doesn't know is that soft-spoken James Ferris does all the writing while gregarious Ken Franklin does all the talking (as in talk shows, personal appearances, book signings).

The arrangement has made them both rich, but Jim wants to try serious writing on his own. The decision enrages the untalented Ken, who depends on Mrs. Melville to maintain his high style of living. Rather than risk exposure and poverty, Ken resolves to kill his partner and collect on the insurance policy they have on each other.

Jim is working on the latest Mrs. Melville novel at their Los Angeles office. It's a Saturday and the building is deserted. Affecting a conciliatory spirit, Ken shows up with a bottle of champagne and apologies for violently opposing Jim's wishes. As a peace offering, Ken says, he's going to take his workaholic partner to his cabin near San Diego. Jim tries to get out of it, saying that he's made plans for dinner with his wife, Joanna. But Ken is as manipulative as he is charming.

Call Joanna and say that you'll be working late at the office, Ken advises. Feeling a little guilty for breaking up the team, Jim agrees. When they get to the car, though, Ken pretends to have forgotten his special lighter. He runs back and tears the office apart, making it look as if the place had been subject to a quick and violent search.

Nearing the cabin, Ken stops at a small store operated by Lily La Sanka, a widow who has a crush on the debonair "writer." He gives her an autographed book and uses the phone to call Joanna. Ken says that he's down at the cabin. He tells Joanna that he and Jim have patched things up. He claims to have left Jim working at the office.

At the cabin, Jim worries that Joanna might be waiting up for him. Ken persuades him to make the call he suggested earlier. Dialing direct, Jim tells Joanna that he's working on the last chapter. As he's talking on the phone, his partner shoots him. Joanna hears the shot and believes it happened at the office. She immediately phones the police.

Officers arrive at the scene and find a ransacked office but no body. Needing a moment of quiet, Joanna goes into the hallway, where she encounters Lieutenant Columbo. Noticing the toll this ordeal has taken on her, the solicitous detective takes Joanna home and fixes her an omelet.

Columbo learns that Jim did all of the actual writing. As he is talking with Joanna, Ken arrives with the perfect alibi: he was in San Diego when Jim was supposedly shot in Los Angeles.

Still, Columbo wonders why Ken didn't grab one of the regular commuter flights when he learned about his partner. Why drive all that way?

Ken is all too willing to help Columbo with his investigation. He tells the lieutenant that Jim was working on a book detailing mob operations. He was going to name names, Ken says. This is obviously a professional hit job.

Jim's body is actually in the trunk of Ken's car. Ken dumps the corpse on his own front lawn. It's a message from the mob, he says. Don't carry on your partner's research.

That's a horrible thing to come home to, Columbo agrees, yet it's remarkable that Ken had the composure to open his mail.

Ken has more to worry about than just Columbo's suspicions. Lily La Sanka happened to look out at the car when he stopped at her store. She saw Jim. She wants $15,000 for her silence. Ken turns on the charm and accepts.

He woos her with champagne and, when Lily's back is turned, moves in for the kill. Picking up an empty bottle, he applies it to her skull with extreme prejudice. The only witness who knew that Jim wasn't in Los Angeles has been removed.

Linking everything together, Columbo has a strong circumstantial case, but he needs something much more damaging to convince a jury. Remembering what Joanna said about Jim's work habits, he sets out on the right track. Jim wrote every idea down on paper.

Summoning Ken to the Franklin and Ferris office, Columbo tells the still smug writer that he's about to be arrested. Ken feigns outrage, but his smirking contempt is tinged by a hint of concern. "Clap me in irons," Ken laughs at the lieutenant who has relentlessly stuck to his trail, "but give me a dime to call my lawyer so I can sue you and your department for false arrest."

Ignoring the outburst, Columbo tells Ken that the second murder was sloppy. Anybody could have planned that. The first murder was brilliant, he continues, but since Ken doesn't have any real imagination, how could he have thought up such an ingenious plan? That murder must have been conceived by someone else—maybe a real mystery writer like Jim Ferris. Sure enough, Columbo has found the entire alibi scheme in the Franklin and Ferris papers. All the details are there, all in Jim's handwriting. That will be enough for a conviction.

Caught in the web of evidence, Ken smiles at his unlikely captor. Resigned, he at least can appreciate the circumstances of his undoing. There's a final note of delicious irony, he tells Columbo. The first murder *was* his idea. It was the only good one he ever had. The plot was so good that Jim could never think of how Mrs. Melville would solve it. Ken had told the idea to Jim several years ago. Who could have guessed that he'd write it down?

The *Columbo* series couldn't have made a classier debut. In many ways, "Murder by the Book" is the finest of all the episodes. Levinson, Link and Bochco would all single it out as their favorite.

Look at the credits for the episode and you'll see why. Nobody knew it at the time, but this was an amazing moment of collaboration. Levinson and Link produced. Bochco wrote it. And the director was some kid named Steven Spielberg.

Bochco would go on to co-create such NBC series as *Hill Street Blues* and *L.A. Law*. Spielberg would direct five of the top-grossing films of all time: *Jaws, Close Encounters of the Third Kind, Raiders of the Lost Ark, Indiana Jones and the Temple of Doom* and *E.T.: The Extra-Terrestrial*.

In 1971, however, Steve Spielberg was a promising young director who had yet to make his first feature. Although only in his mid-twenties, he had already been on the Universal lot for a couple of years. One of his first assignments had been to direct Joan Crawford in a segment of Rod Serling's 1969 *Night Gallery* TV movie pilot.

Like other Universal executives, Levinson and Link were impressed by Spielberg's imaginative short subject *Amblin'*. While preparing to take *Columbo* to series, the producers bumped into the young director and invited him to lunch.

"We were looking for directors," Levinson recalled. "He was a nice young kid and we didn't know what we were doing. I asked him if he would like to direct a *Columbo*, and he said, 'Sure.' It was as simple as that. Then we had to sell him to Falk. People were saying then that Steve was a technical director, that he could handle cameras but not actors. We knew that wasn't true, but we had to convince Peter."

Spielberg had directed a segment of the aborted Levinson and Link series *The Psychiatrist*. They arranged a screening of the episode for Falk, who was quite taken with the direction. He met with Spielberg and agreed to let him direct a *Columbo*.

"Which was interesting because there were a lot of people Peter rejected as directors," Levinson said. "This wasn't the Steven Spielberg of legend. This was just a nice young kid. We used to make jokes about coming down to the set for a milk-and-cookie break with the director."

Yet his youth did cause some very real problems at first. Early in the shooting of "Murder by the Book," Levinson and Link got a phone call from their director.

"Come down to the set," Spielberg told them. "Nobody's talking to me."

Spielberg's ambitious vision had clashed with veteran director of photography Russ Metty's. Even before shooting had started, Metty had disagreed with Levinson and Link's "look" for the show. Having photographed such films as *Touch of Evil* for Orson Welles (whom he called a "nice kid"), Metty believed that *Columbo* should be shot in dark and murky tones. Yes, it was a mystery and, yes, too much television is too bright, but the producers wanted a bright feel. A box of expensive cigars convinced Metty to go with the Levinson/Link vision.

Now he was at odds with Spielberg.

"Russ was a gruff old buzzard," Levinson said, "and a great talent. We were lucky to have him. He says to us, 'Your hot-shot director has me in this room down on Sunset Boulevard which is four walls of glass. Where the hell do you expect me to put my lights?'

"We didn't know what he was talking about. We didn't know anything about lights. And to our eternal credit, we said, 'He's the director. Do what he says.'"

By making Spielberg's ideas work, Metty gave the episode a look that's visually intriguing.

And when such differences were resolved, "Murder by the Book" turned into a very happy set. Falk adored working with Jack Cassidy, also a consummate professional.

"The fun we all had was that this was Link and Levinson that this show was all about: two mystery writers," Levinson explained. "Everyone would say, 'Which of you is the writer and which of you is the talker?' Of course, it's not literally us, but we thought it was a novel idea for a murder. A man kills another man because he would be revealed to be the one without talent. There was a constant string of Link and Levinson jokes made during that show."

When one of the producers was in earshot, Cassidy would ask, "Which one am I playing here, Link or Levinson?"

As if to underscore the idea, the mystery team was given an alliterative ring: Franklin and Ferris. An in-joke was even tossed into the script. The title of the autographed book Ken Franklin presents to Lily La Sanka is *Prescription: Murder.*

While hopes and spirits were high, nobody was prepared for the screening of the first cut of "Murder by the Book." To use a trite show business expression, it knocked their socks off. Spielberg's direction was as clever and inventive as the script.

"Steve had done all sorts of experimental things," Levinson said. "We absolutely loved it. There were only twenty feet cut from his first cut. I think it was of a man crossing a room. That's all that was done to it. I don't think that happened before or since with a project Bill and I worked on."

The same year as "Murder by the Book," Spielberg directed his breakthrough TV movie at Universal—a stunning adaptation of fantasy writer Richard Matheson's story *Duel.* It put him on the

Hollywood map. His first theatrical feature, *The Sugarland Express*, followed in 1974. *Jaws* hit the screen a year later.

"Everybody tries to take credit for Steve Spielberg's success," Levinson commented. "All I can tell you is that we enjoyed working with him. He was extraordinarily gifted. His technique is incredible. We happened to luck into a director who, in terms of visual mastery of the medium, is one of the greatest directors in the history of film. No matter what you think of Steve Spielberg, there's no denying that he has an instinctive genius for film. We didn't know how fortunate we were. We thought that was the norm for directors. We hadn't worked with that many directors, so we were not that impressed."

Indeed, there is a visual richness to "Murder by the Book" that the series would never again achieve. The opening and closing sequences are particularly effective.

When "Murder by the Book" begins, we see Jim at work and Ken driving to the office. You don't the car's engine. You don't hear the noises of the city. The only sound you hear is the clacking of a typewriter. It's an incredibly tense and riveting opening. It immediately established the fact that this series would try to do things differently.

Picking up on the typewriter sound, Billy Goldenberg ran typing rhythms through a synthesizer and integrated the results into his suspenseful musical score. The closing shot is an eerie close-up of the knowing Mrs. Melville (a portrait in Ken and Jim's office).

It would be fair to say that all the elements came together for "Murder by the Book." Martin Milner, familiar to television audiences as policeman Pete Malloy on NBC's *Adam 12*, made a sympathetic and likable murder victim. Barbara Colby brought a lonely and pathetic quality to the role of Lily La Sanka. But it was the late Jack Cassidy who really made things click.

His "preening arrogance," as Bill Link called it, made him the ideal *Columbo* villain. Barry and Grant had been terrific adversaries for Columbo, but Cassidy truly set the standard. He typified everything Levinson and Link wanted in a contrast to Peter Falk.

"There are certain kinds of leading men who play properly against Peter," Levinson said. "You can't have Peter playing against a Jack Klugman or a Martin Balsam. There's no contrast. We needed elegant, slick actors like Robert Vaughn, Jack Cassidy and Robert Culp. Cassidy was the perfect *Columbo* villain because he played murderers of enormous ego who could patronize Columbo. There aren't that many actors who can do that, so we used him more than once."

In fact, Cassidy would be asked back twice more. Only Culp played a *Columbo* murderer as many times.

For all the heavyweight talent working on "Murder by the Book," there was just one artistic debate of consequence. Spielberg wanted to film Lily La Sanka's murder à la Hitchcock. As Ken Franklin approaches with the champagne bottle in hand, the camera cut to a closeup of Lily. Her face contorted in a terrified scream, but there is no sound. Cut to commercial.

Levinson thought the silent touch was confusing. He believed the audience should hear the scream. Link, though, sided with Spielberg, and the majority carried the day.

"I violently disagreed with that," Levinson said, "but that was our only argument. That was it."

Levinson, Link, Bochco, Spielberg, Falk, Cassidy, Goldenberg, Metty—"Murder by the Book" is probably the best episode of the best season of TV's best mystery series.

"I love that one best of all for all kinds of reasons," Bochco said. "It was my first one, and Steve did a wonderful job. We grew up together at Universal. We were like kids on the block. I had never done a script like that before. Dick and Bill knew the style and made enormous contributions. And I love writing for Peter. His kind of humor was right up my alley."

Levinson and Link had led with their best card, but there were still aces in that strong first-season hand.

CASE #4: DEATH LENDS A HAND

(originally aired October 6, 1971)

Written by RICHARD LEVINSON AND WILLIAM LINK
Directed by BERNARD KOWALSKI
Produced by RICHARD LEVINSON AND WILLIAM LINK
Associate producer: ROBERT F. O'NEILL
Story editor: STEVEN BOCHCO
Music Score: GIL MELLÉ
Sunday Mystery Movie Theme: HENRY MANCINI
Director of photography: RUSSELL L. METTY, A.S.C.
Art director: ARCH BACON
Film editor: EDWARD M. ABROMS
Set decorations: RICHARD FRIEDMAN
Unit manager: HENRY KLINE
Sound: DAVID H. MORIARTY
Assistant director: JACK BARRY
Editorial supervision: RICHARD BELDING
Costumes by BURTON MILLER
Main title design: WAYNE FITZGERALD
Titles and optical effects by UNIVERSAL TITLE

CAST

LT. COLUMBO	PETER FALK
INVESTIGATOR BRIMMER	ROBERT CULP
ARTHUR KENNICUT	RAY MILLAND
MRS. LENORE KENNICUT	PATRICIA CROWLEY
KEN ARCHER	BRETT HALSEY
DENNING	ERIC JAMES
MEDICAL EXAMINER	DON KEEFER
CAPTAIN OF DETECTIVES	LEN WAYLAND
CEIL GENTRY	LIEUX DRESSLER
BRIMMER'S SECRETARY	BARBARA BALDAVIN

Synopsis—Communications czar Arthur Kennicut has hired high-priced private investigator Brimmer to determine if his wife is having an affair. She had been, but Brimmer falsifies the report. He tells Kennicut that his wife has a clean bill of health.

Brimmer lets Mrs. Kennicut hear the whole confrontation on an intercom. In exchange for his continued protection, the investigator wants her to be "a good listener." In other words, he hopes to blackmail her into being a pipeline of information about her politically powerful husband. He suggests that she think it over.

That night, Mrs. Kennicut is waiting for Brimmer at his beach house. She has made her decision. The affair was a stupid mistake. She had ended it. She will go to Arthur and tell him the truth. Maybe he will forgive her. Maybe not. Either way, Brimmer can't blackmail her. He's lost his leverage. She wonders how many others have given in to his extortion.

Oh, and no matter how Arthur feels about the affair, he's going to despise Brimmer for lying to him and trying to blackmail his wife. Cornered and enraged, the volatile Brimmer lashes out with the back of his hand. Mrs. Kennicut falls backward, striking her head on a glass table. She is killed.

Brimmer puts the body in the trunk of his car and dumps it near an automobile junkyard on the other side of town.

The first police officers on the scene believe that Mrs. Kennicut was the victim of a robbery gone sour. Arriving late (of course), Lieutenant Columbo observes an odd bruise and cut on the left cheek. It seems to have been made by a ring with a distinctly cut stone. Conclusion Number One: The killer struck out with his left hand. Conclusion Number Two: The killer must be left-handed. Conclusion Number Three: The killer wears a fancy ring.

Arthur Kennicut takes a liking to diligent Lieutenant Columbo, but he's displeased with the lack of progress in the case. He decides to call in an investigator he's used before—Brimmer! So the murderer has been hired to solve a killing he committed.

Columbo notices that Brimmer wears a fancy ring with a distinctly cut stone. He also learns that the investigator is ambidextrous.

Columbo goes to the golf course where Mrs. Kennicut took lessons—many, many lessons. The young teaching pro acts very guilty, but the lieutenant scratches him off the list of suspects. He wears no ring, and his golfer's tan would show if he recently removed one. Under questioning, the golf instructor admits that he had an affair with Mrs. Kennicut.

When Columbo starts nosing too close to the truth, Brimmer offers him a job with his agency.

Columbo has to find a way to get Brimmer to betray himself. He gets an idea from a picture of Mrs. Kennicut. She's wearing glasses. Arthur says she switched to contact lenses. Columbo asks him to have the body exhumed. If the contact lenses aren't on the body, maybe they're at the scene of the murder.

Brimmer learns of Columbo's plan and rushes to the cemetery. His car won't start. He orders it sent to the garage and takes another. He arrives in time to hear that one contact is missing.

It's the longest of long shots, but Brimmer can't take any chances. He carefully combs his rug at the beach house. No contact is found. What about the trunk of his car? He transported the body in the trunk of his car. Brimmer heads for the garage and searches the trunk. There is the contact. He is safe.

Suddenly, the lights click on. Lieutenant Columbo, Arthur Kennicut and several uniformed police officers have been waiting for Brimmer. Regaining his composure, the private detective pretends to be surprised by their suspicions and walks toward a garbage can. Just as he is about to dispose of the contact, a hand clamps down on his wrist. The contact is taken out of his hand by the pursuer he tried to shake, mislead and buy off—Columbo. Having incriminated himself, Brimmer confesses.

Funny thing, Kennicut observes, that Brimmer's car should break down just when Columbo thought of the contact lenses. Yes, Columbo agrees in a mysterious way, but, you know, in his mispent youth, he and his friends learned lots of nasty tricks. One was that a potato stuck in a tailpipe would keep a car from starting.

The first *Columbo* series episode actually filmed is very close in quality to "Murder by the Book." It also is one of only two series episodes scripted by Levinson and Link (although they came up with story ideas for several others).

Edward Abroms' editing, always a big plus for *Columbo*, keeps the story moving at a brisk pace and incorporates visual gems that delight the eye. Levinson and Link would make a point of crediting Abroms with adding a luster to each sequence his deft hand touched. The producers were so pleased with their film editor's efforts that they asked him to direct the last episode of the first season, "Short Fuse."

Taking its cue from *Ransom for a Dead Man*, "Death Lends a Hand" (even the title is fiendishly clever) shows the murder in a manner that's as artful and inoffensive as possible. When Brimmer flies into a rage, the action shifts to slow motion. You see the animal snarl on his face, but the actual blow is left to our imagination. You see Mrs. Kennicut recoiling from the impact, but contact with the table is merely suggested by the clever editing and camera work. In a touch that is positively Hitchcockian, the glass tabletop shatters and crystalizes. We've seen nothing and everything.

Unlike most *Columbo* cases, "Death Lends a Hand" centers on a murder that is not premeditated and carefully planned. The killing is an accident. Still, Brimmer's ruthless nature and cruel temper keep us from developing any sympathy.

Robert Culp's Brimmer lacks the monumental vanity of Jack Cassidy's Ken Franklin, yet there's a controlled fury about this character that makes him somewhat more threatening. Again, Falk was blessed with an actor whose style complemented his.

"There's a nice moment in 'Death Lends a Hand,'" Levinson said. "Culp is eating in his office, and Peter leans over the table and gets his tie in the food. Culp just picked it up and mopped it off. That's not in the script. It just happened on the set."

The experience proved rewarding enough to earn Culp repeat guest-starring offers. Like Cassidy, he would play a *Columbo* murderer three times.

Gracing the episode with his presence is Oscar-winning actor Ray Milland (*The Lost Weekend*), a veteran of such suspense films as *The Ministry of Fear, Circle of Danger, The Thief* and Hitchcock's *Dial M for Murder*. Cast as an iron-willed publisher, he nonetheless lets great love and sorrow show through Arthur Kennicut's stern exterior. Yes, there is the classic *Columbo* parry-and-thrust game being played out by Culp and Falk, but Milland's portrayal gives "Death Lends a Hand" an enormously fascinating three-way tension. Not surprisingly, Milland was invited back the following season to play a guest murderer.

Levinson, Link and Falk had argued about Columbo being introduced as a police officer with an expired driver's license. Falk thought this was taking Columbo's sloppy nature too far. Ironically, the scene Falk finally agreed to shoot was edited out because of time considerations. But a scene left in the final cut shows Columbo on line at the motor vehicle bureau. That's where he gets the idea about Mrs. Kennicut wearing contact lenses. The much-debated setup, though, was gone.

FOOTNOTE **#2**: *The Car*

While "Death Lends a Hand" was in the planning stages, Levinson and Link decided that Columbo should have a dilapidated car to fit his personality. Falk resisted this idea, too. Columbo already had the wife, the cigar and the raincoat. That was enough. No more gimmicks were needed. (Another ironic footnote: Levinson and Link would be annoyed when writers and producers played too heavily on these gimmicks in later seasons).

"We finally talked Peter into looking at cars on the Universal backlot," Levinson said. "Bill and Peter went over to take a look."

"There was an immense selection," Link recalled. "There was every make and model imaginable. Peter didn't like any of them."

"They all looked alike," Falk explained. "There were hundreds and hundreds of cars in this garage. It was the day before we were to start shooting, and they wanted me to pick out a car. As an actor, it was like trying to find the right hat for a part. I finally told Bill, 'I don't see anything. Let's go.' Just as we were walking out, way back in a corner, I just saw the nose of a car sticking out. They said, 'This one doesn't even run. It doesn't even have an engine in it.' I said, 'This is the one.'"

"It looked like an orphan," Link said.

The car was, in fact, a silver Peugeot of ancient vintage.

"Peter," Link said, "why would an L.A.P.D. cop be driving this unique foreign car?"

"Don't worry," Falk assured him, "the audience will like it. It's idiosyncratic."

It was a mess. Much of the trim was missing. There were more than a few dents to be found. The seats were torn. The black convertible top was ripped in places. And the rear-view mirror wouldn't stay in one position. You could say it was love at first sight. Columbo had a car.

You might also say that this car was the closest thing the series had to a regular supporting player. It would appear in most of the forty-three episodes, although travel could force the detective's wheezy wheels to take a much-needed rest ("Dagger of the Mind" is set in England and "Troubled Waters" is set at sea). Twice the car would be involved in accidents: a fender-bender at the beginning of "A Matter of Honor" and the spectacular collision with speeding police cars in "Make Me a Perfect Murder." In several episodes, the car serves as a rich source of humor ("Short Fuse," "Etude in Black," "Negative Reaction"). In the very last Columbo presented on NBC, the car gets a flat tire.

After Columbo ended its NBC run, Falk remained convinced that the car was safely stored on the Universal backlot where he first recognized the automobile that must belong to Lieutenant Columbo. When ABC announced plans to revive Columbo in 1988, Link discovered that Universal had sold the car. Parties in Florida and San Diego claimed to have the original Peugeot. Link guessed that one probably had the "stand-in" car. The car was found in Ohio.

Columbo surveys the wheezy engine of "the car." They were made for each other.

MEMORABLE EXCHANGES ABOUT COLUMBO'S CAR

"Etude in Black" (1972)

MECHANIC: Have you ever thought about getting a new car?
COLUMBO: I already have two cars. Of course, my wife drives nothing special. That's just for transportation. You understand.
MECHANIC: I only work on foreign cars.
COLUMBO: It is a foreign car.
MECHANIC: Oh, I know, but there are limits, man.

"Short Fuse" (1972)

ROGER STANFORD: You mean that old heap out there is yours?
COLUMBO: Oh, yeah. Needs a coat of paint, doesn't it?

"Any Old Port in a Storm" (1973)

VALET: Boy, you sure don't see very many of these things around.
COLUMBO: I've got over 100,000 miles on it. You take care of your car, it'll take care of you.

"Candidate for Crime" (1973)

POLICEMAN: You ever consider getting another car?
COLUMBO: I got another car. My wife drives it. But that's nothing special, just transportation.

"Mind Over Mayhem" (1974)

COLUMBO: I don't want you to work on my car. It's running beautiful.

"A Friend in Deed" (1974)

CHARLIE SHOUP (used car salesman): Yes, indeed. It's a real honey. You
know we don't get to see many of these around anymore—especially
in this condition.
COLUMBO: Well, I try to take good care of it.

"A Deadly State of Mind" (1975)

COLUMBO: But I don't see any European cars here. Only my car.
SERGEANT KRAMER: You've got a European car?
COLUMBO: That's a French car. Yeah, my car's a French car.

CASE #5: DEAD WEIGHT

(originally aired October 27, 1971)

Written by JOHN T. DUGAN
Directed by JACK SMIGHT
Produced by EVERETT CHAMBERS
Executive producers: RICHARD LEVINSON AND WILLIAM LINK
Associate producer: ROBERT F. O'NEILL
Story editor: STEVEN BOCHCO
Music Score: GIL MELLÉ
Sunday Mystery Movie Theme: HENRY MANCINI
Director of photography: RUSSELL L. METTY, A.S.C.
Art director: ARCH BACON
Film editor: RICHARD M. SPRAGUE
Set decorations: RICHARD FRIEDMAN
Assistant director: JACK BARRY
Sound: DAVID H. MORIARTY
Unit manager: HENRY KLINE
Editorial supervision: RICHARD BELDING
Costumes by BURTON MILLER
Main title design: WAYNE FITZGERALD
Titles and optical effects by UNIVERSAL TITLE

CAST

LT. COLUMBO	PETER FALK
MAJOR GENERAL MARTIN HOLLISTER	EDDIE ALBERT
HELEN STEWART	SUZANNE PLESHETTE
MRS. WALTERS	KATE REID
COLONEL ROGER DUTTON	JOHN KERR
HARRY BARNES	VAL AVERY
BERT	TIMOTHY CAREY
TV NEWSMAN	CLETE ROBERTS
OFFICER SANCHEZ	RON CASTRO
FIRST OFFICER	GLEN VERNON
SECOND OFFICER	JIMMY PELHAM
FIRST MARINE CADET	JIM HALFERTY

Synopsis—While sailing off a marina with her ever-critical mother, insecure Helen Stewart believes that she has seen a man in a bathrobe shoot a man in a uniform. The police are skeptical because the window and the house Helen points out belong to retired Marine general Martin Hollister, a beloved war hero.

But Helen's eyes were not playing tricks on her. Hollister had been visited by Colonel Roger Dutton, a Marine procurement officer who had been awarding the general's construction company lucrative military contracts at bargain-basement bids. Dutton had also allowed a fortune in phony cost overruns. The inspector general is starting a full investigation into all contracts, and Dutton feared that it was only a matter of time until his arrangement with Hollister was uncovered.

Rather than wait for the corruption to be traced to his office, Dutton had decided to go AWOL. He had booked passage to Geneva on a flight leaving that day. Hollister, however, wouldn't entertain the idea of a retreat. What if Dutton was discovered in hiding? What if he was forced to testify? What if he sold Hollister out in return for a shorter prison sentence?

Dutton was a risk that Hollister couldn't afford. Picking up the pearl-handled Colt .45 that he carried so many times into battle, the general coolly eliminated the only link to his dirty dealings.

Checking out Helen's report of a murder, Lieutenant Columbo shows up at Hollister's home. Two cadets are busy packing a coffin-size crate. The general explains that he's donating several uniforms, war trophies and military souvenirs for an exhibit at his alma mater, the Marine Military Institute. Hollister, who is about to leave for a testimonial dinner in his honor, puts on a gracious and understanding act for the police lieutenant. He lets Columbo look in any box and every closet.

What about that famous pearl-handled pistol? Unfortunately, Hollister says, that was stolen during the Korean War. A duplicate was made for the exhibit.

Columbo has to admit that there doesn't seem to be much evidence of murder, but Hollister is troubled by the possibility of a witness. He starts romancing Helen, and that makes Columbo suspicious.

When Dutton's body is found floating in a fishing channel, the lieutenant stays on Hollister's trail. It's at the newly opened Hollister Exhibit that Columbo discovers the evidence he needs.

It bothered Columbo that a man who cherishes every small war memento was careless enough to allow his trademark gun to be stolen. Maybe there never was a duplicate made. Maybe the so-called duplicate is the original.

Anybody else, Columbo says, would have thrown that gun away after the killing. But the general's tremendous pride and confidence would not let him part with so dear a memory. His ego demanded a crowning touch: Put the murder weapon on display in a museum where everyone can see it.

The magnificent bravado that carried Martin Hollister to battlefield victories has proved his undoing against Lieutenant Columbo.

If "Death Lends a Hand" was a slight step below "Murder by the Book," "Dead Weight" was a slight step below "Death Lends a Hand."

Although a thoroughly enjoyable *Columbo* episode, "Dead Weight" contains more holes than the one Hollister puts in Dutton.

The mystery fan will first quibble with the caliber of the gun that Hollister uses. In *Ransom for a Dead Man*, Leslie Williams used a .22 so there wouldn't be any traces of a murder in her living room. Hollister uses a .45 at close range. The results wouldn't be pretty. There's a good chance that the bullet would pass through the body and leave lots of evidence behind (lots of blood on Hollister's spic-and-span paneling and carpet). And a man so well acquainted with weapons should know better.

The second lapse in logic is the story about the duplicate gun. Why does Hollister make up that yarn about losing his beloved pearl-handled pistol in Korea? Is it to throw Columbo off the track? If so, it raises a barrage of inconsistencies. It would be easy to check the records. Was the gun reported stolen in Korea? Columbo would wonder why not. And if the gun wasn't stolen, why would Hollister keep it in hiding for more than fifteen years? Could he resist the chance to show it off at every opportunity? There must be plenty of witnesses who have seen the gun passed off as the genuine article. That would bother Columbo.

Okay, say the duplicate gun story wasn't fabricated for Columbo's sake (after all, at the time of the murder, the museum must know it's getting a copy). Then we have to ask why Hollister has been telling this story all these years. He hasn't been planning to use it in a murder. Either way, this gimmick doesn't work.

Several moments are reminiscent of *Ransom for a Dead Man*. A sequence in which Hollister maliciously makes Columbo seasick is little more than a reworking of Leslie Williams' dizzying airplane ride. It does set up one hilarious exchange, however. Hollister wonders how someone named Columbo could be so ill at ease on the water.

"It must have been another branch of the family, sir," Columbo queasily replies.

Still, "Dead Weight" overcomes the plot goofs and repetitions because Jack Smight keeps the focus on the excellent performances. The episode may be mediocre mystery, but it's long on character study. Playing to that strength, Smight's camera remains remarkably station-

ary, allowing the actors to carry the day. He conjures up one or two
unusual angles (an Orson Wellesian shot of Falk, up from the floor so
the ceiling is visible), yet there's a moody static quality to "Dead
Weight" that makes it an effective departure from "Murder by the
Book" and "Death Lends a Hand."

For once, a witness is every bit as fascinating as the murderer.
Suzanne Pleshette, a year away from becoming Emily Hartley on the
long-running *Bob Newhart Show*, plays Helen Stewart as a hard-luck
woman searching for happiness and a little self-confidence. You like
her, and you despise Hollister for exploiting her loneliness.

There's also fine work from Kate Reid, who, thirteen years later,
starred opposite Dustin Hoffman in the Broadway revival of Arthur
Miller's *Death of a Salesman*. Cast as Helen's domineering mother, she
brings depth to a role that easily could have come off as a shrill
stereotype.

Adding a note of authenticity to the episode is the presence of
veteran newscaster Clete Roberts, who actually reported action at
the front during the Korean War. He plays a television newsman de-
scribing Hollister's career. Roberts would make special visits to the
M*A*S*H set, portraying a broadcast journalist assigned to interview
members of the 4077th.

Finally, Eddie Albert is every inch the blood-and-guts war hero. He
carries on the tradition of the classy *Columbo* adversary. His portrayal
of Hollister is at times so chilling that we know why people use the
phrase cold-blooded murderer. His icy resolve makes a particularly
good contrast to Pleshette's warm vulnerability. Albert's grim performance must have come as quite a shock to fans who had just followed
him through six seasons of *Green Acres* (CBS, 1965–71).

FOOTNOTE **#3**: *The Murderers* or *The Quality of Evil*

Jack Cassidy, Robert Culp and Robert Vaughn were the quintessential
Columbo murderers. But you can't have Jack Cassidy, Robert Culp and
Robert Vaughn alternating as the murderer every three episodes.

Even though the field of possible actors was narrowed by the
Columbo formula, the series always attracted high-class villains—from
Eddie Albert to Ruth Gordon, from Janet Leigh to George Hamilton,
from Theodore Bikel to Louis Jourdan. Stars who wouldn't normally
do episodic television would gladly play a murderer on *Columbo*.

"The network was very hard-nosed about having name actors,"
Richard Levinson said. "That didn't turn out to be much of a problem,

The ideal Columbo *murderer—Jack Cassidy.*

because it was thought of as a prestige show. Once the show was a hit, you'd be surprised who wanted to be in it."

Roddy McDowall, a murderer during the first season, voices an opinion echoed by most guest stars: "Villains are always great fun to play, and these were very juicy roles. And remember, the villain got to be on camera and carrying on for twenty minutes before Columbo even showed up. *Columbo* was like *Alfred Hitchcock Presents*. It was very rewarding."

"I don't do a lot of guest-starring stuff," Robert Conrad said. "I'm usually the star of what I do. But I'd make an exception for *Columbo*. I really enjoyed working in a prestige show with quality people."

For the record, only nine of the guest murderers were women and none was black.

"We always talked about women and black actors," Levinson explained. "We talked about Sammy Davis, Jr. playing a real show business type. And we thought James Earl Jones would be perfect. There were no objections that I recall. It just never worked out.

"The network never liked it when we used British actors. The network didn't think that British actors had name value with American viewers. We liked them because they played well against Peter's New

York accent. We always wanted Christopher Plummer, and we never got him."

With that in mind, we submit for your approval (as Rod Serling would have put it) a list of ten actors who never played a *Columbo* murderer—but should have:

1. Christopher Plummer
2. James Earl Jones
3. Anthony Hopkins
4. Orson Welles
5. Hal Holbrook
6. Diana Rigg
7. Anthony Quayle
8. Sammy Davis, Jr.
9. Maurice Evans
10. Glenda Jackson

Notice that this list is limited to reasonable prospects (no one would have expected Olivier or Brando to show up for guest shots) who were active while *Columbo* was on the air. These are the might-have-beens, the could-have-beens and should-have-beens.

In the same spirit, let's try a list of ten actors who never played a *Columbo* murderer—and never should:

1. Edward Asner
2. Jack Klugman
3. Martin Balsam
4. Jack Warden
5. Ernest Borgnine
6. Penny Marshall
7. Robert Blake
8. Redd Foxx
9. Karl Malden
10. Claude Akins

In addition to high-class guest stars, *Columbo* needed high-class professions for the murderers. This would become increasingly difficult for the writers.

The first five killers numbered a psychiatrist, a lawyer, a private investigator catering to wealthy clients, a writer and a general. Now what?

"We were writing villains from the Yellow Pages," Levinson revealed. "We'd go through the book looking for possible occupations. Ironically, many were used in later seasons."

CASE #6: SUITABLE FOR FRAMING

(originally aired November 17, 1971)

Written by JACKSON GILLIS
Directed by HY AVERBACK
Produced by RICHARD LEVINSON AND WILLIAM LINK
Associate producer: ROBERT F. O'NEILL
Story editor: STEVEN BOCHCO
Music Score: BILLY GOLDENBERG
Sunday Mystery Movie Theme: HENRY MANCINI
Director of photography: RUSSELL L. METTY, A.S.C.
Art director: ARCH BACON
Film editor: BUDD SMALL
Set decorations: RICHARD FRIEDMAN
Assistant director: GIL MANDELIK
Sound: JAMES H. ALEXANDER
Unit manager: HENRY KLINE
Editorial supervision: RICHARD BELDING
Costumes by BURTON MILLER
Main title design: WAYNE FITZGERALD
Titles and optical effects by UNIVERSAL TITLE

CAST

LT. COLUMBO	PETER FALK
DALE KINGSTON	ROSS MARTIN
EDNA MATTHEWS	KIM HUNTER
FRANK SIMPSON	DON AMECHE
TRACY O'CONNOR	ROSANNA HUFFMAN
SAM FRANKLIN	VIC TAYBACK
MITILDA	JOAN SHAWLEE
CAPTAIN TYLER	BARNEY PHILLIPS
LANDLADY	MARY WICKES
MATRON	SANDRA GOULD
EVANS	CURT CONWAY
POLICEMAN	CLAUDE JOHNSON
PARKING BOY (JOE)	DENNIS RUCKER

Synopsis—Multimillionaire and greedy art collector Randy Matthews has decided to alter his will. His nephew, powerful art critic Dale

Kingston, will not receive the vast Matthews collection of priceless paintings.

Before the changes can become common knowledge, Dale shoots his uncle and makes it look like the work of art thieves who broke into the Matthews mansion. An electric blanket keeps the body warm while Dale attends the opening of an art gallery exhibit. His young protégée, art student Tracy O'Connor, stays at the mansion and waits for the exact moment when the security guard is scheduled to make his check. After removing the heated blanket, she fires a shot and runs out the back way. The guard rushes in to find a body that's still warm. Dale, who is dropping bon mots at the gallery, has the perfect alibi.

When the police start piecing together what happened, several details bother Lieutenant Columbo. How did the crooks beat the alarm system? He suspects that they had somebody on the inside. Secondly, the security officer heard the sound of high-heels running in the distance. A woman was involved.

Finally, the pattern of the robbery doesn't make any sense. At first, in the hall entrance, the thieves nabbed paintings of lesser value. In the murder room, during what had to be seconds before the killing, the crooks suddenly got smart and selected two valuable Degas pastels. Dale realizes that he staged the break-in badly. And he sees that Columbo won't be easily shaken.

Columbo's theory is that Dale had someone murder his uncle so he could inherit the art collection. The detective is stunned when lawyer Frank Simpson reads Matthews' will. The art treasures have been left to the murdered man's sweet but slightly scattered ex-wife, Edna. Maybe Dale didn't know about the changes, Columbo suggests. Ah, the art critic knew two weeks before the killing. He has a letter from his uncle to prove it.

Dale's plan is much more sinister than Columbo suspected. He shot his uncle and he now intends to frame Edna for the killing. Tracy threw the murder weapon in Edna's backyard, which is walking distance from her former husband's mansion. Dale will nail the case shut by getting the stolen paintings from Tracy and planting them in Edna's house.

Once the paintings have been transferred to his car, Dale picks up a rock and kills Tracy. Columbo is waiting back at the critic's house. He dropped by to look at a few art books.

Columbo notices that Dale is carrying a portfolio. He reaches to look at the paintings inside, but Dale puts him off, claiming fatigue.

The murder weapon is found, and Dale feigns concern for his vulnerable aunt. Edna couldn't kill anybody, he declares. To Dale's disgust, Columbo agrees with him. Edna is a very fragile person, the lieutenant says. He doesn't want to push her too hard. He'd hate to make another mistake. There will be no accusations until the case is airtight.

Edna tells Columbo that Randy had tired of the collection. She had convinced him to leave the paintings to museums and universities. Such lovely works should belong to the people. That's what led to the change in the will.

Dale suggests that Columbo search Edna's house. When he doesn't find anything, Edna can be scratched off the list of suspects. Columbo doesn't see any need for it, so Dale convinces Frank Simpson to go over the policeman's head. He claims it will protect Edna in the event that the district attorney decides to prosecute the person with the best motive.

The police search Edna's house and find the paintings. They immediately start dusting for fingerprints. Columbo tells Dale that he's still the primary suspect. Prove it, Dale demands. We can, Columbo says, with fingerprints.

That won't do any good at all, Dale informs him. His fingerprints would be all over those paintings.

No, not yours, Columbo says, "mine." He reminds Dale about that evening at his home, when he walked in with the portfolio. Columbo wanted to see the paintings inside. He grabbed for them. He touched them.

If Edna had stolen the paintings, how did Columbo's fingerprints get on them? Dale screams entrapment. Columbo must have just touched them now. The detective slowly removes his hands from the pockets of his raincoat. He's wearing gloves.

The first of several *Columbo* scripts written by Jackson Gillis, "Suitable for Framing" compares very favorably to "Murder by the Book" and "Death Lends a Hand." These three episodes are the crème de la crème of the first season.

A crafty writer, Gillis displayed particular cunning when crafting clever *Columbo* clues. It was a gift that Falk, Levinson and Link greatly appreciated and admired.

"Boy, Jackson could come up with some wonderful clues," Bill Link exclaimed. "Dick and I had been working on a clue using fingerprints. We just couldn't get it. We were hitting our heads against the wall. Jackson came up with the idea of the policeman's fingerprints being the pivotal clue. He really bailed Dick and me out on 'Suitable for Framing.' We were ready to kiss him.

"You see, most mystery writers get the ending first. You write backward. But in *Columbo*, you had to start with an interesting villain and

Unaware that one friend is framing another for murder, lawyer Frank Simpson (Don Ameche) tries to figure out where Columbo's investigation is heading ("Suitable for Framing").

a perfect crime. We rarely worked backward from the ending. They were very tough. When *Columbo* got in trouble, it was usually a weak ending. Some are very good. Some are weak. Because of Jackson, 'Suitable for Framing' is one of the best endings."

Nobody pushed for good clues harder than Falk.

"The *Columbo* format made it difficult to turn out scripts," he said. "There are a limited number of writers who can do this. There's a mind-set and a philosophy that make this type of writing tricky. And another big problem is that television is always so frantic. My ideal was to have five or six *Columbo* scripts on the shelf, sitting there. Why can't television have it done in advance? Get them right before you start doing them.

"You have to be careful with *Columbo*. There are real clues and there are things that just have the appearance of being clues. There are real clues that have a genuine ingenuity and a real delight when the audience finds out what they are. The best kind of clue is the type where the audience says, 'Why didn't I think of that?' But at the same time, they're saying, 'Gee, that's clever.' Most clues are fake. They just manipulate. Real clues are hard to come by. They're like hen's teeth. When you get one, the ending is a delicious surprise. It's entertaining, brilliant, unpredictable yet totally convincing and satisfying in every way. They're rare."

Directed by television veteran Hy Averback, "Suitable for Framing" (the fourth pun title in a row) also benefits from one of the strongest all-around casts ever assembled for a *Columbo*. Vic Tayback, later Mel in the movie *Alice Doesn't Live Here Anymore* and the CBS series version (*Alice*), has some nice moments as avant-garde artist Sam Franklin (Falk has a marvelous time in the scene where Columbo, thoroughly flustered and embarrassed by the presence of a nude model, tries to question Franklin). Wonderful character actress Mary Wickes has a cameo as Tracy O'Connor's gossipy landlady. Joan Shawlee, an Abbott and Costello graduate who played Pickles on *The Dick Van Dyke Show*, plays flamboyant art gallery owner Mitilda. Kim Hunter, an Academy Award winner for *A Streetcar Named Desire*, makes an endearing Edna. Don Ameche, who would go on to overcome a ten-year career slump and win an Oscar for *Cocoon*, (1985), is typically stalwart and dignified as Frank. And Ross Martin, best known as Artemus Gordon on *The Wild, Wild West*, is still another worthy addition to Columbo's rogues gallery. Thirty-two years before "Suitable for Framing," twelve-year-old Peter Falk got his first taste of acting while attending summer camp in upstate New York. His dramatics counselor was Ross Martin.

CASE #7: LADY IN WAITING

(originally aired December 15, 1971)

Written by STEVEN BOCHCO
  (from a story by Barney Slater and Ted Leighton)
Directed by NORMAN LLOYD
Produced by EVERETT CHAMBERS
Executive producers: RICHARD LEVINSON AND WILLIAM LINK
Associate producer: ROBERT F. O'NEILL
Story editor: STEVEN BOCHCO
Music Score: BILLY GOLDENBERG
Sunday Mystery Movie Theme: HENRY MANCINI
Director of photography: RUSSELL L. METTY, A.S.C.
Art director: ARCH BACON
Film editor: EDWARD M. ABROMS
Set decorations: RICHARD FRIEDMAN
Assistant director: RALPH FERRIN
Sound: DAVID H. MORIARTY
Unit manager: HENRY KLINE
Editorial supervision: RICHARD BELDING
Costumes by BURTON MILLER
Main title design: WAYNE FITZGERALD
Titles and optical effects by UNIVERSAL TITLE

CAST

LT. COLUMBO	PETER FALK
BETH CHADWICK	SUSAN CLARK
BRYCE CHADWICK	RICHARD ANDERSON
PETER HAMILTON	LESLIE NIELSEN
MRS. CHADWICK	JESSIE ROYCE LANDIS
CHARLES	JOEL FLUELLEN
SECOND DETECTIVE	RICHARD BULL
FIRST DETECTIVE	GARRY WALBERG
HOSTESS	BARBARA RHOADES
HEARING OFFICER	JON LORMER
FRED	FRANK BAXTER
WAITRESS	SUSAN BARRISTER

Synopsis—Family corporation chairman Bryce Chadwick has forbidden his mousy younger sister, Beth, to marry dynamic and ambitious company lawyer Peter Hamilton. Bryce believes that Peter is nothing but a fortune hunter.

There's nothing in Peter's background or character to justify this accusation. In fact, Bryce agrees that the corporation's attorney is honest and dedicated. Bryce just can't accept the notion that someone might be interested in Beth for reasons aside from her money. Since Beth refuses to cut the affair off, he has taken matters into his own hands.

Bryce has sent a letter to Peter. It contains an ultimatum: leave Beth alone or submit your resignation. Bryce is certain that his strategy will force Peter to reveal his true colors.

This interference, however, is not swallowed meekly by his sister. The letter is the last straw for Beth, who was dominated by her father and is now similarly kept under thumb by her brother.

While Bryce is asleep, Beth takes the house key from his key ring. The next day, she puts a burned-out lightbulb in the outdoor lamp over the front door.

Her plan seems foolproof: The servants will be gone that night. Beth will be alone in the house. Bryce will come home late. The front light won't work. He'll be unable to find his key. He'll try to wake up Beth. She'll tell him to come in through the full-length sliding windows in her bedroom. When he does, the burglar alarm will go off and she'll shoot him. Then she'll replace the missing house key on his ring and throw the keys in a bush near the front door, making it look as if Bryce had dropped them there. When the police arrive, Beth will tell them that she had taken pills and was in a deep sleep. Bryce, she will claim, set off the alarm when he came through the window. The alarm woke her up. Frightened and still very drowsy from the pills, Beth will tell the police, she grabbed for the burglar gun she kept in her bedside table. She fired, thinking Bryce was a thief—a case of accidental homicide. The police will surmise that Bryce couldn't find his keys in the dark.

But things go slightly wrong that night. Beth didn't count on the spare key that Bryce keeps in a hanging flower pot. While she is waiting for him to come through the window, Bryce casually walks in her bedroom door. She fires.

Now Beth has to move fast. Peter, just back from a business trip, has read Bryce's letter and is at the front gate. He hears the shots and sprints toward the house.

Beth moves the body near the window. She breaks a window to make it appear as if Bryce had broken in. She sets off the alarm and puts the key back on his ring. She drops the key in the bushes and pockets the bothersome spare. Peter, who was on his way over to have it out with Bryce, arrives in time to call the police.

It certainly looks like an accident, but Lieutenant Columbo is bothered by a few details. There is a late edition newspaper found in the front hall. Where did it come from? A home delivery boy would have brought an earlier edition. Peter says it isn't his. Beth says that she was at home all day. Bryce supposedly came through the window and wasn't in that part of the house.

Then there's the matter of Bryce's shoes. If he marched around the house and climbed through the window, they would have dewy grass and dirt on them.

What bothers Columbo most, though, is Beth's behavior. Overnight, she's been transformed into a cool and confident businesswoman. She quickly assumes command of the family corporation. She gets a new hairstyle. She buys a new wardrobe.

Peter is somewhat dismayed by the "new" Beth. Never interested in her money, he always did love her. Yet it's Peter who supplies the conclusive evidence against Beth. It's in his testimony given at the inquest. He heard the shots. Then he started running. Then he heard the alarm. If it happened the way Beth said, Peter would have heard the alarm first, then the shots.

Once in a very great while, Columbo actually despised a murderer (see "A Stitch in Crime," "An Exercise in Fatality" and "Murder Under Glass"). In these few instances, beyond the challenges of the case, he greatly enjoyed snaring the sneering culprit.

Less infrequently, he genuinely felt sorry for someone pushed into such a dastardly act (see "Any Old Port in a Storm," "Swan Song," "Forgotten Lady" and "The Bye-Bye Sky High I.Q. Murder Case"). "Lady in Waiting" is the first entry in this category.

Although not among the finest of the first season episodes, "Lady in Waiting," like "Dead Weight," overcomes standard mystery plotting through the strength of the performances. Susan Clark, just starting her television career, elicits our sympathy for Beth Chadwick, a victim of arrogance and chauvinism.

Clark would go on to win an Emmy for her work in the TV movie *Babe* and star in the ABC series *Webster*. At the time, though, she was the least known of the guest murderers hired for the 1971–72 season.

"I was under contract to Universal," Clark said, "and if they had told me to sweep the floor, I would have done it. When that script came down, I knew it was a plum. It interested me because it was the mouse that roared. You started off as one character and then became another. It was fun to get into different looks and attitudes.

"Universal had something like fifteen hours of television on the air at that time. You felt like you were on top of the world at that studio.

But nobody thought that *Columbo* was going to become a cult favorite. I knew I was lucky to get the part, but it was just a job."

The actress, like most of the *Columbo* guest stars, has nothing but praise for Falk.

"Peter had a lot of energy," she said. "The show was ahead of its time in a lot of ways, so it was very challenging. Peter loved improvisation. You had to be up to work with him. He didn't compete, but he did test you. If you had it, then everything clicked."

Also contributing fine characterizations to the episode are Richard Anderson (later the boss of both *The Six Million Dollar Man* and *The Bionic Woman*), Leslie Nielsen (in the first of two *Columbo* appearances; interestingly, neither was as a murderer) and Jessie Royce Landis. Echoing Mrs. Walters (Kate Reid) in "Dead Weight," Mrs. Chadwick tells Lieutenant Columbo, "I must say, you hardly look the role."

Still, it's rather amazing that "Lady in Waiting" is any good at all. It was during the filming of this episode that Falk waged his greatest battle with Universal. The studio had promised the actor that he could direct a *Columbo*. Time was running out. This was the fifth of the series' original six-show order. Now the studio executives were adopting the position that Falk had been hired to act, not to direct. The star's reaction took Universal by surprise. He walked off the studio lot and went home.

"That was very exciting," Clark remembered. "He made a point of coming up to me and saying, 'Nothing personal. I think you're a terrific actress, but we have this problem.' He decided to make his contractual ploy right there, so we did what we could without him. They had promised him that he could direct. He knew the writing on the wall. They had kept putting him off. He wasn't born yesterday. He just said, 'Let me know when you're ready to talk.'"

In fact, Falk made a point of courteously explaining his position to the cast and crew.

"It was a delight working with Peter and Susan Clark," director Norman Lloyd recalled. "One day, Peter came up to me and said, 'Now, Norman, I don't want you to take this personally, but I'm having trouble with my negotiations with the studio. I'm not going to be around for a little while.'"

Levinson and Link were again caught in the middle. The producers had been maintaining a tight and feverish schedule (Falk's departure for Broadway loomed closer and closer); now, through no fault of their own, that careful program was disintegrating.

Falk was suspended. There were notes from his doctor, claiming that the actor was too sick to work. There were threats of legal action. Falk would not budge.

"There was this great contention between him and the studio over whether he was going to direct, which created more pressures for us," Levinson said. "Falk shouldn't have won. It was a first-year show. It would have been tough for him to have directed and be on screen so much. And the show wasn't even on the air yet. But he held the studio hostage, and he did it before we knew we had a hit. We said, 'If you want to let him direct, that's your business.' We wanted to get back to work."

What caused Universal to fold? NBC was getting over its early uneasiness about *Columbo*. Network executives were extremely pleased by the footage they were seeing. They were mortified by the idea that there would be no *Columbo* in the fall. They even asked for a seventh episode.

Falk had won. Universal told Levinson and Link to find a script for him to direct.

During the suspension period, the producers had hired an actor, dressed him in the raincoat and filmed scenes from behind. The idea was that Falk would later dub in his voice. It wasn't necessary, yet the measure gave the producers a chance to rib their star.

"When Dick Irving suspended Peter, we got the famous midget—a short guy who looked like Peter from the back," Dick Levinson said. "When Peter came back, I told him, 'We had problems while you were gone. We had to close down.' Peter asked why. I said, 'The midget wants to direct.'"

Despite the delays, Lloyd delivered an atmospheric episode. He had been a producer and director with Alfred Hitchcock's series, so it's not surprising that "Lady in Waiting" has several Hitchcockian touches. Levinson and Link had once worked for producer Lloyd. Lloyd was now working for producers Levinson and Link.

The "Lady in Waiting" war set the pattern for Falk's future skirmishes with the studio. The actor would demand a bigger salary, higher budgets or longer shooting schedules. The studio would fight. The star would wait them out and prevail.

During one of these confrontations, Sheinberg's replacement at Universal made an interesting proposal to Levinson and Link.

"It looked like Peter was only going to do a couple of *Columbos*," Levinson said. "Frank Price, the then-head of television here, came up with the idea of bookending with a Falk *Columbo* at the beginning and a Falk *Columbo* at the end. And in the middle, he'd let four or five other actors play the role. Art Carney as Columbo one week. Orson Welles as Columbo in the next episode. He said, somewhat sardonically, 'It's like Hamlet. Let different actors try to play it.'"

CASE # 8: SHORT FUSE

(originally aired January 19, 1972)

Written by JACKSON GILLIS
  (from a story by Lester and Tina Pine and Jackson Gillis)
Directed by EDWARD M. ABROMS
Produced by RICHARD LEVINSON AND WILLIAM LINK
Associate Producer: ROBERT F. O'NEILL
Story editor: STEVEN BOCHCO
Music Score: GIL MELLÉ
Sunday Mystery Movie Theme: HENRY MANCINI
Director of photography: HARRY WOLF, A.S.C.
Art director: ARCH BACON
Film editor: JOHN KAUFMAN, JR.
Set decorations: CHARLES S. THOMPSON
Assistant director: KEVIN DONNELLY
Sound: MELVIN M. METCALFE, SR.
Unit manager: HENRY KLINE
Editorial supervision: RICHARD BELDING
Costumes by BURTON MILLER
Main title design: WAYNE FITZGERALD
Special photographic effects by ALBERT WHITLOCK
Titles and optical effects by UNIVERSAL TITLE

CAST

LT. COLUMBO	PETER FALK
ROGER STANFORD	RODDY MCDOWALL
DORIS BUCKNER	IDA LUPINO
DAVID BUCKNER	JAMES GREGORY
EVERETT LOGAN	WILLIAM WINDOM
BETTY BISHOP	ANNE FRANCIS
SERGEANT	STEVE GRAVERS
MURPHY	LAWRENCE COOK
NANCY	ROSALIND MILES
FARRELL	LEW BROWN
POLICEMAN	JASON WINGREEN
FERGUSON	EDDIE QUILLAN
PINSTRIPE	STUART NISBET
GIRL	ANNETTE MOLEN

PLAINCLOTHESMAN .... JIM NEUMARKER
MAN .... GEORGE SAWAYA

Synopsis—Boyish but brilliant research scientist Roger Stanford is upset by developments at the Stanford Chemicals plant, a business started by his late father. His uncle, corporation head David "D.L." Buckner, wants to force Roger out and sell the company.

To ensure Roger's cooperation, D.L. has had his nephew investigated. Spying has uncovered some embarrassing stains on the irresponsible Roger's record: gambling, drugs, car theft. It would be a shame if D.L.'s wife, Roger's doting aunt Doris, would see this report.

Doris, like Roger and company attorney Everett Logan, opposes the selling of Stanford Chemicals. D.L. will suppress his findings if Roger uses his influence to change his aunt's mind.

Rather than submit to blackmail, Roger uses his scientific genius to plot his uncle's murder. He rigs a cigar box to explode seconds after the lid is opened. Spare cigars are removed from the glove compartment of his uncle's car, and the box is placed with the rest of the luggage prepared for a short trip. That night, on a dangerous mountain road near a resort, an explosion kills D.L. and his chauffeur.

At the Buckners' home, Lieutenant Columbo learns that D.L. had used his car phone to leave a message for Doris on their answering machine. They can hear D.L. opening his cigar box.

As the tape continues, Columbo notices how agitated Roger has become. He keeps looking at his watch. The message ends just seconds before the explosion, yet a sudden noise caused by Columbo's stumble makes the young man jump in fright. Doris takes his nervousness for concern.

It looks as if the bomb was in the cigar box. Roger has made sure that suspicion will fall on Everett. Just when it looks as if the case is closed, Columbo announces that some startling new evidence has been found. He rushes to the murder area with Roger and Everett.

Columbo is handed a package and they board a tram that will quickly get them to the resort where Doris is waiting. What is the evidence? It is D.L.'s charred yet remarkably intact cigar box.

This is good news, Columbo announces. It means that D.L. wasn't murdered. The limousine's gas tank must have blown up, throwing the cigar box clear. To Roger's horror, the police lieutenant opens the box.

Seconds go by. Roger's panic builds. In a frenzy, he grabs the box and searches for the tube with the bomb. Columbo and Everett look

Columbo confronts boyish murderer Roger Stanford (former child star Roddy McDowall). Despite McDowall's "joyously evil" performance, "Short Fuse" is one of the weaker Columbo episodes.

on knowingly. There is no bomb, of course. This is just a box taken from Everett's office. Columbo has staged this scene to get Roger to incriminate himself.

Although not the last episode aired during the first season, "Short Fuse" was the last to be filmed. And it's the least of the seven.

Levinson and Link had given "Short Fuse" to Edward Abroms to direct. It was their way of saying thank you for the outstanding work he had done as film editor on *Ransom for a Dead Man*, "Death Lends a Hand" and "Lady in Waiting." The fault does not fall on Abroms' shoulders, however. There simply wasn't time to fashion a first-class mystery. This was the seventh episode NBC asked for after the production team had somehow managed to complete the original six-show order ahead of schedule. Yes, with rookie producers at the helm, with the only star walking off, with the artistic battles and the lack of good writers, *Columbo* had wrapped things up with time to spare. Now the network was asking for just one more thing.

"The network was so pleased with what they were seeing that they wanted the seventh," Dick Levinson said. "We were furious. We didn't want to do another one. We had just done all of those pictures in a very short time frame with no scripts ready."

So, "Short Fuse" was shot under even more hectic conditions than the other six.

"It's just not as strong as the others in the first season," Falk commented.

There was little time for the sharpening and polishing that Levinson, Link and Bochco usually brought to a script. As a result, "Short Fuse" (first titled "Formula for Murder") is badly paced. Scenes end abruptly, disturbing the delicate balance.

Yet there are some wonderful moments in the episode. Abroms' direction is at times very clever and inventive. Borrowing a technique used in the *Mystery Movie* credits, he focuses in and out of scenes: blur to sharp, sharp to blur. While hardly a new trick, it enhances the episode (as nicely as Albert Whitlock's photographic effects) because McDowall's character is also supposed to be an avid photographer.

And Abroms' splendid tram finale is a tense bit of claustrophobic suspense. It's a memorable conclusion to one of the less memorable *Columbo* outings.

"Short Fuse" is given badly needed boosts by the typically strong performances of Windom (Burt Gordon in *Prescription: Murder*) and McDowall.

Even though McDowall was in his early forties, the actor could still pass for a man in his twenties. He brings a contagious enthusiasm to the role.

"He was evil as all get-out," McDowall said of Roger Stanford. "He was joyously evil. It was appetizing to play. The role could only work if it was done on a high level of enjoyment. He loved being this son of a bitch. And I loved working with Ida Lupino and Jimmy Gregory."

CASE # 9: BLUEPRINT FOR MURDER

(originally aired February 9, 1972)

Written by STEVEN BOCHCO
   (from a story by William Kelley and Ted Leighton)
Directed by PETER FALK
Produced by RICHARD LEVINSON AND WILLIAM LINK
Associate producer: ROBERT F. O'NEILL
Story editor: STEVEN BOCHCO
Music Score: GIL MELLÉ
Sunday Mystery Movie Theme: HENRY MANCINI
Director of photography: LLOYD AHERN, A.S.C.
Art director: ARCH BACON
Film editors: ROBERT L. KIMBLE, A.C.E. AND CHRIS KAESELAU
Set decorations: CHARLES S. THOMPSON
Assistant director: WILLIAM HOLE
Sound: ROGER A. PARISH
Unit manager: HENRY KLINE
Editorial supervision: RICHARD BELDING
Costumes by BURTON MILLER
Main title design: WAYNE FITZGERALD
Titles and optical effects by UNIVERSAL TITLE

CAST

LT. COLUMBO	PETER FALK
ELLIOT MARKHAM	PATRICK O'NEAL
BEAU WILLIAMSON	FORREST TUCKER
GOLDIE WILLIAMSON	JANIS PAIGE
JENNIFER WILLIAMSON	PAMELA AUSTIN
MISS SHERMAN	BETTYE ACKERMAN
DR. MOSS	JOHN FIEDLER
CARL	JOHN FINNEGAN
GUARD	NICK DENNIS
CLERK	ROBERT GIBBONS
OFFICER WILSON	CLIFF CARNELL
WORKMAN	JIMMY JOYCE

Synopsis—Flamboyant Texas tycoon Beau Williamson returns from a long trip abroad to learn that brilliant architect Elliot Markham has persuaded his wife, young Jennifer Williamson, to fund a revolutionary multi-million-dollar office complex: Williamson City. Beau is not touched (except in his wallet) by the honor. He knows a hustler when he sees one.

A charming sophisticate, Elliot is using the naive Jennifer to get at Beau's money.

In a rage, Beau storms into Elliot's office and smashes the scale model of Williamson City. He then drives out to the construction site and confronts the architect.

"Nobody puts a lasso around my money without my consent," Beau shouts at Elliot. There won't be any money to build cities.

What would happen, Elliot wonders, if something unforeseen were to befall the freewheeling millionaire? Don't get any big ideas, Beau answers. If he dies, the Williamson fortune goes into trust. Jennifer gets a comfortable income, but not enough to fund anything like Williamson City.

The devious architect sees a way out. Elliot goes out to Beau's horse farm and hides in the industrialist's car. When Beau gets into the car, thinking he's alone, Elliot emerges from the back and forces him at gunpoint into a nearby stable. After the door is closed, a shot is heard.

Elliot then drives Beau's car to the airport. Jennifer and friends will assume that the unpredictable Texan just took off on one of his frequent globe-trotting expeditions. If Beau isn't declared dead, Jennifer can spend his money in any manner she thinks fit.

There would be no trouble if it wasn't for Goldie, Beau's bawdy first wife. She's told the police that he is dead. Why? Beau wouldn't have left town without calling her, she says. There can be only one reason: he can't.

Although there is no real evidence of foul play, Lieutenant Columbo investigates. Something bothers him about Beau's car. There are only country music tapes in the car. Goldie and Jennifer both say that's all he listened to, yet the car radio is tuned to a classical music station.

During a visit to Elliot's office, Columbo notices two things: the wrecked model of Williamson City and that the architect likes classical music.

Columbo takes Goldie's claims even more seriously when he learns that Beau didn't show up for an appointment with his heart specialist. The energy cell in his pacemaker needs replacing.

While attending one of Elliot's university lectures, the police lieutenant is intrigued by information about the pyramids of Egypt. The pharaohs would bury architects and workers in the structure to make sure secrets died with them. Could Elliot have dumped Beau's body in a deep excavation on the construction site? Covered by tons of concrete and steel, it would be in a perfect hiding place.

Columbo does some checking and discovers that a hole was filled the day after Beau disappeared. If you're so sure, Elliot tells him, dig it up.

He does. To Columbo's embarrassment, there's nothing to be found. Elliot can't help rubbing in the victory.

That night, Elliot drives to the stables and gets the body. Now he'll dump it into the excavation. The police have already searched there.

But Columbo is waiting for him. He had to ask himself why Elliot kept trying to finesse him into digging up that hole. He's not a stupid man. He'd never do it if Beau was really buried there.

"It's just that music thing that bothered me," Columbo tells Elliot. "Carnegie Hall and Nashville. They don't mix."

When Falk returned from his suspension, he was a hero to the actors at Universal and in television. He had taken on the system and won. Levinson and Link, however, were not feeling so kindly toward their star.

Having been helpless observers to the tug-of-war between star and studio, they were feeling vengeful (their description). With wicked glee, they assigned Falk the most difficult script to direct. Much of the action was set on a construction site, where incessant noise and activity would make rehearsing and filming a maddening treadmill of frustration. Interruptions would be constant as work crews went about their business.

"From the standpoint of difficulties, we gave him the worst one to direct," Levinson said.

Still, Falk surprised his producers. His preparations were impeccable. Despite a cold, he spent long hours and weekends at the Century City location, planning shots and camera angles.

"When he was directing, he called on Spielberg and [close friend John] Cassavetes for advice," Levinson said. "That was one of the first examples of Spielberg helping another director."

Levinson and Link would drive over to Century City so they could smile down on the harried director. Falk would pause long enough to shake his fist at them.

Norman Lloyd also visited the location.

"Peter remained dedicated to quality," he recalled. "He had this dreadful excavation scene, and he wanted twenty-five extras to make it look good. The studio would only give him eight. He paid for the others out of his own pocket."

Levinson and Link had mixed reactions to the finished product.

"Our feeling was that he did a good job directing, but not so good playing the character," Levinson said.

The producers believed that the drain of directing had slightly hurt his performance. They detected a manic quality creeping into his usually low-key portrayal of Columbo.

Perhaps Falk agreed with them. He would gain greater and greater control over the series, but the actor would never again direct a *Columbo* episode.

Actually, Levinson and Link may have been reading Falk's on-location agitations into the characterization. On first viewing, the Columbo of "Blueprint for Murder" doesn't seem noticeably different from the Columbo of "Suitable for Framing" and "Lady in Waiting." Second, third and fourth screenings justify the verdict.

And if not in the same class as "Murder by the Book," "Death Lends a Hand" and "Suitable for Framing," "Blueprint for Murder" is several cuts above "Dead Weight," "Short Fuse" and "Lady in Waiting."

Indeed, "Blueprint for Murder" completely vindicates Falk's demand to direct. Forrest Tucker blazes through his brief stint as a guest victim. Patrick O'Neal makes a wickedly smooth murderer. And Columbo's delightful scenes with Goldie Williamson (Janis Paige) sparkle with genuine affection.

Bochco remains quite fond of "Blueprint for Murder." "I got a big kick out of that one," he said.

It was the most expensive of the seven initial episodes, but budget overruns could be overlooked in the wake of NBC's enthusiasm for the series.

In the final scene, Columbo, having been warned by a doctor to quit smoking, starts to light a cigar. Instead, he throws it away and gets in a waiting police car. No one knew if *Columbo* would be back for a second season, so Levinson and Link probably wanted a fitting finale—just in case.

Summing Up the First Season

Seven *Columbo* episodes had been completed in about five months. Three were outstanding. The other four were miles ahead of the mystery shows being produced for network television.

As Falk's departure for New York approached, Levinson and Link noticed they were getting along better and better with their star. They had battled their way to mutual respect.

While *Prisoner of Second Avenue* was establishing itself as a hit of the Broadway season, *Columbo* was being hailed as the jewel of the fall television season. With the good lieutenant leading the way with regular finishes in the Nielsen ratings service's top-ten shows, *The NBC Mystery Movie* became the fourteenth highest-rated series of the 1971–72 season.

But the ratings only tell part of the story. *Columbo*-mania was sweeping the country. Comedians were latching on to Columbo's catchphrases. Cab drivers in New York were yelling their Columbo impersonations at Falk. Backstage visitors at *Prisoner* were asking about *Columbo*. Stage door mobs pleaded for autographs from Columbo.

By January of 1972, a rumor was making the rounds that the show wouldn't return for a second season. Levinson and Link laughed it off. NBC, Universal and Falk were all eager for more *Columbos*. The producers were at work on scripts for the 1972–73 season. Falk's Broadway contract would end in June, when *Columbo* was scheduled to go back into production.

Levinson and Link, though, had decided against producing the second season. They were tired of the demands made by a series. They wanted to get to work on a TV movie.

"In fact, we got so busy with *That Certain Summer* that we didn't have any time to enjoy the success of *Columbo*," Dick Levinson said. "We had a blockbuster hit and we wanted to wallow in it, but we were already deep into other projects. We were so glad to get out of the series. The only regret was not having time to enjoy its success."

There was one brief moment to wallow—May 6, 1972, the night of the National Academy of Television Arts and Sciences' annual Emmy awards. Because of the rules that year, *Columbo* was up against the

Masterpiece Theatre miniseries *Elizabeth R* in both the Outstanding Dramatic Series and the Outstanding New Series categories. It lost to the British import each time.

Yet Falk won the Emmy for Outstanding Continued Performance by an Actor in a Leading Role in a Dramatic Series. Edward Abroms picked up a statuette for Best Editing. And every writer nominated in the Outstanding Achievement in Drama (Series) category was the author of a *Columbo* episode.

"We all went to the awards together," Dick Levinson recalled. "Steve Bochco and his wife, Jackson Gillis and his wife, Bill, who wasn't married at the time, and my wife and I all sat at the same table. We were competing with each other. We were the nominees. Bill and I thought Bochco was going to get it. We thought 'Murder by the Book' was the best of the first season and it would win the Emmy, so we made a deal. The winners had to take the losers for an enormously expensive lunch. We figured we'd get a good lunch out of it. And we won [for 'Death Lends a Hand'], so we had to take them to lunch.

"My wife was applauding madly until she realized that Steve and Jackson had lost. Of course, I don't feel sorry for Steve Bochco. He's only won about a thousand Emmys."

Actually, Bochco would walk away from *Columbo* with something much more precious than an Emmy—experience.

"We wrote or rewrote just about every show of the first season," Levinson said. "We had to be careful. In one episode, somebody had Columbo giving his address. We cut it out. Another writer gave him a first name. We cut it out. Steve was great at character, but he didn't know structure. He says he learned a great deal about elaborate structuring, which served him well when he did *Hill Street Blues.*"

Yes, Bochco says almost exactly that: "I was so young. It was a formative process for me. Levinson and Link were enormously helpful in showing me how to structure a show. I was no fool. These guys are geniuses. I was twenty-six and I was functioning in a perfect environment. I was observing Bill and Dick as producers. I was getting a massive amount of input. Up to that point, it was the best work experience I'd had in my life. Dick Levinson remained one of my closest friends. I considered him one of my earliest and most influential mentors.

"I think they took me on because they needed a body. The title of story editor was a misnomer. I was a writer. I wrote my fingers off. Bill and Dick were looking over my shoulder all the way. I had never done anything like that before. Professionally, *Columbo* put me on the map. I remember with clarity the disappointment when I didn't win the Emmy, but I also remember being pleased for Bill and Dick."

Bochco learned one other thing from Levinson and Link—something he would remember when launching such innovative series as *Hill Street Blues* and *L.A. Law.*

"I watched them fighting for what they believed in," he said. "At the beginning, NBC had enormous problems with the show. There was always pressure to get Peter on earlier. They couldn't stand it that the people saw the crime right up front. I saw Bill and Dick go to war for what they believed the show should be."

When Falk returned to Universal after leaving Broadway, Levinson and Link told him that they wouldn't be producing the second season of *Columbo.* The actor was upset. He asked them to continue. The partners were caught off guard. Remember the fights and the intrigue? Why did he want them back?

"Because now I trust you," Falk said.

"It took a year to earn his trust and a monster hit," Levinson said.

PART III

THE SECOND SEASON (1972–73)

"That's my specialty, you know—homicide."

—LIEUTENANT COLUMBO
"Etude in Black" (1972)

The Return of the Raincoat

Before leaving to pursue other projects, Levinson, Link and Bochco prepared scripts and established some of the early groundwork for a second season of *Columbo*. The producing duties were put in the able hands of Dean Hargrove, the man who had written and produced *Ransom for a Dead Man*.

Hargrove was a wise and obvious choice to take over for Levinson and Link. He was already well acquainted with the character and, more importantly, Falk trusted him.

Trust was a very prominent word in the *Columbo* star's vocabulary. Falk was mistrustful of networks and studios, so he needed individuals he could rely on to deliver the quality he demanded. There would always be a producer, writer and/or story editor who had his confidence.

Falk had learned to trust Levinson, Link and Bochco. Their places would be taken, in various stages of succession, by Hargrove, Peter S. Fischer, Roland Kibbee, Edward K. Dodds, Everett Chambers, Jackson Gillis and, finally, by the actor's old friend from the *Trials of O'Brien* days, Richard Alan Simmons.

Most of these men were writers. Considering how much Falk appreciated a strong script, that isn't surprising.

Not only was Hargrove a writer and producer with Columbo experience, he was a Universal veteran who enjoyed the challenges of producing. *Columbo* had been a debilitating trial for Levinson and Link. Hargrove found it much smoother sailing.

"It wasn't at all frustrating for me," he said. "There were always changes to be made and every script was rewritten to some extent, but I don't recall any serious clashes with Peter over material. Peter is a very idiosyncratic actor, so where he was difficult was time. Production was slowed down. But the proof is in the performance. The show was so successful that the studio swallowed the time and budget overruns."

Hargrove was in a position to see a trend develop that few others ever noticed or admitted to noticing.

"A lot of people started blaming their own failings on Peter," he said. "If things weren't going right, they'd say, 'Well, we have a difficult star.' Peter got a lot of bad raps for things he didn't deserve. He never said anything about that."

And if the sailing was a bit smoother during the second season, Hargrove knew it was because the route had been charted by Levinson and Link.

"The first year is always the most difficult," he explained. "I had the benefit of coming in after they had established the show. *Columbo* was a very popular show, so it was very helpful to my career. And it was a great experience."

Each of the remaining thirty-six *Columbo* episodes would carry the credit line, "Created by Richard Levinson and William Link." The team's official involvement with the series, however, was over. Still, they would keep a careful eye on the programs and continue to serve as unofficial, unbilled creative consultants. Well, not exactly creative consultants—more like ombudsmen.

"We had styled it, so Falk continued to call on us," Levinson said. "We would have lunch at the Universal commissary after every one of the new shows aired. And we'd discuss them. We didn't always agree with the people who came after us. In later years, other cops were deferential to Columbo. We hated that. I said, 'Never play him with subordinates. Always play him with superiors.' We also disagreed with too many close-ups."

Although the *Columbo* style was indeed set, changes were in store for the second season. Overjoyed with the popularity of its *Mystery Movie* slate, NBC moved the *Columbo/McCloud/McMillan and Wife* wheel to 8:30 P.M. Sundays for the 1972–73 season. A fourth detective, Richard Boone as *Hec Ramsey*, was added to the mix, but ol' Hec never quite caught on with the viewers. He lasted two seasons.

With *The NBC Sunday Mystery Movie* a sure winner for the season, the network filled the vacated Wednesday time slot with another Universal mystery package, *The Wednesday Mystery Movie*. This wheel consisted of George Peppard as *Banacek*, Richard Widmark as *Madigan* and James Farentino in *Cool Million*.

In fact, largely due to the influence of *Columbo*, there were character cops running all around prime time by the fall of 1973: *Banyon, Cannon, Barnaby Jones, The Magician, Shaft, The New Adventures of Perry Mason, Toma, Griff, Hawkins, Tenafly, The Snoop Sisters* and *Kojak*.

"*Columbo* ushered in the era of the character cop," Levinson said. "Columbo was the shabby man in elegant surroundings. Kojak was the elegant man in shabby surroundings. Columbo's cigar became Kojak's lollipop."

The Wednesday Mystery Movie didn't duplicate the original wheel's success, but a word about *Banacek*. Peppard's series may have had the most intricate and baffling mysteries of any detective show on television. Yet that's only half of the equation. Long on plotting, *Banacek* came up a little short on character. Thomas Banacek was a likable enough fellow. He just didn't have Columbo's enduring appeal. Several seasons later, Tom Selleck's long-running *Magnum, P.I.* would reverse the formula. While the stories were nothing to write home about, Thomas Magnum had charm to spare. The moral: It's better to have a strong character than strong writing when you want to last on commercial television. *Columbo* was blessed with both.

Television lives by another rule: If it works, steal it. So it was hardly shocking when ABC launched its own mystery wheel in 1972. *The Men*—Robert Conrad in *Assignment Vienna*, Laurence Luckinbill in *The Delphi Bureau* and James Wainwright in *Jigsaw*—flopped after one season. The moral: The Copy is rarely as sharp as The Original.

NBC had nervously suggested changes before *Columbo* had reached the air. Now that the series was a hit, the network pushed through a demand that would haunt the show.

NBC reasoned that if *Columbo* was a hit at ninety minutes, it would be an even bigger hit at two hours. *Columbo* spent the rest of its existence bouncing between the two running times. This wasn't the total creative "disaster" that Levinson and Link describe in *Stay Tuned*, but it was an unfortunate mistake.

The consensus is that *Columbo* worked best as a ninety-minute show.

"Against all of our advice," Dick Levinson said, "they pushed the show to two hours. They did it for financial reasons. You could charge more for more commercials. That part of it made good business sense, especially with an expensive show. It was easier to justify going over budgets. But the show was bloated at two hours. It was too long for this show to hold."

Link, Bochco, Hargrove and Falk agreed with him.

"*Columbo* was crisp at ninety minutes," Bochco said. "It worked best at ninety minutes. At two hours, it was a bit indulgent and inflated."

"I always thought they were too long at two hours," Hargrove commented. "*Columbo* was difficult enough to sustain over ninety minutes without having to add thirty minutes."

Still, even though *Columbo* was a natural ninety-minute series, the two-hour experiments were not all failures. After all, Hargrove had demonstrated in *Ransom for a Dead Man* that the format could be sustained over two hours. And some of the longer *Columbo* episodes, certainly "Any Old Port" and "Troubled Waters," rank with the series' best efforts.

But the point remains that *Columbo* was as innately a ninety-minute show as *The Twilight Zone* was a thirty-minute show. When Rod Serling's classic fantasy series ballooned to sixty minutes for its brief fourth season in 1963, there were a few outstanding scripts, but most seemed padded and a bit forced. The same judgment applies to *Columbo* at two hours: some gems, most burdened with unnecessary baggage.

"Some of the two-hour shows are all right," Falk said. "As a rule, you were safer at ninety minutes. You can tell the story better in ninety minutes."

For his part, Falk was overjoyed to be back playing a character he had truly grown to love. The actor was as eager to return to *Columbo* as viewers were for more episodes.

Between the Emmy ceremonies and the fall 1972 start of the second season, Falk made perhaps the most memorable of his many outrageous visits to Johnny Carson's *Tonight Show*. Carson repeatedly asked him about his rather humorous acceptance speech at the Emmys. Falk kept dutifully answering questions that the *Tonight Show* host never posed.

What about the Emmy speech? Falk told about the change in time slots. What about the Emmy speech? Falk told about the plot of the first new episode. What about the Emmy speech? Falk told about the jump from ninety minutes to two hours.

Finally, Carson asked a question about *Columbo*. "Oh, look, John," Falk deadpanned, "I don't want to plug the show."

Carson would have his revenge by doing a wickedly funny Mighty Carson Art Players spoof of *Columbo*. Each time the criminals in the skit thought they were rid of the pesky police lieutenant, he (Carson in wig and raincoat) would show up in a filing cabinet, closet or fireplace to ask just one more thing.

About ten years later, Peter Scolari would do a similar Columbo turn for an episode of ABC's *Bosom Buddies*. Falk had made Columbo part of our collective pop-culture consciousness.

CASE # 10: ETUDE IN BLACK

(originally aired September 17, 1972)

Written by STEVEN BOCHCO
    (from a story by Richard Levinson and William Link)
Directed by NICHOLAS COLASANTO
Produced by DEAN HARGROVE
Associate producer: EDWARD K. DODDS
Executive story consultant: JACKSON GILLIS
Music Score: DICK DE BENEDICTIS
Sunday Mystery Movie Theme: HENRY MANCINI
Director of Photography: HARRY WOLF, A.S.C.
Art director: ARCH BACON
Film editor: BUDD SMALL
Set decorations: JOHN MCCARTHY
Assistant director: BRAD ARONSON
Sound: EDWIN S. HALL
Unit manager: HENRY KLINE
Editorial supervision: RICHARD BELDING
Music supervision: HAL MOONEY
Costumes by GRADY HUNT
Special photographic effects by ALBERT WHITLOCK
Main title design: WAYNE FITZGERALD
Titles and optical effects by UNIVERSAL TITLE

CAST

LT. COLUMBO	PETER FALK
MAESTRO ALEX BENEDICT	JOHN CASSAVETES
JANICE BENEDICT	BLYTHE DANNER
LIZZI FIELDING	MYRNA LOY
JENIFER WELLES	ANJANETTE COMER
PAUL RIFKIN	JAMES OLSON
BILLY	JAMES MCEACHIN
MIKE ALEXANDER	DON KNIGHT
THE HOUSE BOY	PAT MORITA
SAM	MICHAEL PATAKI
DR. BENSON	MICHAEL FOX
AURDREY	DAWN FRAME
DURKEE	CHARLES MACAULAY

EVERETT .... GEORGE GAYNES
TV DIRECTOR .... WALLACE CHADWELL

Synopsis—Young and talented concert pianist Jenifer Welles is threatening to go public with details of her affair with brilliant symphony orchestra conductor Alex Benedict. Since Alex's strong-willed mother-in-law, Lizzi Fielding, is the chairman of the symphony board, he cannot risk the scandal.

Alex leaves his expensive foreign car at a garage and has his wife, Janice, drive him to the nearby Hollywood Bowl, where he is to conduct a young people's concert that night. While everyone believes that the maestro is taking a usual pre-performance nap in his dressing room, he is actually sneaking off the premises and to the garage. Already dressed in his tuxedo, Alex gets to his car (through the garage's bathroom window left open during his earlier visit), leaves unnoticed and drives to Jenifer Welles' apartment.

He asks her to play something by Chopin. When Jenifer's back is turned, Alex picks up a heavy ashtray and wraps it in a towel. He knocks his mistress unconscious and drags the body into the kitchen. He makes it appear as if she committed suicide, falling and striking her head when fumes from the gas oven overcame her. But the conductor doesn't notice that the flower he always wears in his lapel has fallen under the piano.

That night, when Jenifer fails to show up for the concert, Alex pretends to be in one of his typical fiery rages. He picks up the phone and angrily tries to call her. Janice notices that her husband knows the number by heart.

It certainly looks like suicide to the police, especially when they find the note Alex left in her typewriter: "I'm sorry for the trouble I'm causing, but life for me is no longer worth living." It was typed on Jenifer's personal stationery.

Jenifer's former lover, symphony musician Paul Rifkin, can't believe that this vibrant, beautiful woman could commit suicide. Lieutenant Columbo agrees with him. As usual, little things bother him.

Why would someone with everything to live for take her own life? Why didn't she save her pet cockatoo, Chopin? And the bump on the head is pretty severe. Somebody could have hit her.

Alex shows up to answer some routine questions. Picking up the lost boutonniere, he makes as if it just fell off his lapel. Facing television reporters as he leaves the house, the conductor is certain that he's removed the only piece of incriminating evidence.

Paul tells Columbo that Jenifer broke off their romance because she had started seeing a powerful man whose identity had to be kept secret. The police lieutenant suspects Alex.

First there's the matter of the maestro's car. The mechanic says that there was nothing really wrong with it, and the odometer showed an unexplainable nine extra miles on the morning after Jenifer's death. Nine miles is, of course, the exact distance of a round trip from the garage to Jenifer's apartment.

Then there's the suicide note. The police haven't removed the note from the typewriter in which it was found. But trying to type over an individual letter by striking the same key, Columbo notices that the letter he's typed doesn't match the existing print. It means that somebody typed the suicide note, took it out of the machine and then rolled it back in. Why would someone about to take her own life do that?

All of this is very interesting, as Alex points out, but it doesn't prove anything. Columbo gets his proof when he learns that the young people's concert was taped by the local public television station.

The tape shows that there is no flower in Alex's lapel during the concert. Where is it? It fell off, Alex says. But you picked up a flower at Jenifer's apartment on the night of the murder, Columbo reminds him.

Caught, Alex tries to bluff his way out. He says he didn't pick up a flower at Jenifer's apartment. He says it's only Columbo's word against his.

Columbo shows him a second piece of film—news footage of Alex leaving Jenifer's apartment on the night of the murder. There's a flower on his lapel, plain as day. Where did it come from? When Janice refuses to lie for him, Alex acknowledges that he's been trapped by "a great detective."

Even though it contains one of the series' best clues and finest guest murderers, "Etude in Black" is the first and most grievous example of an episode damaged by the two-hour running time.

"I like 'Etude in Black,' with an asterisk," said author Steven Bochco. "I wrote a ninety-minute version and it got me an Emmy nomination. They made Dean Hargrove rewrite it, expanding it to two hours. That hurt it."

Levinson concurred: "It was done as a ninety-minute show. That version was shown in Canada, and it was a hundred times better than the two-hour one."

"The ninety-minute version was sharply paced," Hargrove explained. "Adding thirty minutes was to the detriment."

Unfortunately, it's the two-hour version that remains in syndication. Obviously protracted, it reduces the effectiveness of Bochco's tautly written script and the sterling direction of Nicholas Colasanto (who would later endear himself to viewers as the foggy Coach on NBC's *Cheers*).

Still, "Etude in Black" emerges as one of the two best episodes of the second season. And that's hardly damning it with faint praise. As Bochco pointed out, "It was still a terrific show. I don't think the quality dipped at all when Dean took it over."

The episode gave Falk the opportunity to play opposite one of his closest friends, John Cassavetes. In 1970, director Cassavetes had made a feature film titled *Husbands*, which starred actor Cassavetes and his buddies Falk and Ben Gazzara. In 1974, director Cassavetes made a feature film titled *A Woman Under the Influence*, which starred his wife, Gena Rowlands, and Peter Falk. Both Gazzara and Rowlands would be involved with future episodes of *Columbo*.

But Cassavetes' appearance in "Etude in Black" goes beyond mere buddy casting. At this point in his career, the actor/director wasn't doing much episodic television and the series was fortunate to get him. He made a delicious counterpart to Falk, heightening the tension of the verbal chess match. Their scenes play on a level of high enjoyment.

Always ready to savor a good clue, Falk was delighted with the flower ploy concocted for "Etude in Black." Certainly Hargrove remembered it when he delivered the pilot TV movie of his lawyer/mystery series, *Matlock*, to NBC in 1986. The pivotal clue, presented in a courtroom scene, was remarkably similar.

"Yes, it was the same device," Hargrove admitted. "Good clues are hard to come by, and those kinds of devices are constantly being reused."

"Well," Levinson sighed, "you can't copyright a clue."

By 1986, *Columbo* had become something of a yardstick for television mysteries. The advertisements for *Matlock* carried the line, "Not since *Columbo* has catching a killer been this clever!"

FOOTNOTE #4: *Dog*

"Etude in Black" also deserves a special place in *Columbo* lore because it marks the debut of Dog, Columbo's pet basset hound. Dog had his origins in NBC's persistent demands for another continuing character.

Weary of the badgering, Levinson and Link merrily decided to comply with the network's wishes. They talked to Bochco, who was writing the opening episode of the second season.

"The network wanted a young cop to be his sidekick," Levinson recalled. "Bill, Bochco and I said, 'Let's give him a dog.' It was just a contemptuous swipe at the network."

Echoing his reaction to the car idea, Falk resisted the idea of a dog. This really was too much.

"Nick Colasanto loved the idea," Falk said. "My reaction was, he has the coat, the cigar, the car, the wife. That's enough. He doesn't need anything more. Nick said, 'Can I show you the dog?' I said, 'Well, if you want to, Nick, but I tell you, I'm against it.' Then he brought in the dog. I said, 'You're right. That's Columbo's dog.' There was no name you could give this hound—just Dog."

Magnificently lethargic and so ugly that he was cute, Dog would only bark and run at the worst possible times.

According to the "Etude in Black" script, Columbo found Dog at the pound and decided to adopt him. He spends much of the episode trying to come up with a name for him.

"I was thinking of watching him and giving him a name to fit something he did," Columbo tells the veterinarian, "but all he does is sleep and drool. This dog needs a name that will give him some stature. He needs all the help he can get."

Dog hardly became a regular character, but he does make splendid appearances in such episodes as "Forgotten Lady," "Playback," "Now You See Him," "Try and Catch Me" and "Make Me a Perfect Murder." We learn that Dog enjoys ice cream, watching television and swimming in a neighbor's pool (a vision mercifully left to our imaginations).

The original Dog, Levinson and Link relate in their book *Stay Tuned*, died and was replaced by an equally passive pooch. Because of the almost inert nature of the role, they write, the change went unnoticed.

Yet the new dog did create some problems for Falk.

"The second dog was much younger than the original," the two-legged actor said. "So they had to put makeup on the second dog to make him look older. Now I'm no time at all in makeup—one, two, three and I'm ready to start shooting. I'd go in early in the morning. I'm sitting in one makeup chair, and they're making up the dog right next to me. I'm out in no time and waiting to start because the dog is still in makeup."

CASE # 11: THE GREENHOUSE JUNGLE

(originally aired October 15, 1972)

Written by JONATHAN LATIMER
Directed by BORIS SAGAL
Produced by DEAN HARGROVE
Associate producer: EDWARD K. DODDS
Executive story consultant: JACKSON GILLIS
Music Score: OLIVER NELSON
Sunday Mystery Movie Theme: HENRY MANCINI
Director of photography: HARRY WOLF, A.S.C.
Art director: ARCH BACON
Film editor: SAM E. WAKMAN, A.C.E.
Set decorations: JOHN MCCARTHY
Assistant director: FOSTER H. PHINNEY
Sound: EDWIN S. HALL
Unit manager: HENRY KLINE
Editorial supervision: RICHARD BELDING
Music supervision: HAL MOONEY
Costumes by GRADY HUNT
Main title design: WAYNE FITZGERALD
Titles and optical effects by UNIVERSAL TITLE

CAST

LT. COLUMBO	PETER FALK
JARVIS GOODLAND	RAY MILLAND
TONY GOODLAND	BRADFORD DILLMAN
SERGEANT FREDERIC WILSON	BOB DISHY
CATHY GOODLAND	SANDRA SMITH
GLORIA WEST	ARLENE MARTEL
KEN NICHOLAS	WILLIAM SMITH
GROVER	ROBERT KARNES
DRIVER	MILTON FROME
WOMAN	PEGGY MONDO
OFFICER	RICHARD ANNIS
SOUND MAN	LARRY WATSON

Synopsis—Young Tony Goodland is desperate to win back his unfaithful wife, Cathy. Money is the key to her heart, but Tony's comfortable income isn't enough to keep Cathy from stepping out with muscular, well-tanned skiing instructors.

Acidic Jarvis Goodland proposes a way out of Tony's problems. Jarvis, a collector and grower of rare orchids, is the co-administrator of a huge trust fund set up for his nephew. The money can only be touched under extraordinary circumstances. Prompted by his uncle, Tony agrees to fake his own kidnapping.

Jarvis calls Cathy and says he's a mobster warning Tony about paying gambling debts. That night, Jarvis and Tony go to an isolated road running along a canyon. They fire a shot into Tony's Jaguar, making it look as if he were forced off the road and abducted. They then push the car into the canyon.

A note arrives demanding $300,000 in ransom money. Lieutenant Columbo has been called in on the case. He has an assistant— super-efficient, eager-to-please Sergeant Freddy Wilson. A straight-A graduate of the academy, Wilson is up on all the latest technology and crimefighting techniques. Columbo is resistant to the idea until Wilson tells him that Captain Ritchie says he's "fast becoming a legend in the department."

The only way for Jarvis to raise so much money is to break Tony's trust fund. He does so, and, at a rendezvous point, he hands the money over to the "kidnapper" (Tony in a stocking mask).

Later, Jarvis double-crosses Tony and shoots him with the same .32 caliber pistol he used to fire at the Jaguar. This was his plan all along. Jarvis needs money to support his expensive hobby. Tony unwittingly helped his uncle set up a seemingly perfect alibi.

Columbo has his doubts about the case. The path of the bullet found in the car would have passed through the driver. And the skid marks indicate that a bigger, heavier car was chasing the Jaguar. How could it overtake Tony's faster and lighter automobile?

Columbo's suspicions seem justified when Tony's close friend, Gloria West, tells him that the murdered man had been confident of having enough money to win his wife back.

Checking out the people connected with the case, Columbo learns that Jarvis once scared off intruders with a .32 pistol, the type of gun used to kill Tony. Jarvis pretends that he can't find the gun.

Knowing that a ballistic test will prove that his .32 fired the fatal shot, Jarvis takes his pistol and plants it in Cathy's house. He takes the .32 she keeps for protection and tells Sergeant Wilson that this is the gun Columbo was asking about. Jarvis then makes veiled comments about Cathy, leading the zealous Wilson to demand a search of her home.

They find the murder weapon, of course, but Columbo is busy in

Jarvis Goodland's greenhouse. Jarvis had said that when he fired at the intruders with his .32, he only hit a mound of dirt. Columbo has been searching that mound with a metal detector. He has found a bullet.

He now has a nice collection of three bullets. The first was pried from the seat in Tony's car. The second was taken from his body. The third is from the mound of dirt. All three were fired by the same gun.

One of two *Columbo* episodes directed by the talented Boris Sagal, "The Greenhouse Jungle" is nicely plotted but a bit choppy. Ray Milland, so effective as Arthur Kennicut in the previous season's "Death Lends a Hand," is surprisingly less memorable as a murderer. There were marvelous subtleties in his portrayal of Kennicut. His Jarvis Goodland, however, is more heavy-handed. He delivers his lines in a persistent bellow that becomes increasingly tiresome.

Falk's performance, though, is a delight. Some actors grow weary of playing the same role week in and week out. By the time "The Greenhouse Jungle" was shot, Falk had already completed the equivalent of ten movies as Columbo, yet the character seems fresher than ever.

Levinson and Link worried about Columbo wearing out his welcome. The formula was too stylized, they argued, and the repetition could lead to self-parody. What was once innovative could soon become stale and predictable. On the other hand, they pointed out, some network executives believe that audiences like predictability. The wise guys say that familiarity breeds content.

What nobody could predict was Falk's continuing devotion to the character. He approached the forty-fifth episode with the same enthusiasm and diligence that he brought to *Prescription: Murder*. Each excursion in the raincoat was like a musician playing a different variation on the same theme.

Every once in a while, the writers would like to toss a curve into the *Columbo* formula. Jonathan Latimer, a mystery veteran whose credits include the 1942 version of Dashiell Hammett's *The Glass Key*, makes the first experiment in "The Greenhouse Jungle." In the previous ten mysteries, we see the murder committed before Columbo makes his entrance. In Latimer's script, although we wait the usual length of time to see our hero, the lieutenant makes his first appearance before the murder is actually committed. This nice twist is played so smoothly that we hardly notice the change of pattern.

Adding to the fun of "The Greenhouse Jungle" is Bob Dishy as Sergeant Freddy Wilson. Dishy was one of Falk's "old, old friends," and the fun they had on the set is quite apparent on the screen. More than three years later, the actor would revive his Wilson role with equally entertaining results.

Oddly enough, Freddy Wilson was just the type of regular character that NBC wanted so badly for *Columbo*. His presence in "The Greenhouse Jungle" would whet any network executive's appetite. He then disappears and resurfaces three seasons later, driving frustrated network types to dash their heads against the handiest walls.

CASE # 12: THE MOST CRUCIAL GAME

(originally aired November 5, 1972)

Written by JOHN T. DUGAN
Directed by JEREMY KAGEN
Produced by DEAN HARGROVE
Associate producer: EDWARD K. DODDS
Executive story consultant: JACKSON GILLIS
Music Score: DICK DE BENEDICTIS
Sunday Mystery Movie Theme: HENRY MANCINI
Director of photography: HARRY WOLF, A.S.C.
Art director: ARCH BACON
Film editor: TERRY WILLIAMS
Set decorations: JOHN McCARTHY
Assistant director: BRAD ARONSON
Sound: EDWIN S. HALL
Unit manager: HENRY KLINE
Editorial supervision: RICHARD BELDING
Music supervision: HAL MOONEY
Costumes by GRADY HUNT
Main title design: WAYNE FITZGERALD
Titles and optical effects by UNIVERSAL TITLE

CAST

LT. COLUMBO	PETER FALK
PAUL HANLON	ROBERT CULP
ERIC WAGNER	DEAN STOCKWELL
EVE BABCOCK	VALERIE HARPER
COACH LARRY RIZZO	JAMES GREGORY
WALTER CANNELL	DEAN JAGGER
SHIRLEY WAGNER	SUSAN HOWARD
RALPH DOBBS	VAL AVERY
LOS ANGELES ROCKETS	LOS ANGELES LAKERS
MISS JOHNSON	KATHRYN KELLY WIGET
MR. FREMONT	RICHARD STAHL
DEPUTY CORONER	DON KEEFER
PLAINCLOTHESMAN	CLIFF CARNELL
BOX ATTENDANT JIMMY	JOE RENTERIA
SERGEANT HERNANDEZ, L.A.P.D.	IVAN NARANJO

* * *

Synopsis—Paul Hanlon is the general manager of the lucrative Wagner sports empire, a business that includes the Los Angeles Rockets football team. The greatest threat to his power is posed by owner Eric Wagner, an irresponsible swinger who cares little about the operation.

It is a Sunday afternoon and the Rockets have a home game. Paul believes he can murder Eric and set up a perfect alibi.

Sitting in his private luxury box at the stadium, Paul telephones down to the locker room and starts an argument with head coach Larry Rizzo. He demands that the coach come up to see him at halftime.

When the game starts, Paul calls Eric, reminding the young playboy that they're flying to Montreal that night to look at a hockey team. Eric was asleep, groggy from the previous evening's festivities. Paul tells him to take a few laps in the pool.

The crafty general manager then dresses himself as an ice cream vendor and uses one of the Ding-a-ling trucks to drive to the Wagner house. Before getting there, Paul stops and calls Eric from a phone booth. He uses a portable radio to make Eric think he's still in his private box. Eric tells Paul that he's in the pool.

Arriving at the Wagner house, Paul takes a large chunk of ice from the truck's storage section. He approaches the pool and knocks Eric unconscious with the ice. Eric floats face down in the pool. The murder weapon will soon melt away, and the police will think Eric bumped his head while diving. Before leaving, Paul uses a hose to wash away his muddy footprints from around the pool. He gets back to his box in time to meet Larry Rizzo at halftime.

Lieutenant Columbo notices water around the pool. The coroner suggests that this splashed out while Eric was diving. But there's no chlorine in the water on the deck. It's fresh water from the hose. Where did it come from?

After hearing the Wagner family lawyer, Walter Cannell, make angry comments about Paul's ambitions, Columbo suspects that the general manager was involved in some way with Eric's death. But Paul was in his private box at the stadium. The lieutenant has to find a way to break Paul's alibi.

Columbo believes he's on the right track when his surveillance team nabs a private detective, Ralph Dobbs, breaking into the Wagner house. He's trying to remove bugging devices placed in the home telephones. Who hired him? Columbo is shocked to discover it was Cannell, who doesn't trust Paul. The detective's taped conversations include Paul's Sunday exchanges with Eric. They substantiate his alibi.

An interview with prostitute Eve Babcock, an operative for Ralph Dobbs, shows Columbo where he went wrong. Paul knew about the bugs. He knew the detective's tapes would help him.

Again and again, Columbo listens to the tapes, trying to hear a sound that shouldn't be heard. Then it hits him. He hasn't been listening for a sound that should be on the tape and isn't—the chiming clock in Paul's office.

Even though Robert Culp is acknowledged as one of the best *Columbo* murderers, "The Most Crucial Game" is one of the series' weakest entries. The strong cast—Culp, Dean Stockwell, Valerie Harper, James Gregory, Dean Jagger, Val Avery—can't overcome the script's sloppy nature.

In the previous episodes, Columbo always had a strong reason for suspecting the murderer. In *Prescription: Murder*, Ray Fleming didn't call out to his wife after coming home from a long trip. In "Murder by the Book," it was that Ken Franklin didn't fly home after hearing of his partner's disappearance. In "Lady in Waiting," it was the presence of a late edition newspaper in the house. As Falk said, "It couldn't be magic. Columbo had to have reason to suspect the murderer."

In "The Most Crucial Game," however, both the clues involving Paul Hanlon and the motive for murder are weak. And at the end, although Columbo has cleverly managed to break Paul's alibi, he's still a long way from proving that Paul is the murderer. There's no weapon. There are no witnesses. There's only solid proof that Paul was away from his box when he made the second phone call to Eric. Okay, that doesn't look good, yet it's not enough to make a district attorney move.

By the second season of *Columbo*, several scribes and viewers had criticized the series on the grounds that the lieutenant's cases often relied on entrapment and circumstantial evidence. Some of his findings, they claimed, wouldn't stand up in a court of law.

"The Most Crucial Game" seems an odd place to take a stand against these indictments, but the fact remains that such detractors completely missed the point. *Columbo* never was meant to be a realistic depiction of a Los Angeles police lieutenant's career. *Columbo* is escapist fantasy where good persists and eventually triumphs over evil. It is a puzzle—a game of wits. Catching the villain is what's important, not whether the writers play along with the rules of reality.

Columbo is a state of mind. He has no real-life counterpart in the Los Angeles Police Department. Levinson and Link point out in *Stay*

Prostitute Eve Babcock (Valerie Harper) mistakes an amused Columbo for a customer ("The Most Crucial Game").

Tuned that they deliberately avoided the mundane and gritty duties a policeman faces. Columbo would not be running down city alleys or participating in drug busts. He would not be asked to solve street murders or engage in shoot-outs.

Columbo was the American equivalent of the British drawing room mystery. He owed more to Agatha Christie and Dorothy L. Sayers than to Joseph Wambaugh and *Dragnet*. Levinson and Link said that they created a mythical Los Angeles and landscaped it with the stately mansions they had found in the mystery literature of their youth.

The trouble with "The Most Crucial Game" is that it doesn't play fair according to these fantasy rules. Columbo only succeeds in tripping up Paul Hanlon. He doesn't have him completely trapped at the conclusion. As a result, this episode doesn't offer the high degree of satisfaction that the formula promises.

It is interesting to note that "The Most Crucial Game" is credited to John T. Dugan, the author of the previous season's "Dead Weight," another episode that suffers from holes in the plot.

For the first time, a *Columbo* murderer from an earlier season made a return visit to the series. Unfortunately, "The Most Crucial Game" is a less than ideal script for an ideal *Columbo* villain. It would be the feeblest of Culp's three turns as an adversary for the lieutenant. (Actors weren't the only things recycled on *Columbo*. The set used for the Wagner house is a remodeled version of Ken Franklin's "Murder by the Book" living room.)

If not a classic *Columbo*, "The Most Crucial Game" does contain one of the series' most memorable exchanges. Columbo sidles up to Walter Cannell (veteran character actor Dean Jagger) and confidentially asks if he might pose a rather personal question. The audience expects a big break in the case.

"What'd you pay for those shoes?" Columbo asks.

"I think about sixty dollars," the attorney answers.

"I stepped into some water yesterday. I ruined mine. You don't know where I could get a pair that looks like that for around sixteen or seventeen?"

"That was Peter," Levinson said. "He just came up with that."

There's also the priceless scene where prostitute Eve Babcock (Valerie Harper, already well known as Rhoda Morgenstern on CBS's *The Mary Tyler Moore Show*) mistakes Columbo for a customer. So, even with the flaws, "The Most Crucial Game" has managed to win a special place in the hearts of *Columbo* fans.

CASE # 13: DAGGER OF THE MIND

(originally aired November 26, 1972)

Written by JACKSON GILLIS
   (from a story by Richard Levinson and William Link)
Directed by RICHARD QUINE
Produced by DEAN HARGROVE
Associate producer: EDWARD K. DODDS
Executive story consultant: JACKSON GILLIS
Music Score: DICK DE BENEDICTIS
Sunday Mystery Movie Theme: HENRY MANCINI
Directors of photography: HARRY WOLF, A.S.C., AND
   GEOFFREY UNSWORTH
Art director: ARCH BACON
Film editor: RONALD LAVINE
Set decorations: JOHN MCCARTHY
Sound: EDWIN S. HALL
Assistant director: DAVID M. DOWELL
Unit managers: KENNY WILLIAMS AND HENRY KLINE
Editorial supervision: RICHARD BELDING
Music supervision: HAL MOONEY
Costumes by GRADY HUNT
Special photographic effects by ALBERT WHITLOCK
Main title design: WAYNE FITZGERALD
Titles and optical effects by UNIVERSAL TITLE

CAST

LT. COLUMBO	PETER FALK
NICHOLAS FRAMER	RICHARD BASEHART
LILLIAN STANHOPE	HONOR BLACKMAN
SIR ROGER HAVERSHAM	JOHN WILLIAMS
TANNER	WILFRID HYDE-WHITE
DETECTIVE CHIEF SUPERINTENDENT	
WILLIAM DURK	BERNARD FOX
JOE FENWICK	ARTHUR MALLET
FROM LONDON—SPECIAL	
GUEST STARS	JOHN FRASER AND RICHARD PEARSON
THE DIRECTOR	HARVEY JASON
MR. JONES	RONALD LONG

[handwritten annotations: "inspector at airport" above JOE FENWICK line; "(pathologist)" above GUEST STARS line; "(sgt. O'Keefe)" below THE DIRECTOR line]

MAID .... VERONICA ANDERSON

CUSTOMS MAN .... HEDLEY MATTINGLEY

COUNTRY CONSTABLE .... JOHN ORCHARD

CONSTABLE .... PETER CHURCH

GARDENER .... WALKER EDMISTON

INSPECTOR SMYTHE .... GERLAD S. PETERS

MISS DUDLEY .... SHARON JOHANSEN

Synopsis—The marquee at London's Royal Court Theatre proclaims the following night's grand opening: Sir Roger Haversham presents Nicholas Framer and Lillian Stanhope in William Shakespeare's *Macbeth*. Actually, light and lobby posters tell us very little about the real drama going on inside the walls of this venerable theater.

Desperate to get back into the limelight, husband-and-wife team Nick and Lilly view this production of *Macbeth* as their comeback vehicle. With Nicky's blessing, Lilly has been playing up to the largely retired Sir Roger, manipulating him into reopening the Royal Court and backing the Shakespearean tragedy.

Sir Roger learns the truth just before the dress rehearsal. He confronts Lilly in her dressing room. When Nicky comes in, Sir Roger angrily admits that he's been taken by "a ham and a tart." He threatens to close the show and expose them.

There is a scuffle. Lilly's string of stage pearls is broken. As Nicky wrestles with Sir Roger, Lilly picks up a heavy jar of cold cream from her dressing table and throws it. Sir Roger slumps to the floor, dead.

It was an accident, Nicky says. It was self-defense. Yes, Lilly answers, but who's going to believe that mild-mannered Sir Roger Haversham attacked anybody? They hide the corpse in Lilly's stage trunk and go on with the dress rehearsal.

During a break, Lilly is horrified to see the stage doorman, Joe Fenwick, working on the heater near her trunk. She gets him to leave. After the dress rehearsal, Nick and Lilly take the trunk out to Sir Roger's country estate. Since nobody knew that Sir Roger was in London, they arrange the body at the foot of a long staircase. The police will think Sir Roger fell to his death.

The next morning, representatives of Scotland Yard are at Heathrow Airport, waiting for the arrival of a Pan American 707 jet carrying some "great detective from Los Angeles."

Detective Chief Superintendent William Durk is going to show Columbo the Yard's latest techniques. His tour of the legendary facilities is interrupted, though, by a call to Sir Roger's estate. Sir Roger, it turns out, was a distant cousin of Durk's wife.

Poking around the mansion, Columbo notices a few bothersome details. It was assumed that Sir Roger was reading before heading downstairs. But the book found open and face down by his favorite reading chair is a valuable first edition of *Alice in Wonderland*. Why, the American visitor asks, would someone leave such a priceless volume in a manner that could break the spine?

Where are his reading glasses? They were found in the jacket Sir Roger was wearing. They are not even scratched. If he fell down all those stairs, wouldn't they have been smashed?

And there's the little matter of Sir Roger's car. It gets washed every day, yet it shows the spots of having traveled through rainy weather. There has been no rain in the country since the last washing, but it did rain in London the previous night.

Sir Roger's funeral is held at the Royal Court Theatre, where Lilly puts on quite a show of grief. When Columbo and Durk put in an appearance, she discovers that the police know Sir Roger's death was not an accident. She and Nick decide to help the authorities along. They drive out to Sir Roger's estate and ask the butler, Tanner, if he has seen a rare edition of *Macbeth* in the library. Columbo and Durk arrive and ask about the book.

Nick says he loaned it to Sir Roger. It is a copy that belonged to Sir Henry Irving, and the great actor had scribbled notes about the play on every page. Robbery must have been the reason behind Sir Roger's death, Durk concludes. But why, Columbo asks, with so many other priceless works around him, would a thief just take one book?

Columbo attends the opening of *Macbeth,* and backstage he learns that there was a scuffle in Lilly's dressing room on the night of the dress rehearsal. He also finds one of the pearls that fell when Lilly's stage necklace was broken.

Lilly claims that the necklace was broken during a tiff with Nick. Bouncing between dressing rooms, Columbo compares stories. Nick and Lilly have agreed on every detail.

Gee, that's funny, Columbo tells them. He and his wife can never agree on anything. Nick and Lilly not only agree on everything, they use the same language in recalling the event.

Leaving the theater, the acting couple is shocked by the sight of Joe Fenwick carrying Sir Roger's distinctive umbrella. They quickly put together what happened. On the night of the murder, Sir Roger put his umbrella in a corner of Lilly's dressing room to dry. When Joe came in to fix the heater, he mistakenly left his umbrella and took Sir Roger's with him. Nick and Lilly realize they must switch them back or there will be proof that Sir Roger was in London and at the Royal Court on the night of his murder.

Nick follows Joe to a pub and buys the doorman several drinks. When he leaves, Sir Roger's umbrella is in hand. Columbo sees Joe leaving the pub in a downpour. He is surprised to find out that Nick spent his triumphant opening night buying Joe drinks. And he's curious about Joe's missing umbrella.

Nick and Lilly go back to Sir Roger's estate, but Tanner tells them that the wax museum took the producer's hat, coat and umbrella (really Joe's umbrella) for an exhibit honoring this production of *Macbeth.*

They leave just as Columbo arrives. Tanner lies about the couple's visit. With a head start, Nick and Lilly are able to switch the umbrellas in the wax museum's basement.

The next morning, Tanner is knocking at Nick and Lilly's door. He needs employment. They need his silence. Rather than count on his loyalty, Nick kills Tanner, making it look as if the butler took his own life by hanging. He also leaves several valuable books hidden near the body.

The police now think that Tanner murdered Sir Roger and that guilt drove him to suicide. Columbo won't give up. At the opening of the wax museum's *Macbeth* exhibit, he meets with Durk, Nick and Lilly. He tells them how Sir Roger really died. What about proof? Well, Columbo says, the umbrella in the exhibit could tell the story. If it was in the dressing room when the pearl necklace broke, maybe one of the pearls fell into it. Sure enough, a lone pearl rolls out of the opened umbrella. By now quite mad, Nick babbles his way to incrimination. Lilly tells them what happened.

Now it's Durk's turn to be curious. There was little chance of a pearl dropping into that umbrella, the detective chief superintendent says. How did Columbo know it would be there? With a pearl in hand, Columbo asks Durk if he had ever tried to get the attention of a pretty girl in the third or fourth grade. The lieutenant coughs and casually uses his thumb to flip the pearl into a goblet held by the wax figure of Nick.

Great fun from first shot to last, "Dagger of the Mind" is one of the few two-hour episodes that sustains the expanded running time. It also represents something of a turning point for the second season. "The Greenhouse Jungle" and "The Most Crucial Game" were lackluster outings by the first season's standards. With "Dagger of the Mind," however, Hargrove and company hit their stride. They finished the second season with five strong shows.

Intricately plotted, the Jackson Gillis script of a Levinson and Link concept relies a great deal on atmosphere. The London location shots remind us of Columbo's debt to Agatha Christie and Sherlock Holmes. Indeed, the very idea of turning Columbo loose in the stiff-upper world of Great Britain plays like a loving homage to his literary heritage.

Richard Quine's direction calls for grand touches and grand performances that fit the story's theatrical nature. And it doesn't hurt that *Macbeth* is considered a jinx play. The title, of course, is taken from Shakespeare's tragedy. Macbeth at the beginning of Act II:

> "Art thou not, fatal vision, sensible
> To feeling as to sight? or art thou but
> A dagger of the mind, a false creation,
> Proceeding from the heat-oppressed brain?"

(The title "Dagger of the Mind" also was used for a first season (1966–67) episode of NBC's *Star Trek*.)

Between murders, Nicky quotes from the end of Act I: "False face must hide what the false heart doth know." Both quotations are appropriate.

Basehart and Blackman seem to be having a terrific time chewing up the scenery as a third-rate Liz and Dick, and the overall mood is greatly enhanced by the presence of such stalwart English actors as John Williams (who made memorable appearances in Hitchcock's *Dial M for Murder* and *To Catch a Thief*), Wilfrid Hyde-White and Bernard Fox (the latter two would make second *Columbo* appearances).

Curiously enough, "Dagger of the Mind" is one of the very few episodes that Falk doesn't like. The notion of sending Columbo to England just struck him as too much of a network-inspired gimmick.

"That wasn't one of my favorites," the actor said after refreshing his memory with a list of all forty-five titles. "The network also wanted very badly for *Columbo* to shoot an episode in Japan. Why? I don't know. They thought it was a terrific idea."

In later seasons, Richard Levinson would wince when "other cops were deferential to Columbo." A pattern of elevation certainly started to emerge in the second season. In "The Greenhouse Jungle," Freddy Wilson says that Columbo is "fast becoming a legend in the department." In "Dagger of the Mind," we see that the department thinks enough of Columbo to send him for a session with Scotland Yard.

But Levinson and Link came up with the idea for "Dagger of the Mind." So, in at least some small way, they helped this elevation process along.

Still, it only makes sense that Columbo would be gaining some respect from his superiors and his fellow officers. No matter how humble he is, how long could the guy go on solving impossible cases without recognition?

Usually, television takes the opposite route. *McCloud* is a good example. The good marshal kept tackling one tough assignment after another, yet irascible Chief Clifford never stopped treating him like a first-rate nuisance. After seven seasons, you'd think the chief would get a clue. You'd think he would stop shouting long enough to see what a fine lawman he has in McCloud.

Why shouldn't Columbo's abilities be recognized? And, really, it doesn't hurt the character at all. No matter how the world around him acts and reacts, Columbo is the same. That's the important thing. He knows the score, and he continues to shuffle along to the beat of his own drum.

CASE # 14: REQUIEM FOR A FALLING STAR

(originally aired January 21, 1973)

Written by JACKSON GILLIS
Directed by RICHARD QUINE
Produced by DEAN HARGROVE
Associate producer: EDWARD K. DODDS
Executive story consultant: JACKSON GILLIS
Sunday Mystery Movie Theme: HENRY MANCINI
Director of photography: HARRY WOLF, A.S.C.
Art director: ARCH BACON
Film editor: BUDD SMALL
Set decorations: JOHN McCARTHY
Sound: EDWIN S. HALL
Assistant director: DAVID M. DOWELL
Unit manager: HENRY KLINE
Editorial supervision: RICHARD BELDING
Music supervision: HAL MOONEY
Costumes by GRADY HUNT
Main title design: WAYNE FITZGERALD
Titles and optical effects by UNIVERSAL TITLE

CAST

LT. COLUMBO .... PETER FALK
NORA CHANDLER .... ANNE BAXTER
JERRY PARKS .... MEL FERRER
DR. FRANK SIMMONS .... KEVIN MCCARTHY
MR. FALLON .... FRANK CONVERSE
JEAN DAVIS .... PIPPA SCOTT
EDITH HEAD .... HERSELF
DIRECTOR .... SID MILLER
SERGEANT JEFFRIES .... WILLIAM BRYANT
PAUL .... JOHN ARCHER
GATE GUARD .... JACK GRIFFIN
JOE .... ROBERT E. MEREDITH
SERGEANT FIELDS .... BART BURNS

Synopsis—Former movie queen Nora Chandler keeps her career barely alive with occasional roles in a television series or network film.

It is a far cry from her glory days, when she was married to Al Cumberland, the man who built the studio.

Cumberland died in a boating accident twelve years ago, but Nora continues to live in the cottage built for her on the studio lot. Although this property is quite valuable, she has resisted all of studio head Fallon's attempts to buy it.

Nora is shocked and hurt to learn that her personal secretary of eighteen years, Jean Davis, has agreed to marry caustic Hollywood gossip columnist Jerry Parks. In addition to sniping at Nora in print, Jerry has been blackmailing the aging actress. He knows that some creative accounting was done during a picture she produced for herself in Italy. Her juggling of the books cost the studio two million dollars. Wouldn't Fallon just love to have that little bit of information?

Knowing that Jean is to meet Jerry at a bookstore where he'll be signing copies of his latest book, Nora gives her secretary some errands to run. Nora takes a studio car and drives to the bookstore. After seeing Jerry and Jean together, Nora drives out to the columnist's house. She pours a can of gasoline on the carport and splashes a trail of fuel to the hill behind the house. When Jerry's car pulls into the driveway, she strikes a fatal match. The automobile goes up in flames.

Later, the police interrupt Nora's dinner with news of an accident at Jerry Parks' home. As they're telling her the details, Jerry walks in. Jean was driving his car. Nora faints.

Lieutenant Columbo visits Nora in her studio cottage. He notices pictures of the star and her late husband. He notices they are about the same height. He notices the double-eagle Shriner's ring her husband wore. He notices the ornate fountain in her cottage's garden. It doesn't work. She says it was a set piece from one of her movies.

Since Jean was killed in Jerry's car at Jerry's house, Columbo is working under the assumption that Jerry was the intended target. Who would want to see the columnist killed?

Jerry cavalierly tells Columbo that he has many enemies. How about Nora Chandler? The gossipmonger laughs and asks who would be interested in a sliding actress. But Jerry does tell the lieutenant that Al Cumberland's casting couch practices were notorious.

Actually, Jerry has his own suspicions. Meeting Nora at a restaurant, he says that the police would be interested in knowing that she had a wonderful motive for killing him. Columbo surprises them, and they quickly pretend to be having a friendly chat. At the studio, Nora confesses that she lied to the police. The actress tells Columbo that Jerry thinks she had a good reason for wanting him out of the way. It isn't so, she claims. Get him to tell you what he knows, Nora demands.

A humorous interlude from "Requiem for a Falling Star": Former movie queen Nora Chandler (Anne Baxter) tries to get Lieutenant Columbo to spruce up his wardrobe.

Copyright © by Universal City Studios, Inc. Picture courtesy of MCA Publishing Rights, a division of MCA Inc.

With search warrant in hand, Columbo orders the columnist to open his files. There is the proof of Nora defrauding the studio. To everyone's surprise, Fallon's boss, corporation chairman Frank Simmons, tears up the document. He's known about it for ten days. He's faithful to Nora, and they've made an "arrangement." So the actress didn't have a motive.

Maybe, Jerry says mysteriously, and maybe he has something else. Nora looks shaken, but she accuses him of bluffing to save face.

Nora thinks that she is safe. Her confidence crumbles when Columbo says that he now believes Jean was the real target all along. She was driving Jerry's car because she got a flat tire at the bookstore. But the tire doesn't have a leak and no amount of experimenting can make it go flat.

Someone had to make the tire go flat by letting the air out. Someone wanted Jean to take Jerry's car. And it had to be someone who knew where Jean was heading that night.

But why would Nora want Jean dead? Columbo gets an idea from watching an old Nora Chandler movie. In one scene, the actress is dressed as a man to set up an alibi.

Meanwhile, Nora realizes she must get the police back to thinking that Jerry was the intended victim. Again taking a car from the studio, she almost runs him down in the street.

Columbo goes to the studio and shows Nora an envelope with her initials on it. Jerry was found unconscious with this on him, he says. It contains a double-eagle Shriner's ring. What can it mean?

Nora runs back to her cottage and throws open the glass doors to the garden. Columbo walks in and turns on the light switch. He had to see what she would do after looking at the ring. He knows the truth now. Nora killed Jean because the secretary knew that Al Cumberland didn't die in a boating accident. Nora killed her husband in the cottage and buried his body in the garden. Dressed in her husband's clothes, she had taken the boat out and everyone assumed there had been an accident. They were the same height. Who could tell from a distance? The photograph on Nora's wall and the scene from the movie had helped Columbo make the connection, especially after the actress looked frightened when Jerry hinted that he might know more.

Checking the studio records to confirm his suspicions, Columbo learned that Nora had ordered the fountain the day before her husband's disappearance.

Jean knew all this, and Nora was afraid she'd tell Jerry Parks. When Nora saw the Shriner's ring, she thought Jerry had somehow found out. She had to rush and check the garden.

The fountain, it turns out, bothered Columbo from the start. Everything else was in perfect working order. Why didn't the fountain run? Then it hit him. In order to get the fountain to run, someone has to lay water pipes. And in order to lay water pipes, you have to dig up the lawn.

William Link never ceased to be amazed by the Jackson Gillis touch when it came to clues. "Requiem for a Falling Star" (working title "Murder by Starlight") contains several beauts. Like most Gillis scripts, it is crafty, cunning and clever.

"The Greenhouse Jungle" had altered the already familiar *Columbo* formula by having the lieutenant enter before the murder was actually committed. Gillis tries another twist. We know who the murderer is. We know who the victim is. But we're not sure who the victim was supposed to be. So, in addition to the usual howzhegonnacatchhim (or her) mystery, Gillis gives us a second guessing game to play.

Helping maintain a sense of continuity for the series, Gillis served as executive story consultant for the second season. His expertise was worth every penny. Bochco was not replaced as story editor, and Hargrove was doing much of the ever-necessary rewriting. The expert eye of Gillis was always welcome.

The casting of Anne Baxter as a "falling star" is an especially fitting

Hollywood touch because the actress made such an impression as a scheming "rising star" in director Joseph L. Mankiewicz's Oscar-winning *All About Eve* (1950). In that classic motion picture, Baxter's character did everything short of murder. In "Requiem for a Falling Star," her more sympathetic character commits that more heinous crime. In addition to being sharp, her Nora Chandler is not above using her acting abilities to charm or deceive Columbo. For his part, the lieutenant's determination is mixed with a fondness for this aging member of Tinseltown royalty.

Humor was a constant and important ingredient in *Columbo* (although Richard Levinson would object when the comedy became too broad, too cute or too prevalent). There are several priceless moments in "Requiem for a Falling Star."

Legendary costume designer Edith Head tries to spruce up Columbo's wardrobe by suggesting a new tie. Columbo tries to get his wife to talk with Nora on the phone.

And there's a scene that must have had the Universal executives sneering with appreciation.

"Avoid actors," barks Frank Converse as studio boss Fallon. "They'll kill you."

After the wars Falk had put Universal through, the advice must have seemed sage indeed. But Gillis kept his tongue in his cheek for a few more lines. Columbo is surprised to learn that a man as young as Fallon is running the studio.

That's all right, Fallon tells him. "I would never typecast you as a detective, either."

An appearance by Jack Webb (*Dragnet*) had been announced for the episode when it was in the planning stages, but it didn't work out.

Because of the care taken by Falk and the men who succeeded Levinson and Link, *Columbo* rarely suffered from continuity problems (dialogue that conflicts with an earlier episode or runs contrary to the spirit of the character). "Requiem for a Falling Star" has the dubious distinction of possessing one of those few goofs. Columbo tells Nora Chandler that he's never been on a movie set before. Of course, he confronted Joan Hudson on a set in *Prescription: Murder*.

He'd again be on a studio lot in 1976's "Fade in to Murder." The lieutenant ended up on television sets in "Suitable for Framing," "Double Shock" and "Make Me a Perfect Murder."

Since Columbo was routinely matching wits with the rich and powerful of Los Angeles, it's only logical that his work would sometimes take him into the world of show business. Episodes like

"Requiem for a Falling Star" allowed directors to merely set up their cameras on the bustling crossways of the Universal studio lot.

When Nora leaves Columbo for a press conference, she is stepping into the Universal commissary. When Fallon says goodbye to Columbo, he is stepping into the famous MCA/Universal Black Tower.

CASE #15: A STITCH IN CRIME

(originally aired February 11, 1973)

Written by SHIRL HENDRYX
Directed by HY AVERBACK
Produced by DEAN HARGROVE
Associate producer: EDWARD K. DODDS
Executive story consultant: JACKSON GILLIS
Music Score: BILLY GOLDENBERG
Sunday Mystery Movie Theme: HENRY MANCINI
Director of photography: HARRY WOLF, A.S.C.
Art director: ARCH BACON
Film editor: ROBERT L. KIMBLE, A.C.E.
Set decorations: JOHN MCCARTHY
Assistant director: FOSTER H. PHINNEY
Sound: EDWIN S. HALL
Unit manager: HENRY KLINE
Editorial supervision: RICHARD BELDING
Music supervision: HAL MOONEY
Costumes by GRADY HUNT
Main title design: WAYNE FITZGERALD
Titles and optical effects by UNIVERSAL TITLE

CAST

LT. COLUMBO	PETER FALK
DR. BARRY MAYFIELD	LEONARD NIMOY
DR. EDMUND HIEDEMAN	WILL GEER
SHARON MARTIN	ANNE FRANCIS
MARSHA DALTON	NITA TALBOT
HARRY ALEXANDER	JARED MARTIN
NURSE MORGAN	ANETA CORSAUT
DETECTIVE FLORES	VICTOR FLORES
PAUL	KENNETH SANSOM
DR. SIMPSON	MURRAY MACLEOD
DR. MICHAELSON	LEONARD SIMON
TOM	RON STOKES
CLEANING WOMAN	PATSY GARRETT

Synopsis—Dr. Barry Mayfield is a brilliant young heart surgeon on the staff of a major Los Angeles hospital. He and the hospital's senior heart specialist, the revered Dr. Edmund Hiedeman, are working on a drug that will combat transplant rejection.

Veteran nurse Sharon Martin believes that Mayfield is a cold opportunist who would like to take all of the credit for the research project. She doesn't know how right she is.

Mayfield is impatient. He's afraid that others will beat them to the recognition. But Hiedeman defends his colleague, extolling his virtues as a surgeon and a researcher. At the same time, Mayfield is plotting Hiedeman's murder.

Hiedeman is due to have a valve replacement operation. Instead of using the permanent black suture, Mayfield substitutes white dissolving suture that's been dyed black. In a few days, the dissolving surgical thread will start to give way. The new valve will separate, and everyone will assume that Hiedeman died of heart failure.

Mayfield's perfect murder goes smoothly until Sharon notices that the suture has a funny texture. That night, she confronts Mayfield with her suspicions. If Hiedeman dies, she says, he would take over the research project. Mayfield calmly tells her to take her suspicions to an expert and have the suture examined. Sharon calls a laboratory and makes an appointment for eight o'clock the following morning.

In the hospital parking lot, Mayfield is waiting for her with a tire iron. After the evil deed is done, the surgeon removes the incriminating suture from Sharon's pocketbook. He then drives to her apartment and hides two bottles of morphine under the bathroom sink.

The obvious conclusion is that Sharon was dealing hospital drugs and somebody killed her for them. Lieutenant Columbo walks into Dr. Mayfield's office just as he's getting the news. The detective is amazed by the physician's concentration. His voice registers shock, yet Mayfield continues to set his desk clock.

Several other things about the case bother Columbo. From what everyone tells him, Sharon wasn't the type to be dealing drugs. And the killer made sure to wear gloves. It doesn't exactly sound like a desperate drug user. And there are no fingerprints on the morphine bottles. Wouldn't Sharon's be on them if she put them under the sink?

Columbo also is curious when several people tell him that Sharon was upset after Dr. Hiedeman's operation. If everything went so well, why was she upset?

Even more puzzling is the note found in Sharon's pocketbook: "MAC meet at 8 a.m." Who is Mac?

Mayfield sees that he must push Columbo back in the wrong direction. He contacts Sharon's roommate, Marsha Dalton, and gets her to remember a Vietnam veteran Sharon was helping to get over a drug dependency. With hinting and prodding, Marsha remembers that his name was Harry Alexander. She runs off to tell Columbo, but he seems more interested in the fact that it was Mayfield who helped her remember.

Columbo goes to see Harry, who says he hadn't seen Sharon in six months. He claims he's straight. Columbo believes him.

Mayfield thinks something drastic has to be done. He breaks into Harry's apartment and waits for him. When Harry walks in, Mayfield chloroforms him into unconsciousness and injects a massive dose of drugs into his system. In a narcotic haze, Harry falls to his death.

That should convince you of his guilt, Mayfield tells Columbo. Not really, the policeman answers. Harry Alexander was left-handed and the drugs were injected into his left arm. Conclusion: somebody else wielded the needle.

During a visit to Hiedeman's hospital room, Columbo spots the initials MAC on a piece of metal. They stand for Marcus and Carlson Medical Supply Company. Sharon wasn't writing a man's name at all. She had made an appointment to see a chemist at Marcus and Carlson.

The hospital mostly buys bedpans, scissors, clamps and tweezers from Marcus and Carlson. The only thing it buys from that company with a chemical base is suture. So, upset after Dr. Hiedeman's operation, Sharon was making an appointment about suture. The trail leads to Mayfield, who laughs at Columbo.

Slamming a water pitcher on Mayfield's desk, Columbo angrily tells the doctor that he'd better take good care of Dr. Hiedeman. Because if Hiedeman dies, there will have to be an autopsy to see if it was merely heart failure or dissolving suture.

Realizing he must get rid of the evidence and save Hiedeman, Mayfield spikes the elderly doctor's medication. It looks as if the new valve must be failing. Mayfield quickly orders a second operation.

As the surgery is drawing to a close, Columbo and several other officers rush into the operating room. Mayfield blows up and pushes Columbo aside. But all of the suture found is normal. None of the dissolving kind is located anywhere.

Columbo is about to leave when it hits him. Mayfield never loses his cool. Why did he get upset in the operating room? Why did he push Columbo?

After all, Columbo says, "the only thing we didn't search was me." He reaches into his pocket and pulls out the dissolving suture Mayfield put there when he shoved him.

The only episode written by Shirl Hendryx, "A Stitch in Crime" is one of the series' finest outings.

Leonard Nimoy, who had spent three years as Mr. Spock on *Star Trek* and two seasons as Paris on *Mission: Impossible*, makes a virulently brash and cocky opponent for Columbo.

"That was one of the projects the studio offered that I was interested in," Nimoy explained. "Being under contract with that studio and not being assigned to play a lead in a series, I was concerned about doing a lot of guest roles as the guest heavy. I told Sid Sheinberg that I didn't mind doing a *Columbo*, but I didn't want to come out of the studio as the killer of the year. That was my main concern. But I had no qualms about doing *Columbo*. I thought the series was very well done.

"I had a great time working with Peter Falk. I found him a challenging and delicious actor to work with. Playing opposite a good performer, you play your top game. It's a challenge that makes you rise to the occasion."

Mayfield emerges as one of the very few murderers Columbo actually dislikes. Dropping the courteous front for a startling moment, Columbo subjects the haughty doctor to an outburst of sincere indignation. Rare as they were, such interludes greatly displeased Richard Levinson.

"I think Peter wanted his moment as an actor," Columbo's co-creator related, "and I thought it was a mistake. Peter pointed out that we had Columbo lose his temper in the pilot [*Prescription: Murder*, where the lieutenant yells at Joan Hudson]. He seemed to, but he didn't really. That was an act calculated to get a reaction."

Two seasons later, writer and story editor Peter S. Fischer would similarly have Columbo get mad at a murderer. Again having worked up some hostility for an adversary, the policeman has another genuine moment of anger with Milo Janus (Robert Conrad) in 1974's "An Exercise in Fatality." Again Levinson would object.

Still, these moments are so effective and intriguing because they are infrequent. They are teasing flashes of a Columbo who remains hidden behind all that servility.

"A little more of that might not have been bad," Falk argued. "That grounds him and makes him human."

Fischer sided with Falk and laughed off Levinson's objections: "Haven't you figured out that Levinson hates for actors to show emotion on screen? I liked it when Columbo got mad. And it wasn't a ploy. He was really mad. He suddenly dropped the bullshit about being stupid and ineffectual. Those were moments when we saw what he was really like."

If Columbo was moved to anger in every episode, such scenes would have no power at all. The fact is, however, that you could count these outbursts in the entire series and not use all the fingers of one hand.

One of the series' grimmest pieces of black humor appears in "A Stitch in Crime." Columbo arrives on the murder scene tired, unshaven and hungry. He has with him a hard-boiled egg. He keeps looking for a place to crack it.

The murder weapon, a tire iron, is about to be removed. Wait a minute, Columbo says. Hold that out here, he tells a subordinate officer. He studies the black object for a second and then gently taps his egg on it.

CASE #16: THE MOST DANGEROUS MATCH

(originally aired March 4, 1973)

Written by JACKSON GILLIS
  (from a story by Jackson Gillis, Richard Levinson and
  William Link)
Directed by EDWARD M. ABROMS
Produced by DEAN HARGROVE
Associate producer: EDWARD K. DODDS
Executive story consultant: JACKSON GILLIS
Music Score: DICK DE BENEDICTIS
Sunday Mystery Movie Theme: HENRY MANCINI
Director of photography: HARRY WOLF, A.S.C.
Art director: ARCH BACON
Film editor: LARRY LESTER
Set decorations: JOHN MCCARTHY
Sound: EDWIN S. HALL
Assistant director: DAVID M. DOWELL
Unit manager: KENNY WILLIAMS
Editorial supervision: RICHARD BELDING
Music supervision: HAL MOONEY
Costumes by GRADY HUNT
Technical advisor: CHARLES CLEMENT
Main title design: WAYNE FITZGERALD
Titles and optical effects by UNIVERSAL TITLE

CAST

LT. COLUMBO	PETER FALK
EMMET CLAYTON	LAURENCE HARVEY
TOMLIN DUDEK	JACK KRUSCHEN
MAZOOR BEROZSKI	LLOYD BOCHNER
LINDA ROBINSON	HEIDI BRUHL
SERGEANT DOUGLAS	PAUL JENKINS
DR. BENSON	MICHAEL FOX
PROPRIETOR	OSCAR BEREGI
ANTON	MATHIAS REITZ
FIRST REPORTER	DROUT MILLER
SECOND REPORTER	MANUEL DEPINA
DR. SULLIVAN	STUART NISBET

NURSE .... ABIGAIL SHELTON
WORKMAN .... JOHN FINNEGAN

Synopsis—American grand master Emmet Clayton is anxious to prove he is the greatest living chess player. Some experts have suggested that he would have never become world champion if the top Soviet player, Tomlin Dudek, hadn't been forced into inactivity by ill health.

All those doubts will soon be erased, though. Clayton's former fiancée, Linda Robinson, now a close friend of Dudek's, has arranged a match in Los Angeles.

The evening before the match, Clayton notices Dudek slipping away from the hotel. Curious, he follows his opponent to a French restaurant in the neighborhood.

It turns out that Clayton's jovial challenger is eluding the watchful eye of his coach, Mazoor Berozski. Since Dudek is a diabetic, his diet is strictly controlled by a protective entourage. He is trying to secretly satisfy his love for cooked snails.

After some verbal jousting, the two grand masters play an impromptu game of chess on the checkered tablecloth. They use salt and pepper shakers, snail shells and condiment bottles as the pieces. When Clayton loses, he is crushed. He realizes that he can't possibly beat Dudek. Alone and tortured by this shattering realization, he throws his hearing aid against a wall in his hotel room.

Rather than face the humiliation of public defeat, Clayton uses his formidable powers of strategic planning to map out a way to murder Dudek. In order for his scheme to work, Clayton must make it look as if Dudek was accidentally killed while running out on the match.

Early the following morning, Clayton calls Dudek and pretends to be upset. He asks the Russian to meet him in the lobby. When Dudek heads for the elevator, Clayton slips into his room and hastily packs a bag. Using a Russian accent, Clayton already has made plane reservations and summoned a cab for Dudek.

Downstairs, Clayton lures his opponent near the basement disposal machine used to grind the hotel's garbage. The American tells Dudek that he's upset about a romance gone sour. A woman has misunderstood his intentions. His thoughts are in a shambles. She's a native of Dudek's country, Clayton adds.

The understanding Russian offers to postpone the match. Clayton, who knows what Dudek is saying by reading his lips, asks him to write a note of apology to the woman so it will be in her language. What should he write? "I'm sorry. I was wrong. I'm very ashamed."

When the words are written, Clayton pushes Dudek into the trash machine.

The police make the natural assumption. Dudek panicked before the match and, while sneaking out through the hotel's basement, slipped into the machine. Even Berozski accepts the premise when Clayton arrives with a note in Dudek's handwriting and native language. Clayton says the note had been pushed under his door. It says, "I'm sorry. I was wrong. I'm very ashamed."

Clayton expresses great sorrow over the loss. Excuse me, Lieutenant Columbo says, you're talking like Tomlin Dudek is already dead. He's unconscious and in critical condition, but he's still alive.

Several details bother Columbo (as if you didn't know). Dudek wears dentures. His hastily packed bag, though, contains a regular toothbrush. It would seem that somebody else packed his bag. And if somebody else packed his bag, maybe the accident wasn't accidental.

Then there's the matter of the note. It was delivered in an official envelope, yet it wasn't written on official stationery. In fact, the type of paper it was written on can't be found anywhere in Dudek's room.

A policeman notices that the shirt Dudek wore the night before smells of garlic. Nothing on his prescribed diet had garlic and Berozski knows that Dudek slipped out of the hotel the previous evening, so Columbo has area restaurants checked.

The trail leads to the site of Dudek and Clayton's improvised chess game. Clayton claims that he won the match. He says that the defeat obviously shook Dudek's confidence and that's the reason the Russian tried to run away.

Of course, Clayton can't allow Dudek to recover. At the hospital, the chess champion sees Linda Robinson holding a list of medicines to be brought from Dudek's hotel room. He casually glances at the list, which doesn't make Linda at all suspicious. But Clayton has a photographic memory. He goes to Dudek's room and replaces several bottles. An hour after receiving his usual injections, Tomlin Dudek is dead.

Columbo has a strong circumstantial case. Dudek's note was written with an ink that's identical to the type in the pen Clayton always carries. Linda Robinson confirms that Clayton saw the medicine list. And Dudek recorded all of his games, including the one in the restaurant. His journal says that white won, and the restaurant's proprietor remembers that it was Dudek who made the first move with a salt shaker. He played white and won the game.

Columbo needs one more piece of incriminating evidence. He gets it when Dog almost falls into the trash machine. Don't worry, the workmen say, he wouldn't have been hurt too badly. There's a safety device on the entrance of the machine. If something goes in while it's running, the machine shuts itself off automatically. A button on the control panel restarts it.

That's the missing clue, Columbo tells Clayton. If a man wants to kill another man by pushing him into a trash machine and the thing suddenly stops, why doesn't he just go back and turn it on again? Columbo remembers that Clayton said his hearing aid wasn't working on the morning of the match. Clayton didn't turn the machine back on for the simple reason that he didn't hear it stop. Along with all the other trivial evidence, the murderer had to be a deaf man.

In 1973, chess was enjoying a resurgence of popularity thanks to American grand master Bobby Fisher's victory over Soviet champion Boris Spassky. Levinson, Link and Gillis noticed the headlines and concocted this splendid encounter for Columbo. Since the episodes usually resembled a verbal chess match, the theme seems all the more appropriate.

Directing the most enjoyable "Most Dangerous Match" was Edward M. Abroms, the talented film editor whom Levinson and Link rewarded with a directorial assignment in the first season. Fortunately, "The Most Dangerous Match" provided him with a far better script. Abroms responded by delivering an episode that moves beautifully from the eerie opening dream sequence to the final confrontation between Falk and guest star Laurence Harvey.

"After Levinson and Link left the show," Falk said, "we would get their input about the episodes over lunch. I remember in the show about the chess champion, I had certain problems with the clues. I didn't think it was strong enough. I talked to them about it on the phone, and one of them came up with the idea of the salt shaker and the game in the restaurant."

As a chess grand master with incredible powers of observation and total recall, Laurence Harvey registers as one of the most Machiavellian of the Columbo murderers. His Emmet Clayton will do anything to preserve his standing. Still, beneath the cold and confident exterior, Harvey's performance hints at the tremendous insecurities that lurk in this brilliant strategist. It's quite a contrast. Columbo acts insecure, but he's sure of his tactics. Clayton acts boldly, but he's plagued by doubts.

The Columbo team was getting very good at throwing curves into the formula. In "The Greenhouse Jungle," Columbo enters before there's been a homicide. In "Requiem For a Falling Star," the audience didn't know if the murderer got the right victim. In "A Stitch in Crime," the first premeditated murder is still taking place when Columbo enters to investigate a second killing. In "The Most Dangerous Match," the villain thinks he has succeeded, but his victim remains barely alive when Columbo is summoned. Yet the trickiest curve of the second season was saved for last.

CASE #17: DOUBLE SHOCK

(originally aired March 25, 1973)

Written by STEVEN BOCHCO AND PETER ALLAN FIELDS
    (from a story by Jackson Gillis, Richard Levinson and
    William Link)
Directed by ROBERT BUTLER
Produced by DEAN HARGROVE
Associate producer: EDWARD K. DODDS
Executive story consultant: JACKSON GILLIS
Music Score: DICK DE BENEDICTIS
Sunday Mystery Movie Theme: HENRY MANCINI
Director of photography: HARRY WOLF, A.S.C.
Art director: ARCH BACON
Film editor: LARRY LESTER
Set decorations: JOHN MCCARTHY
Sound: EDWIN S. HALL
Assistant director: BRAD ARONSON
Unit manager: HENRY KLINE
Editorial supervision: RICHARD BELDING
Music supervision: HAL MOONEY
Costumes by GRADY HUNT
Main title design: WAYNE FITZGERALD
Titles and optical effects by UNIVERSAL TITLE

CAST

LT. COLUMBO	PETER FALK
DEXTER AND NORMAN PARIS	MARTIN LANDAU
CLIFFORD PARIS	PAUL STEWART
LISA CHAMBERS	JULIE NEWMAR
MRS. PECK	JEANETTE NOLAN
MICHAEL HATHAWAY	TIM O'CONNOR
DETECTIVE MURRAY	DABNEY COLEMAN
MRS. JOHNSON	KATE HAWLEY
YOUNG LAWYER	MICHAEL RICHARDSON
SECOND DETECTIVE	ROBERT ROTHWELL
OLDER LAWYER	GREGORY MORTON
STICKMAN	TONY CRISTINO

*   *   *

Synopsis—Elderly and wealthy Clifford Paris is about to be married to the much younger Lisa Chambers, a fellow physical fitness enthusiast. Unhappy about the impending nuptials, his nephew Dexter, the host of a television cooking show, watches as Clifford fences with family attorney Michael Hathaway.

After the vigorous match, Clifford decides to take a bath. The housekeeper, Mrs. Peck, is settling down to watch a medical drama on television. Dexter approaches his soaking uncle with a wedding present. It's an electric mixer. He turns it on and says, "You're going to get a real charge out of this." With that, he tosses the whirring appliance into the tub. There is a nasty crackling noise as the electrical shock kills the master of the house. Meanwhile, the lights and Mrs. Peck's television set go dark. About fifteen seconds later, the TV picture returns (even if the people are a trifle purple) and gloved hands are switching the house alarm back on.

Lisa arrives and finds Clifford's body slumped over the handlebars of his exercise bike. It looks as if he had a heart attack while in the midst of a typically strenuous workout. But the hysterical Lisa calls the police, screaming murder and claiming that everyone was after his money.

So it's Homicide's droopy Lieutenant Columbo who arrives and immediately incurs the wrath of the meticulously neat Mrs. Peck. When a cigar ash falls in the wrong place, she screams, "You must belong in some pigsty."

The penitent lieutenant retreats to the bathroom and tries to spruce up. He notices that the towel in the hamper is damp and the soap in the tub is wet, even though the tub is dry. Mrs. Peck does the laundry every day at three, so, despite someone's efforts to clean up the bathroom, it's obvious that Clifford took a bath after fencing with Michael Hathaway. That bothers Columbo. Why would someone exercise, take a bath, then immediately start to exercise again?

The autopsy reveals that Clifford Paris died of ventricular fibrillation caused by a severe psychological or physical shock. The lights going off for fifteen seconds suggest electrical foul play to Columbo. The lieutenant's assistant, Murray, finds a distinctive footprint outside Mrs. Peck's window. It was made by a special type of shoe—for someone with flat feet. Flamboyant Dexter seems like the logical suspect until his brother, conservative bank executive Norman, arrives. They are identical twins, right down to their flat feet.

Could Dexter have pitched an electrical appliance into his uncle's tub? Or could it have been Norman, pretending to be Dexter, wielding the fatal appliance? At the bank, stuffy Norman is all too willing to suggest that his estranged brother is the likely killer. He calls Dexter an unreliable, low-life sponger. Norman says that the high-living Dexter probably wanted to get his hands on their uncle's three-million-dollar estate.

When Columbo visits Dexter on the set of his cooking show, the gourmet host argues that Norman is not without motive. He asks Columbo if he has the time for a quick flight to Las Vegas. Norman is a compulsive gambler. He owes one casino $37,000.

Columbo has two suspects with equally good motives.

Michael Hathaway drops a bombshell when he tells Norman that Clifford did leave a will. Lisa Chambers is to get the bulk of the estate. Clifford changed his will because he wanted Lisa to be sure that he knew she wasn't marrying him for money. Without that document, Norman and Dexter would split the fortune and Michael would make a tidy sum managing the estate. The brothers agree to keep Michael as business manager—if he can get Lisa's copy of the will away from her.

But when the lawyer arrives at Lisa's apartment, he sees that she has been pushed from her balcony. She is dead, and in his rush to leave with the will, Michael runs straight into the arms of the police. He says that Dexter set him up.

Columbo summons the twins to their uncle's house. Everything finally fits together. They start in the bathroom. The way the sunken tub is situated, one person couldn't have lifted out a wet body. There's no place to get the proper leverage. Secondly, Mrs. Peck claims that the lights were out for only fifteen seconds. After throwing a mixer into the tub, however, Columbo needs sixty-seven seconds to run to the basement and replace the fuse. And how did the murderer get into the house when the alarm was on?

There's only one conclusion: Dexter and Norman were in it together. One of them was already in the house and shut the alarm off for the other. One of them killed their uncle while the other waited near the fuse box. They both lifted the body out of the tub and staged the heart attack scene.

The brothers claimed that they never talked to each other, yet the telephone company's records show that Dexter and Norman had talked about twenty times in the last ten days. That's a lot of calls for brothers who aren't on speaking terms. The only thing that brought them together was murder.

"Double Shock" lures you into thinking that it's a typical *Columbo*. All of a sudden, a second Martin Landau shows up and we have a traditional whodunit on our hands.

Guest star Martin Landau cooks up an improvised scene with Peter Falk for "Double Shock."

"Every once in a while, we talked about doing a departure," said Richard Levinson, who sketched out the original story with Link and Gillis. "They wanted an occasional variation on the format, so we did it with 'Double Shock.'"

Landau, like Nimoy, had been a resident master of disguise on *Mission: Impossible.* One of the reasons the episode works so well is his ability to make the Paris twins so distinctive.

No fewer than five writers (six if you count Hargrove's rewriting) worked on "Double Shock," yet one of the best scenes was ad-libbed. During the filming of his cooking show, Dexter Paris calls Lieutenant Columbo onto the set. The police officer has a grand time before the cameras and demonstrates—not for the first or last time—that he is probably more at home in the kitchen than Mrs. Columbo.

"We had a set that was very receptive to ideas," Falk said. "Some scenes were improvised. That one was almost totally improvised because the nature of the scene allowed it. For Columbo, there was this sudden delight about being called out of the audience and being made the center of attention."

In fact, the series' humorous nature hit a particularly playful streak in "Double Shock." Jeanette Nolan is wonderful as Mrs. Peck, the outraged housekeeper who battles to keep her television operating and her temper under control. Again and again during the episode, her fury with Columbo puts the detective in danger of becoming the third murder victim.

Summing Up the Second Season

Levinson and Link had battled to finish seven *Columbo* episodes for the rookie season. Dean Hargrove delivered eight, including a couple of two-hour shows, for the second season.

If *Columbo* had been a smash hit in the 1971–72 season, it was a mega-hit in the 1972–73 season. With *Columbo* ranking first or near first for each of the eight weeks it aired an original episode, *The NBC Sunday Mystery Movie* became the nation's sixth-most-watched series.

A week after "Double Shock" aired, a story by Jeff Greenfield appeared on the front page of *The New York Times* arts and entertainment section. Titled "Columbo Knows the Butler Didn't Do It," the article noted how dinner parties were being adjourned early and telephone calls interrupted so fans wouldn't miss the first five minutes of each *Columbo* mystery. While paying tribute to the charm of Falk's characterization, the author launched a debate by declaring that much of the series' appeal could be chalked up to class antagonism.

Richard Levinson sighed when the subject was brought up about ten years later: "All of a sudden, Columbo was being called a proletariat hero. People were reading in some grand philosophical message. The real reason we played him against the rich was for contrast, not to make any kind of statement."

Still, even though they were no longer officially connected with the series, all of the attention gratified Levinson and Link.

"People were rearranging their schedules to be home for *Columbo*," Levinson recalled. "In the second year, the intellectual community latched on to it. The letters we got from professors, academics and scholars were enormously satisfying. We are very proud of that series. If you're lucky, once or twice in a lifetime you get an international hit like *Columbo*."

About a month after Greenfield's article appeared, Columbo made his second appearance on the cover of *TV Guide*. The series was shut out at the Emmys in 1973; the rules had again put *Columbo* in the same category as British imports for *Masterpiece Theatre*.

The second season of *Columbo* coincided with the building of headlines about the Watergate scandal. Who could get to the bottom of the break-in? Humorist Art Buchwald, in one of his syndicated columns, sent Lieutenant Columbo into the White House.

Also in 1973, the film version of William Peter Blatty's horror novel, *The Exorcist*, was released, and several people noticed the similarities between Lieutenant Columbo and Lee J. Cobb's overly polite Lieutenant Kinderman. Since the book was published in May 1971 (four months before the series premiered), there were suggestions that this was another case of television stealing a character.

Levinson and Link irritably explained that Columbo made his debut more than a decade before *The Exorcist* saw print. *Prescription: Murder* was made into a TV movie in 1968. *Ransom for a Dead Man* aired March 1, 1971.

When informed of all this, the film's director, William Friedkin, reportedly said, "Well, two heads with a single brilliant thought."

Five years later, Friedkin directed a film called *The Brink's Job*. It starred Peter Falk.

PART **IV**

THE THIRD SEASON (1973–74)

"Just point me in the right direction. I'll find him. I'm good at that."

—LIEUTENANT COLUMBO
"Any Old Port in a Storm" (1973)

The Lucky Third

The third season of *Columbo* saw a tremendous influx of talent at the top. With Edward K. Dodds as associate producer and Jackson Gillis as story consultant, Dean Hargrove had produced all eight of the second season's episodes. It was a herculean chore.

Gillis helped get the third season rolling, then left for other projects. It didn't completely end his association with the series. His name would be on outstanding entries in both the fourth and fifth seasons.

Hargrove found a compatible partner for the third season: Roland Kibbee. The team of Hargrove and Kibbee sat at the top of the hierarchy as executive producers. The episodes they didn't produce were handled by Douglas Benton, Robert F. O'Neill (the gifted associate producer from the first season) or Dodds (who also returned as associate producer for several episodes).

Even without Levinson, Link, Bochco and Gillis, there were producers and writers who knew the *Columbo* formula very well indeed. Kibbee and Benton were newcomers, but Hargrove, O'Neill and Dodds (who had been unit manager on *Prescription: Murder*) were intimately acquainted with the Emmy-winning lieutenant. And of the eight directors hired for the third season, four had seen action with the series.

Writers—the lack of good ones, that is—would always be a problem for *Columbo*, so the entry of Peter S. Fischer in the third season was of particular significance.

"I didn't have time to write original stories," Hargrove recalled. "We were constantly looking for promising scripts. We got some spec material (on speculation and not assigned by a producer) from Peter Fischer, and I liked it a lot. His stuff was so good that we made him the story editor for the fourth season."

Fischer would actually be given the same lofty title that Gillis had held during the second season: executive story consultant. But the job was story editor.

Aptly enough, the series' first story editor, Steven Bochco, was instrumental in getting Fischer involved in *Columbo*.

"When I came out to California," said Fischer, a native of Flushing, New York, "one of the first people I met was Steven Bochco. He and

I played in the same poker game on Thursday nights. I was a big *Columbo* fan, so I wrote a spec *Columbo* script for my own amusement and enjoyment. It was a very good script, too. I gave it to Steve and he gave it to Hargrove and Kibbee. They read it and liked it, but, meanwhile, I got a job working on another series called *Griff* [ABC, 1973–74]—the late, unlamented *Griff*. Bochco and I did it together. He was the producer. He called me up and asked me if I wanted to be story editor. We had a lot of laughs while the *Titanic* was sinking."

Griff, which starred Lorne Greene, had a run that paralleled the third season of *Columbo*. While Bochco's series was struggling to find an audience, however, Hargrove was wooing Fischer for *Columbo*.

"Dean asked me if I would write a script for *Columbo*," Fischer explained. "They were in trouble on scripts. Dean said, 'We liked your spec script. What else do you have? Do you have any other thoughts?' And I came up with 'Publish or Perish.'"

Two of Fischer's scripts were produced for the third season. The young writer gave the talent pool just the boost it needed. He understood the character and he liked it. Like Gillis, he had a splendid knack for clues. Like Levinson and Link, he had a good mind for mysteries. And Falk liked him.

"You could tell from the start that Peter Fischer had a real feel for the show," Falk said. "You start with Levinson and Link. They created it. What we missed when Dick and Bill left was a writer who could ride herd on the scripts. Dick and Bill were gone. Bochco was gone. So Peter greatly helped the show. He made fantastic writing contributions."

Under Hargrove and Kibbee's direction, the *Columbo* unit actually improved on the strong second season.

In fact, the third season—the lucky third—compares very favorably with the outstanding first season. Considering how entrenched the *Columbo* format had become in the public viewing consciousness after two TV movies and two seasons, the freshness of these episodes is quite remarkable.

There is an ironic footnote to this shining season: for the second year in a row, *Columbo* was scheduled against *Mannix*, the two-fisted CBS detective series created by Levinson and Link. A top-ten show during the 1971–72 season, *Mannix* faded badly when forced to battle for ratings with *The NBC Sunday Mystery Movie*. Mike Connors' private eye would make something of a comeback during the 1974–75 season, yet CBS had seen enough. The network canceled the violent program after its eighth year.

Richard Boone's *Hec Ramsey* returned as the fourth member of the *Sunday Mystery Movie* wheel. *Hec* continued to struggle, as did the revamped *NBC Wednesday Mystery Movie* wheel: Widmark's *Madigan*, James McEachin in *Tenafly*, Dan Dailey and James Naughton in *Faraday and Company* and Helen Hayes and Mildred Natwick as *The Snoop Sisters*.

Unable to duplicate the *Columbo/McCloud/McMillan and Wife* success on Wednesday nights, NBC made the *Wednesday Mystery Movie* the *Tuesday Mystery Movie* in January 1974. They had tried to reinvent the wheel and the experiment had failed. NBC gave up on a second *Mystery Movie* package. There would be only one wheel rolling for NBC in the fall of 1974.

CASE #18: LOVELY BUT LETHAL

(originally aired September 23, 1973)

Written by JACKSON GILLIS
   (from a story by Myrna Bercovici)
Directed by JEANNOT SZWARC
Produced by DOUGLAS BENTON
Executive producers: DEAN HARGROVE AND ROLAND KIBBEE
Associate producer: ROBERT F. O'NEILL
Executive story consultant: JACKSON GILLIS
Music Score: DICK DE BENEDICTIS
Sunday Mystery Movie Theme: HENRY MANCINI
Director of photography: HARRY WOLF, A.S.C.
Art director: LOYD S. PAPEZ
Film editor: LARRY LESTER
Set decorations: GEORGE GAINES
Sound: TERRY KELLUM
Assistant director: JACK DORAN
Unit manager: KENNY WILLIAMS
Editorial supervision: RICHARD BELDING
Music supervision: HAL MOONEY
Costumes by GRADY HUNT
Wardrobe furnished by SAKS FIFTH AVENUE
Main title design: WAYNE FITZGERALD
Titles and optical effects by UNIVERSAL TITLE

CAST

LT. COLUMBO	PETER FALK
VIVECA SCOTT	VERA MILES
KARL LESSING	MARTIN SHEEN
DAVID LANG	VINCENT PRICE
SHIRLEY BLAINE	SIAN BARBARA ALLEN
DR. MURCHESON	FRED DRAPER
FERDY	GINO CONFORTI
JERRY	COLBY CHESTER
LAB ATTENDANT	BRUCE KIRBY
SERGEANT	JOHN FINNEGAN
BURTON	DICK STAHL
FINGERPRINT MAN	MARC HANNIBAL

POLICEMAN .... DAVID TOMA
FASHION MODERATOR .... LAYNE MATTHESS

Synopsis—Legendary cosmetics queen Viveca Scott finds that her
Beauty Mark empire is being threatened by arch rival David Lang. Her
hopes for survival rest on the development of a revolutionary cream
formula that actually helps remove wrinkles. The early tests by Beauty
Mark's chief chemist, Dr. Murcheson, are encouraging.

Viveca is horrified to learn that Karl Lessing, Murcheson's young
assistant and her former lover, has pirated the formula. He intends to
sell it to David Lang.

What Karl doesn't know is that Viveca has a spy in the enemy
camp—David Lang's private secretary, Shirley Blaine. She tells
Beauty Mark's founder and chairman that David is going to give
$200,000 to a mysterious Mr. Smith.

Viveca goes to Karl's beach house and demands the return of
Murcheson's formula. Still bitter about their breakup, he tells his boss
that the formula is not written down anywhere. He takes the unique
eight-sided sample jar from the flour tin where it was hidden and
casually tosses the rest of the magical cream to Viveca. It won't do her
any good, he claims. The formula is only in his head.

"It's mine," Viveca says.

"Is it?" Karl asks contemptuously.

"You stole it," she shouts.

"Prove it," he answers.

Seeing that Karl has the upper hand, she writes down a financial
offer on the back of a television magazine. He laughs at her. Driven to
desperation, Viveca suggests a personal and business partnership.
Enjoying her humiliation, he turns her down.

Enraged, Viveca grabs Karl's microscope and hits him over the
head. He is dead. She takes the jar and runs.

Lieutenant Columbo is on the scene the next morning. He notices
the octagonal shape in the flour tin and the picture of Viveca Scott on
the dead man's dart board. He also sees the figures written on the TV
magazine. Somebody jotted them down with a black eyebrow pencil.

Feeling the carpet, he tells the other officers to be careful. There's
broken glass from somewhere.

The police learn that Karl, although he had less than $300 in the
bank, had made reservations for Paris and the Riviera.

In the personnel offices of Beauty Mark, Columbo finds that Karl's
file is the only one that has been carelessly shoved in backward. Few

people had access to those files, so his suspicions about Viveca are becoming stronger.

In the research labs of Beauty Mark, Columbo learns about the company's use of special containers to code research products. Each experiment gets a different shape jar, close in size to the octagonal outline left in Karl's flour tin.

When Columbo tells Viveca about the figures scrawled with an eyebrow pencil, she says that indicates a brunette. She's a redhead and redheads don't use black eyebrow pencils. But later he discovers that she uses a black eyebrow pencil to paint on her trademark beauty mark.

The lieutenant's case becomes stronger when he adds the fact that Karl Lessing, using the name of Smith, had met with David Lang.

Columbo isn't the only one putting things together. Shirley realizes what happened and she's decided to blackmail Viveca. Viveca pretends cooperation while slipping the secretary a cigarette laced with poison. Minutes later, the drug takes effect and Shirley is killed in a car accident.

What finally solves the case is the case of poison ivy developing on Viveca's hand. She hasn't been out of state and poison ivy doesn't exist in the Los Angeles area. Where did she get it?

Oddly enough, Columbo, too, has developed poison ivy on his hand. They got it in the same place—Karl Lessing's beach house. The chemist had been working with poison ivy. A sample was on the slide in his microscope. Viveca got her poison ivy when she wielded the microscope as a weapon. Columbo got his when he touched the shattered remains of the slide in the carpet.

Although beautifully acted, "Lovely but Lethal" has a relatively weak conclusion. Columbo's case rests on the fact that both he and Viveca have developed poison ivy. Of course, she could always claim that her infection was caused by shaking hands with him! While this is a nifty clue, it isn't conclusive. Hargrove and Kibbee actually led the third season with their weakest card.

Still, the cast is strong, even by *Columbo* standards. In addition to Vera Miles (*The Searchers, The Wrong Man, Psycho*) as a cosmetics queen whose regal exterior conceals a mental makeup capable of murder, the episode features Vincent Price, Martin Sheen and Fred Draper.

Sheen, who was six years away from his performance in Francis Ford Coppola's *Apocalypse Now*, was quite willing to do anything that had Levinson and Link's names on it. The year before "Lovely but Lethal," he had starred with Hal Holbrook in a landmark TV movie written by

The title "Lovely but Lethal" refers to cosmetics legend Viveca Scott (Vera Miles), who can't turn around without being confronted by the tenacious Lieutenant Columbo.

the team, *That Certain Summer*. A year after the episode, he would star in their TV movie *The Execution of Private Slovik*. In 1984, he was featured in *The Guardian*, a drama they wrote for Home Box Office.

"I just adore them," Sheen said in 1985. "It's just that simple. They're just such good and decent and bright and funny guys. I laugh around them all the time. They're very humane. I would work for them wherever, whatever."

There was one other reason Sheen agreed to accept a relatively small role in "Lovely but Lethal."

"I wanted to meet Vincent Price," he explained. "Even though I knew I had no scenes with him, I knew I'd get to meet him. That was my thrill. He's one of my favorite actors. We had great fun together. That's my favorite memory of that whole show."

"Well, I became an enormous fan of Martin Sheen," Price said about a week later. "I loved the show, so I was very pleased to be asked to be on it."

CASE # 19: ANY OLD PORT IN A STORM

(originally aired October 7, 1973)

Written by STANLEY RALPH ROSS
   (from a story by Larry Cohen)
Directed by LEO PENN
Produced by ROBERT F. O'NEILL
Executive producers: DEAN HARGROVE and ROLAND KIBBEE
Music Score: DICK DE BENEDICTIS
Sunday Mystery Movie Theme: HENRY MANCINI
Director of photography: HARRY WOLF, A.S.C.
Art director: ARCH BACON
Set decorations: JOHN M. DWYER
Assistant director: JOE BOSTON
Unit manager: WILBUR MOSIER
Film editors: BUDD SMALL and LARRY LESTER
Sound: DAVID H. MORIARTY
Editorial supervision: RICHARD BELDING
Music supervision: HAL MOONEY
Costumes by GRADY HUNT
Main title design: WAYNE FITZGERALD
Titles and optical effects by UNIVERSAL TITLE

CAST

LT. COLUMBO	PETER FALK
ADRIAN CARSINI	DONALD PLEASENCE
RIC CARSINI	GARY CONWAY
KAREN FIELDING	JULIE HARRIS
JOAN STACEY	JOYCE JILLSON
FALCON	DANA ELCAR
MAITRE D'	VITO SCOTTI
THE DRUNK	ROBERT DONNER
STEIN	ROBERT ELLENSTEIN
BILLY FINE	ROBERT WALDEN
LEWIS	REGIS J. CORDIC
ANDY STEVENS	REID SMITH
OFFICER	JOHN MCCANN
FRENCHMAN	GEORGE GAYNES
STEWARD	MONTY LANDIS

AUCTIONEER .... WALKER EDMISTON
CASSIE MARLOWE .... PAMELA CAMPBELL

Synopsis—Half-English and half-Italian Adrian Carsini is about to be named the wine industry's man of the year. Although a dedicated winemaker and ardent collector, Adrian is a poor businessman. Such lack of regard for profit infuriates his young half-brother, Ric, a high-living playboy who enjoys auto racing, scuba diving and parachute jumping.

The family wine business and the money were left to Adrian. The land that Carsini Wineries sits on, however, legally belongs to Ric.

On the Sunday that Adrian and his devoted secretary, soft-spoken Karen Fielding, are about to leave for a New York business trip, Ric stops at the winery to announce that he's getting married for the fourth time. He's short of cash, but that's only going to be a temporary situation. Ric says that he's decided to sell the Carsini land to competitors who specialize in notoriously cheap mass-market wines.

Adrian, who has known true happiness at the winery, is appalled and infuriated. In a blind rage, he picks up a heavy object from his desk and knocks Ric unconscious.

Karen is in her outer office briefly, but Adrian sends her home. He then takes Ric's body into his private wine cellar and shuts off the air-conditioning unit. Securely tied up, Ric will suffocate while Adrian is in New York City.

After hiding Ric's beloved red sports car, Adrian heads for the airport. When he returns to the West Coast several days later, he takes Ric's body from the wine vault and dresses it in scuba gear. Packing a folding bicycle, he drives the sports car to a deserted stretch of beach. He dumps the body into the ocean and pedals back to the winery.

In the meantime, though, Ric's fiancée, Joan Stacey, has filed a missing person report with the police. When there's no officer in the missing person's office, she winds up talking to a Lieutenant Columbo. He's with Homicide, yet he agrees to do some checking for her.

"I see he's an Italian and we Italians have got to stick together," Columbo tells her.

The Coast Guard spots Ric's body and the police make the natural assumption. Ric hit his head while scuba diving. The oxygen in his tanks ran out and he suffocated. The coroner agrees that it was death by suffocation and fixes the date of the "accident" as Tuesday.

Adrian, of course, was in New York at the time. It certainly looks like an accident, but several details bother Lieutenant Columbo.

The top of Ric's sports car was down. It rained Tuesday. Why would someone leave the top down when it was raining, especially on an expensive car that the owner kept in top condition? And there are no water stains in the car.

Just as troubling are the results of the autopsy. Ric hadn't eaten for two days before his death. Why would someone weaken himself by fasting for two days and then do something as strenuous as scuba diving? Joan and Ric's friends tell Columbo that the younger Carsini brother was a superb athlete and a big eater.

Columbo suspects Adrian of somehow being involved with his brother's death. To better understand his adversary, the beer-drinking lieutenant takes a crash course in basic wine knowledge. He learns about breathing, decanting and sediment.

While showing Columbo his private collection of priceless wines, Adrian explains that air conditioning is necessary to keep the vault at a safe temperature. Excessive heat will cause oxidation and spoil the wine.

Columbo asks if someone could get trapped in the vault. When he persists, Adrian offers to leave and shut the door. Seemingly satisfied, the lieutenant walks out a few seconds later.

Columbo is stumped by the fact that Adrian was the last person to see Ric alive. Ric was at the winery on a Sunday and supposedly went scuba diving on Tuesday. Why didn't anyone see him for two days? The winery guard saw Ric arrive, but he never saw the younger Carsini brother leave.

Karen covers for her boss by telling Columbo that, yes, she did see Ric leave the winery on Sunday.

Pretending to be penitent for his "unwarranted suspicions," Columbo invites Adrian and Karen out for an expensive dinner at an ultra-swanky restaurant. Adrian is impressed by the policeman's wine selection. He is stunned when the restaurant has a rare vintage dessert wine.

But his pleasure turns to fury when his discerning palate deduces that the wine has been ruined by oxidation.

Leaving the restaurant, Columbo expresses admiration for Adrian's tasting skills. It's amazing what heat can do. While they were in New York, the lieutenant says, there was an unbelievable heat wave. The temperature shot up to 109 degrees.

While driving home, Karen makes it clear that she will no longer be merely an employee. Without her lies, Columbo would still suspect Adrian. She'll use this power for blackmail.

Vintage Columbo, *"Any Old Port in a Storm" finds the good lieutenant seeking answers from winemaker Adrian Carsini (Donald Pleasence) and his secretary, Karen Fielding (Julie Harris).*

There's an even sadder fate ahead for Adrian. After emptying the bottles from his wine vault, he heads for the rocky cliffs where the police found Ric's car. One by one, he throws the cherished wine into the ocean. Columbo is watching him.

The detective realized that, without air conditioning, the heat in Adrian's wine vault must have jumped to more than 150 degrees. The wine was oxidized.

How could he be sure? Well, when left alone in Adrian's vault, Columbo took the liberty of borrowing a bottle. That was the wine served to them at the restaurant.

The irony is not lost on Adrian. He is one of the few men in the country who could have told Columbo that the dessert wine had been exposed to extreme heat.

"Do I get a confession?" Columbo asks.

Yes, Adrian answers, this actually is a great weight off his shoulders.

He tells the lieutenant that Karen had extortion plans. Columbo realizes how much it hurts to destroy these precious wines. He drives Adrian back to the winery and shows him the dessert wine he has brought along, knowing this would be the end of the case.

"You've learned very well, Lieutenant," Adrian says.

Genuinely touched, Columbo answers, "That's the nicest thing anybody's ever said to me."

Like "Dagger of the Mind," "Any Old Port in a Storm" is one of the few two-hour episodes that doesn't seem padded. But "Any Old Port in a Storm" is a far better effort than the very entertaining "Dagger of the Mind."

Indeed, "Any Old Port" easily earns a mention with the very best *Columbo* episodes: "Murder by the Book," "Death Lends a Hand," "Suitable for Framing," "A Stitch in Crime."

Perhaps Columbo never felt so unhappy about catching a murderer. In the course of his investigation, the dogged lieutenant comes to appreciate Adrian Carsini's love of the vineyards and honored traditions.

"I'm very fond of that episode," Falk commented. "Columbo liked the Donald Pleasence character a lot. That character had the same obsession with excellence that Columbo had. Columbo might have been a slob with clothes, but he had a respect and admiration for excellence. The job has to be done properly. He doesn't like sloppiness in the job. Columbo was delighted by that guy. He admired him."

And Pleasence made a splendidly engaging and eccentric adversary for Falk's splendidly engaging and eccentric hero.

Thrust into the world of winemaking, Columbo seems more Italian than ever before.

"We gave him an Italian name, but, remember, Irish-faced Thomas Mitchell played Columbo on stage," Richard Levinson said. "Falk would bring in the Italian aspects."

More and more, Columbo dropped hints about his Italian heritage. In one of the last episodes, "Murder Under Glass" (1978), we discover he has a rough command of Italian.

"Any Old Port in a Storm" is the first episode to feature an amusing cameo appearance by veteran character actor Vito Scotti. The versatile performer did such a wonderful job as the fussy maitre d', he was brought back to play a fashionable Beverly Hills tailor in the very next episode, "Candidate for Crime." There would also be memorable appearances as a mortician in "Swan Song" and a derelict in "Negative Reaction."

"Vito Scotti is a good friend and a terrific actor," Falk said. "We

Adrian Carsini (Donald Pleasence), the murderer Columbo most regretted catching.

were glad to use him whenever we could. He was terrific as the waiter, the old bum, the funeral parlor director."

Cast in the relatively minor role of Billy Fine is Robert Walden, the actor who would later achieve fame as reporter Joe Rossi on CBS's *Lou Grant* and ex-football kicker Joe Waters in the witty Showtime pay-cable sitcom *Brothers.*

In its first season, *Columbo*, a series that broke many of commercial television's hard-and-fast rules, lived by its own set of strictly enforced rules. These were set down by the character's creators, Richard Levinson and William Link. And most were observed until the show ended its prime-time run. Never give Columbo a first name. He doesn't carry a gun. Don't show him at home. Never show his wife. These you might call commandments, and they were kept.

But producers and writers who followed Levinson and Link didn't feel as obligated to observe the lesser laws of the first season. Levinson and Link had decreed that Columbo never be shown in his office, yet that's where we first see him in "Any Old Port in a Storm." It doesn't hurt the episode at all.

Vintage *Columbo* from opening credits to last, "Any Old Port in a Storm" is at the same time clever, poignant and funny. If there's a sense of tragedy to the conclusion, there's also a mischievous spirit running throughout the tautly paced two hours. Nowhere is that more apparent than in the scene at the bar. Columbo is trying to hear something but a drunk (played by Robert Donner) keeps trying to strike up a conversation. Finally, the inebriated fellow hits Columbo with one of his own trademark lines: "I'm sorry that I bothered you."

FOOTNOTE #5: *Columbo's Theme Song*

In addition to the presence of Vito Scotti, "Any Old Port in a Storm" contains another delightful first. This episode marked the introduction of the song "This Old Man" (the children's nick-nack-patty-whack tune), which Columbo hums while making a phone call at the winery. He hums it again in "Candidate for Crime" and the rest, as they say, is history. The melody became as much a part of *Columbo* as the car, the dog and the wife.

It became something like Columbo's unofficial theme song. After a while, the music arrangers started working the tune into the scores of different episodes. All of this reached a magnificent conclusion in "Murder Under Glass." In a montage scene, a parade of waiters serves a stunning array of food to a smiling Columbo, marching to the lively accompaniment of a grandly arranged version of "This Old Man" (although producer Richard Alan Simmons had wanted the "Colonel Bogey March").

Again, Falk was responsible.

"I just used to like to sing it," he explained, "and one day it came out of Columbo. It's a song that absolutely tickles me. That just happened. I whistled it in a couple of shows. It just evolved. It's such a silly little tune."

CASE # 20: CANDIDATE FOR CRIME

(originally aired November 4, 1973)

Written by IRVING PEARLBERG, ALVIN R. FRIEDMAN and
   ROLAND KIBBEE, & DEAN HARGROVE
   (from a story by Larry Cohen)
Directed by BORIS SAGAL
Produced by DEAN HARGROVE and ROLAND KIBBEE
Associate producer: EDWARD K. DODDS
Music Score: DICK DE BENEDICTIS
Sunday Mystery Movie Theme: HENRY MANCINI
Director of photography: WILLIAM CRONJAGER
Art director: JOHN WM. CORSO
Set decorations: WILLIAM J. MCLAUGHLIN
Assistant director: WALT GILMORE
Unit manager: BRAD ARONSON
Film editor: ROBERT L. KIMBLE, A.C.E.
Sound: EDWIN S. HALL
Editorial supervision: RICHARD BELDING
Music supervision: HAL MOONEY
Costumes by GRADY HUNT
Main title design: WAYNE FITZGERALD
Titles and optical effects by UNIVERSAL TITLE

CAST

LT. COLUMBO	PETER FALK
NELSON HAYWARD	JACKIE COOPER
HARRY STONE	KEN SWOFFORD
VICTORIA HAYWARD	JOANNE LINVILLE
LINDA JOHNSON	TISHA STERLING
MR. CHADWICK	VITO SCOTTI
SGT. VERSON	ROBERT KARNES
SGT. ROJAS	JAY VARELA
DEPUTY COMMISSIONER	REGIS CORDIC
HARRIS	SANDY KENYON
DIRECTOR	JACK RILEY
DR. PERENCHIO	MARIO GALLO
HIGHWAY PATROLMAN	JUDE FARESE
TV ANCHORMAN	CLETE ROBERTS

Synopsis—With election day close at hand, Nelson Hayward finds himself in an extremely tight race for a Senate seat from California. Since the candidate is known for his tough stands against organized crime, campaign manager Harry Stone has manufactured stories about death threats against Nelson. Although only a ploy to drum up badly needed votes, the strategy is effective enough to earn Nelson a constant curtain of police protection. One of the Los Angeles officers assigned to this detail is a homicide lieutenant named Columbo.

Knowing that the death threats are completely phony, Nelson cavalierly dismisses them when answering questions from reporters. He won't be intimidated.

Actually, it's crude Harry Stone who is intimidating Nelson. Harry knows that the married candidate is carrying on an affair with campaign worker Linda Johnson. It's political dynamite. It has to be ended.

Harry has become too powerful. He knows too much. He pulls too many strings. Nelson tells his campaign manager that he'll stop seeing Linda, but he can't just tell her over the phone. She might do something rash—something that will lead to scandal. Harry grudgingly sees the wisdom in this.

Nelson says he has an idea. He pretends to call Linda, asking her to meet him at his beach house. But how can he slip away from the hotel? The police are watching his every step. Nelson convinces Harry to put on his hat and jacket. When the police see Harry drive away in Nelson's clothes, they'll assume it's the candidate. They'll give a panicked chase, and the confusion will allow Nelson to sneak away unnoticed.

The two plan to meet at the beach house. Harry easily loses the police, who believe that he's Nelson, and drives to the rendezvous point. Nelson is waiting for him in the garage. The politician shoots his campaign manager three times. He puts a watch on the dead man's wrist, sets it ahead to 9:20 and smashes the crystal against the garage floor.

The senatorial candidate then drives to his other house, where guests have arrived for a surprise party in honor of his wife's birthday. The festivities start at 8:30. About an hour later, Nelson goes into the study and calls the police. Disguising his voice, he tells them they can find Nelson Hayward's body in the garage of his beach house.

It doesn't take long for the first officers on the scene to figure out what happened. Harry dressed as Nelson and lured the police away from the hotel so the candidate could enjoy his wife's party. Mobsters followed Harry to the beach house, thinking he was Nelson, and shot him down. The broken watch sets the time of death at 9:20. The phone call backs that up.

The commissioner puts Columbo in charge of the murder investigation. A number of things bother the lieutenant. First, he notices that the engine of the car Harry was driving is cold. Police were on the scene moments after the shooting supposedly occurred, so the engine should still be warm.

Then there's the broken watch itself. Harry bought all of his clothes with only one thing in mind: durability. He was a rugged man with rugged tastes. Wouldn't he wear a watch that was almost impossible to break? Yet the watch on his wrist is a flimsy model with a fragile crystal. It doesn't fit him.

And the street light across from the garage is out. Without that, how did the killer have enough light to shoot Harry?

Finally, where did the killer call from? The call came in minutes after 9:20, but the only phone in the area is in a garage that was closed on the night of the shooting.

Columbo also learns that Nelson had ordered an identical jacket to the one he gave Harry to put on.

Nelson realizes that Columbo is on his trail. The only way to avert suspicion is to arrange an attempt on his life. His plan seems ingenious. Taking the gun he used to shoot Harry, the candidate goes into his hotel room and says he needs some time to make private phone calls. When alone, he goes out on the balcony and puts a silencer on the gun. He shoots through the window, aiming as if to hit somebody on the phone. Nelson draws the blinds, puts the gun back in his briefcase and gives it to Linda to put in the office safe. Then Nelson and his wife, Victoria, go off to vote.

That night, with campaign workers in the outer room, Nelson again excuses himself to make some private calls. This time, he sets off a firecracker on the balcony. Everyone rushes in. There was the sound

of a shot. There's a bullet hole in the glass window. There's a hole in the wall near the phone.

Columbo arrives and says the man that fired the shot is still in the room. Nelson is furious. There's no gun in the room. All that the police have to do, the candidate says, is dig out the bullet and see if it matches the ones found in Harry's body.

No, Columbo tells him, they've already done that. There is no bullet in the wall. It's in the lieutenant's pocket. And it was fired from the same gun that killed Harry Stone.

You see, Columbo explains, he had asked to be told when Nelson was alone. Officers reported to the lieutenant when the candidate went in to make his private calls that afternoon. Columbo was in the press suite, 616, which is next door to Nelson's room, 615. He waited for the phone light to come on. When it didn't come on, Columbo had to ask himself what Nelson was doing all that time. When Nelson and Victoria went to vote, Columbo went in and found the bullet. That bullet was removed from the wall three hours before Nelson claims that somebody fired it at him.

Despite the splendid payoff and fine work by former child star Jackie Cooper, "Candidate for Crime" is only moderately successful. Like "Etude in Black," it is a two-hour episode that should have been held to ninety minutes. Several scenes are mercilessly padded. Others are unnecessary.

What makes these shortcomings all the more frustrating is that "Candidate for Crime" is so tantalizingly close to being one of the high-caliber *Columbo* stories. Skillfully using dozens and dozens of extras, director Boris Sagal ("The Greenhouse Jungle") effectively creates the hectic atmosphere of a campaign in its last days.

The pacing, however, is severely damaged by the need to pump the episode to two hours. Tighter scenes and an editor's scissors would have lifted "Candidate for Crime" several notches.

Yet the episode does have one of the series' most memorable openings. After nineteen mysteries in which we waited about twenty minutes for Columbo to appear, his face appears in the first few seconds of "Candidate for Crime." The lieutenant already has been assigned to the team protecting Nelson Hayward. Then he disappears and the episode proceeds according to formula.

"That was nice," Falk said. "You're not supposed to see him for twenty minutes and, all of a sudden, he's the first thing you see."

A Peter S. Fischer script had yet to be produced for *Columbo*, but the writer was watching the show very carefully. He was just delighted with the "Candidate for Crime" opening.

"It's terrific," Fischer laughed. "You're watching the credits and there he is. Your reaction is, 'Wait a minute. What's he doing here? He's not supposed to show up for twenty minutes.'"

CASE # 21: DOUBLE EXPOSURE

(originally aired December 16, 1973)

Written by STEPHEN J. CANNELL
Directed by RICHARD QUINE
Produced by DEAN HARGROVE AND ROLAND KIBBEE
Associate producer: EDWARD K. DODDS
Music Score: DICK DE BENEDICTIS
Sunday Mystery Movie Theme: HENRY MANCINI
Director of photography: WILLIAM CRONJAGER
Art director: JOHN W. CORSO
Set decorations: WILLIAM MCLAUGHLIN
Assistant director: PHILLIP COOK
Unit manager: BRAD ARONSON
Film editor: RONALD LAVINE
Sound: WILLIAM BEARDEN
Editorial supervision: RICHARD BELDING
Music supervision: HAL MOONEY
Costumes by GRADY HUNT
Main title design: WAYNE FITZGERALD
Titles and optical effects by UNIVERSAL TITLE

CAST

LT. COLUMBO .... PETER FALK
DR. BART KEPPLE .... ROBERT CULP
VICTOR NORRIS .... ROBERT MIDDLETON
MRS. NORRIS .... LOUISE LATHAM
TANYA BAKER .... ARLENE MARTELL
ROGER WHITE .... CHUCK MCCANN
PRESS PHOTOGRAPHER .... DENNY GOLDMAN
FIRST DETECTIVE .... JOHN MILFORD
FILM EDITOR .... GEORGE WYNER
BALLISTICS MAN .... RICHARD STAHL
PATTERSON .... FRANCIS DESALES
HOUSEKEEPER .... ALMA BELTRAN
DETECTIVE MARLEY .... DENNIS ROBERTSON
SECOND DETECTIVE .... HARRY HICKOX
MRS. HALSTEAD .... ANN DRISCOLL
NORBERT .... E.A. SIRIANNI

FIRST DETECTIVE .... MANUEL DEPINA
TECHNICIAN .... THOMAS BELLIN
NARRATOR .... PETER WALKER
RECEPTIONIST .... MARY BETH SIKORSKI

Synopsis—Dr. Bart Kepple is a brilliant motivational research scientist, but he's also something of a blackmailer. A certain Tanya Baker is quite proficient at getting Kepple's male clients into compromising positions. One of these clients, powerful Victor Norris, has decided that he will no longer be a victim of extortion. The married Norris is threatening to expose Kepple.

The author of several books on motivational research and its use in selling, Kepple is an expert on the use of subliminal cuts. These are one-frame pictures edited into motion pictures or commercials. They go by so fast that the human eye doesn't realize what it has seen, but the picture or message does register with the subconscious mind, leaving behind a strong mental suggestion. If, for instance, subliminal cuts of hot buttered popcorn were edited into a movie, it would make more people think of popcorn. The popcorn sales would go crazy. (A somewhat disreputable selling tool, it works well enough for the government to frown on its use.)

Several clients are gathering at Kepple's research institute to see a film he has put together on advertising and the art of selling. Norris is one of those businessmen. Before the guests start arriving, Kepple calls Mrs. Norris and tells her that he is Tanya Baker's boyfriend. He says that her husband is having an affair with Tanya. He claims to have proof. He asks her to meet him later that night.

At a reception, Kepple makes sure that Norris eats plenty of his beloved caviar—a very salty snack. What Norris doesn't know is that the film he is about to see has been salted with subliminal cuts. The screening room is warm and Kepple has edited shots of iced tea and soft drinks into scenes of deserts.

When everyone has left his office, Kepple takes a pistol from his cabinet and goes to the screening room. From the stage, he tells the audience that the film has no narration, so he'll read the script from behind the curtain.

He actually has recorded his narration, and the tape will make everyone think that he was behind the curtain during the entire run of the film. When Norris inevitably gets up to go to the water fountain, Kepple is waiting for him.

The early evidence seems to cast suspicion on Mrs. Norris. Having been called away from her home by Kepple, she has no alibi for the time of the shooting. And there's a motive: Victor was having an affair with Tanya Baker.

Kepple, on the other hand, would appear to have the perfect alibi. People heard him narrating the film when Norris was shot, and none of the guns in his office match the caliber of the pistol used to kill Norris.

But details about the murder bother Lieutenant Columbo. How could the murderer know that Victor Norris, out of all the people in the screening room, would get up and go to the water fountain? How could he know when Norris would leave the screening room? It doesn't make sense that a gunman, even Victor's wife, would wait in the lobby and hope that Norris would come out alone.

And Mrs. Norris doesn't seem like a killer. If she had planned to murder her husband, wouldn't she at least have tried to arrange a better alibi?

After reading Kepple's books, Columbo learns all about subliminal stimulus. Yet the institute's screening room projectionist, Roger White, also has figured out how Kepple killed Norris. He heard the splices going through the projector. He wants $50,000 for his silence. Kepple agrees to the terms, but later goes to the theater where Roger works and kills him.

Columbo has to find a way to get Kepple to expose himself. During another screening at the institute, Kepple becomes panicky and bolts for his office. He removes something hidden in a lamp just as Columbo emerges from his hiding place.

Kepple is holding a calibration converter, an instrument that fits into the barrel of a pistol. It will convert a .45 into a .22. That's a nice touch, Columbo says.

Then Kepple realizes how Columbo caught him. The lieutenant had a photographer take several pictures of him snooping around Kepple's office, including one by the lamp. They were edited into the film. A subliminal cut made Kepple think that Columbo may have found the converter. He had to check. The crafty detective had used the scientist's own methods against him. The irony isn't lost on Kepple.

"I'll tell you one thing, Lieutenant," he laughs, "you have to admit, you never would have solved it without using my technique."

"That's right, Doc," Columbo agrees. "If there was a reward, I'd support your claim to it."

A cunningly crafted mystery, "Double Exposure" is the only *Columbo* episode penned by Stephen J. Cannell. In 1973, the writer

Columbo is bewildered by his talk with the widow (Louise Latham) of the man murdered in "Double Exposure."

was under contract at Universal and dying (figuratively speaking, of course) to write for the series.

"I always loved the show," Cannell explained. "I always wanted to write a *Columbo*, but other commitments kept getting in the way. Then there was a writers' strike and I had all this time on my hands. When I was in college, I had written a thesis on subliminal cuts. I found that thesis while I was cleaning out my garage, and I thought it was a terrific idea for a *Columbo*. So, during the strike, I wrote it on spec. I did it just for the heck of it. I was entertaining myself. I swung by Dean Hargrove's office and said, 'Here, I was bored and wrote this during the strike. If you like it, use it.'"

Cannell isn't indulging in idle praise when he says that he was a

Columbo fan. He followed the show with an expert eye during its first two seasons.

"I was an avid viewer of the series," he said. "It was my perception that it worked best in the first year when the premise was that an urbane, sophisticated man or woman, for reasons of complete personal gain or jealousy, would commit a perfect murder—an intelligent murder. He was completely sure of himself and along would come this shambling guy in a raincoat. At first amused by this little guy, the murderer slowly would realize that he had a major intellect on his hands. It became mano a mano. That led to the classic scene where Columbo and the murderer would sit opposite each other and the murderer says, 'You think I committed this murder.' And Columbo says, 'Aw, gee, if I ever made you feel like that . . .' And the guy would say, 'Cut the shit. You know and I know that I did this, but you'll never prove it.' So Columbo would force him into a second move—a stupid move—that would incriminate him. In the second season, I saw more crimes of passion. I thought it should be a cold-blooded, sophisticated, planned murder."

He kept to that vision in "Double Exposure," the third and final *Columbo* episode featuring Robert Culp as a murderer.

"Robert Culp was exactly the guy I pictured," Cannell said. "But I never said to anyone, 'Gee, Robert Culp would be perfect for this.'"

And perfect he was. It was the actor's third appearance in as many seasons. More than seven years later, Culp would play Bill Maxwell in writer/producer Stephen J. Cannell's ABC series *The Greatest American Hero.*

In between "Double Exposure" and *American Hero,* though, Cannell would launch a detective series that, like *Columbo,* is hailed as one of the medium's finest efforts. If *Columbo* represents television's best mystery influenced by the G.K. Chesterton/Agatha Christie school, then *The Rockford Files* is its equivalent in the Raymond Chandler school. Starring James Garner as private detective Jim Rockford, the series lasted six seasons (1974–80).

Cannell sees a few similarities between *Columbo* and *The Rockford Files.*

"Both were stylish blendings of a great actor with strong writing and a strong concept," he explained. "Remove any one of those elements and you wouldn't have a classic. They were both really well executed shows. And each was a case of the right actor in the right part. Garner and Falk were ideal for those roles. *Rockford* wouldn't have worked without Garner. The same is true of *Columbo* and Falk. Of course, you can't overlook the genius of Levinson and Link. They're masters at mystery. They came up with a concept that was artful and cerebral. It had talk instead of action, and the talk was done so well that you didn't need action. It was a brilliant show."

It's unfortunate that Cannell didn't write more *Columbo* episodes. He certainly understood the show, and he concocted a marvelous duet for Falk and Culp. In fact, his dialogue underscores the idea that we're watching a game. When Columbo tries a particular ploy, Kepple answers by saying, "I'll play." In other scenes, the give-and-take becomes less and less veiled.

Cannell's script artfully advances the game in absorbing fashion. Falk and Culp rise to the occasion.

The Rockford Files, which premiered the fall after "Double Exposure" aired, signaled the start of Cannell's rise as one of television's most powerful writer/producers. His many series have included *Chase*, *Baa Baa Black Sheep* (also known as *The Black Sheep Squadron*), *City of Angels* (another Chandleresque detective show), *Tenspeed and Brownshoe*, *The A-Team* (which helped NBC climb out of the ratings basement), *Hardcastle & McCormick*, *Riptide*, *Hunter*, *Stingray*, *Wiseguy*, *21 Jump Street* and *J.J. Starbuck*.

A footnote for *Columbo* trivia fans: "Double Exposure" was the first episode in which Columbo refers to a previous case. He enters and says that he was "working late on that Hayward case" (i.e. Nelson Hayward of "Candidate for Crime").

CASE # 22: PUBLISH OR PERISH

(originally aired January 18, 1974)

Written by PETER S. FISCHER
Directed by ROBERT BUTLER
Produced by DEAN HARGROVE AND ROLAND KIBBEE
Associate producer: EDWARD K. DODDS
Music Score: BILLY GOLDENBERG
Sunday Mystery Movie Theme: HENRY MANCINI
Director of photography: WILLIAM J. CRONJAGER
Art director: JOHN W. CORSO
Set decorations: WILLIAM MCLAUGHLIN
Assistant director: ROBERT GILMORE
Unit manager: BRAD ARONSON
Film editor: ROBERT L. KIMBLE, A.C.E.
Sound: WALLACE BEARDEN
Editorial supervision: RICHARD BELDING
Music supervision: HAL MOONEY
Costumes by GRADY HUNT
Main title design: WAYNE FITZGERALD
Titles and optical effects by UNIVERSAL TITLE

CAST

LT. COLUMBO	PETER FALK
RILEY GREENLEAF	JACK CASSIDY
ALLEN MALLORY	MICKEY SPILLANE
EILEEN MCRAE	MARIETTE HARTLEY
EDDIE KANE	JOHN CHANDLER
JEFFREY NEAL	JACQUES AUBUCHON
LOU D'ALLESANDRO	GREGORY SIERRA
DAVID CRASE	ALAN FUDGE
SGT. YOUNG	PAUL SHENAR
WOLPERT	JACK BENDER
SECURITY GUARD	TED GEHRING
RESTAURANT OWNER	VERN ROWE
LAB TECHNICIAN	LEW PALTER
LOCKSMITH	GEORGE BRENLIN
PALMER	J.S. JOHNSON
WALTER	MAURICE MARSAC

Synopsis—Allen Mallory, the author of five bestselling detective novels, has decided to leave Riley Greenleaf's publishing house. His agent, Eileen McRae, has convinced him that he can write serious fiction for rival publisher Jeffrey Neal.

Enraged by the defection, Riley hires demolitions expert Eddie Kane to kill Allen. In addition to collecting on a huge life insurance policy, Riley will make sure that Allen never writes for another publisher.

Riley secures Eddie's services by promising that he'll publish the Army veteran's how-to book on explosives. Riley gives Eddie a key to Allen's office and a pistol. The gun belongs to Riley and his fingerprints are all over it. The key also belongs to Riley. After shooting Allen, Eddie is to drop both near the scene of the murder.

The publisher's devious plan is to draw suspicion to himself and then demolish it with an airtight alibi.

Riley shows up at a publishing party and makes what appear to be drunken threats. He staggers off to establish an alibi. Later that night, while Eddie is shooting Allen, Riley is getting himself thrown out of a bar. He also gets into an accident in the bar's parking lot. He insults a couple and tells them to call his insurance agent in the morning.

Allen's body is discovered the next morning. Riley, of course, is the early suspect. He made threats to Allen. The murder weapon has his fingerprints on it. And his key was found near the door of Allen's office.

But before the day is out, the couple gets in touch with Riley's insurance agent and confirms that he wasn't anywhere near Allen's office when the author was shot. Lieutenant Columbo has to admit that it looks as if someone is out to frame Riley for the writer's murder.

Riley tells Columbo that he had no idea what Allen's latest book was about. Eileen says the novel, *Sixty Miles to Saigon*, dealt with a prisoner of war in Vietnam. The story was so promising that Universal had purchased the film rights for Rock Hudson. The studio, though, didn't want the central character killed off, so Eileen suggested an alternate ending acceptable to the author.

Meanwhile, Columbo tells Riley that there's no question about someone trying to incriminate him. Riley's key, which was left near

Mickey Spillane, creator of detective Mike Hammer, appears as writer Allen Mallory in "Publish or Perish."

Copyright © by Universal City Studios, Inc. Picture courtesy of MCA Publishing Rights, a division of MCA Inc.

the body, doesn't fit the lock to Allen's office. Allen had had the locks changed about three weeks ago, the lieutenant says. How did the murderer get in the room? Even Riley is stumped by that one. He thought the old key would work when he gave it to Eddie. Anyway, Columbo tells the publisher, when they find the person with the new key, they'll have the murderer.

Riley had intended all along to get rid of Eddie, but now he must be sure that the police think he is the murderer. Riley has a new key made and heads for Eddie's apartment. He gives the hired gunman drugged champagne. While Eddie is out, Riley uses his typewriter to compose a fake letter—supposedly written nine months before by Eddie to Riley. It is the outline for a novel titled *Sixty Miles to Saigon*.

The publisher takes the original copy of the letter and puts the carbons in Eddie's metal filing cabinet. Riley places the key to the new lock on Eddie's key ring and leaves a detonation device behind. Eddie is killed, and it appears that the explosion was an accident—an experiment gone wrong. Columbo finds the key and the outline.

Riley tells Columbo that, yes, Eddie Kane did send him the outline for the novel. The publisher claims that Allen saw it and thought it would make a great book. He says that he intended to pay Eddie for his idea, but the veteran was outraged. The logical conclusion is that Eddie killed Allen for stealing his idea.

Eileen has to admit that the synopsis found in Eddie's apartment is identical to Allen's manuscript. In fact, she says, it almost reads like Allen dictated it. That gives Columbo an idea.

The next day, Riley is summoned to Allen's office. Columbo tells the publisher about the evidence against him. First there's the key found on Eddie's ring. It fits the lock on the door, all right, but that lock was changed after Allen's murder, not before. It was changed by Columbo, and the only person he told about the change was Riley. How did Eddie end up with a key to a lock that Columbo had ordered?

You see, Columbo explains, Eddie didn't need a key on the night of the murder. Why not? The door was open.

The lieutenant also has found the man who transcribed the tapes Allen made while working on his books. He admits that Riley has been paying him enormous sums for the contents of *Sixty Miles to Saigon.*

Why is that so damaging? Well, the synopsis that Riley claims Eddie sent to him contains the alternate ending suggested by Eileen McRae. How can an outline written nine months ago include an ending that was only invented last week?

The first Peter S. Fischer script produced for *Columbo,* "Publish or Perish" was cleverly directed by Robert Butler ("Double Shock"). The second of three episodes featuring the definitive *Columbo* villain, Jack Cassidy, the complex ninety-minute outing is full of twists and turns and crests and curves.

Ironically, while "Candidate for Crime" should have been pared back to ninety minutes, "Publish or Perish" could have been extended by a half hour. Fischer hadn't quite mastered the specifics of writing for *Columbo,* and his original script contained too much action.

"It was just too long," Fischer explained. "But instead of cutting out too much, they did an interesting thing. At the same time, they showed on the screen both Jack Cassidy in the bar and the murderer killing Mickey Spillane. Otherwise, there would have been no way to show it all."

The parallel action shots work quite nicely, especially since the technique was new to the series. The "explosive" opening credits are another effective touch. Each credit is punctuated by an explosion set off by Eddie Kane—really gets things off with a bang.

"The direction and editing really enhanced that script," Fischer said. "Had they shot what I gave them, it would have been too long and maybe harder to follow. They made it work, although I think it was a nightmare for the editors."

It's difficult to imagine a better Riley Greenleaf than Cassidy, yet the young writer originally envisioned a far different actor in the role.

"I had written that character for Jack Klugman," Fischer revealed. "I wanted the publisher to be much seedier, not the typical elegant *Columbo* villain. Dick [Levinson] said it works best when you take the scruffy little guy with the blue collar and put him up against diamond studs." In fact, Klugman was one of the actors Levinson had said should never be a *Columbo* murderer.

"I think everybody connected with the show thought Culp and Cassidy were just perfect," Falk said. "Terrific actors. But there wasn't one that we had on the show that I had a problem with—not one."

By all accounts, "Publish or Perish" was a very happy set.

"I didn't have a great part," Mariette Hartley commented, "but it was great fun working with Peter and Jack Cassidy. They worked very hard, but it was loose. Jack Cassidy would chase me around the set. He was just terrible in a wonderful sort of way."

The episode also benefits from the presence of Mickey Spillane, author of the Mike Hammer detective novels. An author of popular detective fiction was playing the author of popular detective fiction in a detective series.

Columbo makes his second reference to the Hayward case ("Candidate for Crime"), and the episode even indulges in an obvious in-joke. Hartley's character, Eileen McRae, says that Universal (the *Columbo* home studio) wants to buy Allen Mallory's novel for Rock Hudson (star of *McMillan and Wife*, one of the *Columbo* companion series on *The Sunday Mystery Movie*).

CASE # 23: MIND OVER MAYHEM

(originally aired February 10, 1974)

Written by STEVEN BOCHCO, DEAN HARGROVE AND ROLAND KIBBEE
  (from a story by Robert Specht)
Directed by ALF KJELLIN
Produced by DEAN HARGROVE AND ROLAND KIBBEE
Associate producer: EDWARD K. DODDS
Music Score: DICK DE BENEDICTIS
Sunday Mystery Movie Theme: HENRY MANCINI
Director of photography: WILLIAM J. CRONJAGER
Art director: JOHN W. CORSO
Set decorations: WILLIAM MCLAUGHLIN
Assistant director: PHILLIP COOK
Unit manager: BRAD ARONSON
Film editor: RONALD LAVINE
Sound: WALLACE BEARDEN
Robot furnished by BILL MALONE
Editorial supervision: RICHARD BELDING
Music supervision: HAL MOONEY
Costumes by GRADY HUNT
Main title design: WAYNE FITZGERALD
Titles and optical effects by UNIVERSAL TITLE

CAST

LT. COLUMBO .... PETER FALK
DR. MARSHALL CAHILL .... JOSE FERRER
PROF. HOWARD NICHOLSON .... LEW AYRES
NEIL CAHILL .... ROBERT WALKER
MARGARET NICHOLSON .... JESSICA WALTER
STEVE SPELBERG .... LEE H. MONTGOMERY
ROSS .... LOU WAGNER
MURPH .... ART BATANIDES
MOTEL MANAGER .... DARRELL ZWERLING
FARNSWORTH .... CHARLES MACAULAY
CORONER .... JOHN ZAREMBA
FIELDS .... WILLIAM BRYANT
WHITEHEAD .... BERT HOLLAND
PLAINCLOTHESMAN .... ED FURY

JEFF .... JEFFERSON KIBBEE
LADY SCIENTIST .... DIANNE TURLEY
MALE SCIENTIST .... WILLIAM CHRISTOPHER
RECEPTIONIST .... DEIDRE HALL
FIRST REPORTER .... DENNIS ROBERTSON
OFFICER .... LUIS MORENO

Synopsis—Young Neil Cahill's theory of molecular power is about to win him scientist of the year honors. His demanding father, Dr. Marshall Cahill, head of the Cybernetic Research Institute think tank, is justifiably proud.

But Professor Howard Nicholson, an elderly chemist at the Institute, has files that prove Neil stole the theory from the late Dr. Carl Finch. If Neil doesn't confess the fraud, Howard will expose him.

Howard, however, doesn't blame Neil. The responsibility, he says, belongs to Marshall, who has pressured and bullied his son.

"He stole the work of a giant to win the approval of a tyrant," Howard comments.

Marshall will not let his son be touched by scandal. Howard must be eliminated.

That night, Marshall is supposed to be programming war game exercises at the isolated console of an Institute computer. He arranges to have the sophisticated MM-7 robot sit in for him. He then takes the Institute car assigned to his assistant, Ross, and drives to Howard's house.

After Howard's much younger wife, psychologist Margaret Nicholson, leaves for an all-night encounter session, Marshall uses the car's horn to lure his colleague into the driveway. He runs Howard down and takes the body into the living room. Marshall sets things up to make it look as if Howard was killed by drug users after the heroin he tested for the government. He then returns to the Institute and completes the war games. Marshall later notices a tell-tale dent in the car he drove, so he backs into the vehicle with his own car, covering the evidence.

The coroner says that Howard might have been worked over with a baseball bat.

Disheveled Lieutenant Columbo notices several details that indicate the scene has been staged. There's a streak of shoe polish about halfway up the door to the room where Howard's body was found. The polish is from one of Howard's shoes, which proves that somebody carried the body into the room. Besides, Margaret left Howard working in his garage laboratory. The body was left in the living room.

If Howard was in the garage and the robbery took place in the garage, why would the body be in the living room? And the drugs were stolen from a canister marked only with the chemical formula for heroin. A drug user probably wouldn't know that.

The pipe Howard was smoking when Margaret left is missing. Columbo finds fragments of it in the driveway. The coroner tells him that the dead man's injuries are consistent with those of a hit-and-run victim.

What most fascinates Columbo, however, is the match he's found in a living room ashtray. The room was cleaned the night before and only three people were in it afterward: Howard, who smoked a pipe but used a special lighter; Margaret, who doesn't smoke; and the murderer. The match is burned almost all the way down, and Columbo, of all people, knows what that suggests: a cigar smoker. Marshall shows up to offer Margaret his sympathies. Before he leaves, he pulls out a cigar.

Poking around at the institute, Columbo meets boy genius Steve Spelberg, designer of the MM-7 robot. Steve tells the policeman how a robot can be programmed to do almost anything a man can do. Steve is delighted by the lieutenant's company. He tells Columbo that it's the second time in a week that someone has actually treated him like a kid. When was the first time? On the night of Howard's murder, Marshall arranged for Steve to attend a drive-in movie.

Margaret discovers that Columbo is going through Howard's files. The folder for Carl Finch is missing. It's the only thing missing. Maybe that's what the murderer was after all the time. Columbo senses that Margaret, a bad liar, knows more than she's telling. Being Neil's psychologist, she is aware that he plagiarized Finch's theory.

Tortured by guilt and prompted by Margaret, Neil confesses to his theft. Columbo knows that Marshall murdered Howard, but he has no real proof. Instead, with Neil's admission, the lieutenant has a strong case against the murderer's son.

Hoping it will push Marshall to confess, Columbo arrests Neil. He had motive: Howard knew about Finch's work and Neil's scientific theft. He had opportunity: Neil was on the grounds of the Institute when Howard was murdered. And he had means: Neil had checked out one of the Institute's cars. It also doesn't look good that Margaret, a beautiful woman married to an older man, was constantly seen in young Neil's company. A jury just might believe that Neil had more than one motive. Finally, Neil has no way of substantiating his alibi.

Knowing that Neil very well could be convicted of murder,

Marshall runs after Columbo and confesses. If Marshall committed murder to protect his son, Columbo reasoned, maybe he would confess for the same reason.

"How did you know?" Marshall asks.

It was that match, Columbo tells him. "I was looking for a cigar smoker, and there you were."

An idea first sketched out by Steven Bochco (working from a story by Robert Specht), "Mind Over Mayhem" was beautifully fleshed out by Hargrove and Kibbee. Without having to strain to reach the dreaded two-hour limit, director Alf Kjellin delivered a tautly paced blend of mystery and humor.

The guest cast is one of the series' best. Playing the head genius in a colony of geniuses, Jose Ferrer (an Oscar winner for *Cyrano de Bergerac*) is magnificently disdainful of the blue-collar Columbo. Fine performances also are contributed by Lew Ayres, Jessica Walter, Robert Walker, Lee H. Montgomery, Dog and a modified version of Robby the Robot (the familiar science-fiction figure that appeared in the 1956 film *Forbidden Planet* and episodes of *The Twilight Zone* and *Lost in Space.*). Playing minor roles in the episode are two future series stars: William Christopher (who would soon achieve fame as Father Mulcahy on the long-running M*A*S*H) and Deidre Hall (a daytime soap opera performer and Jessie on *Our House*).

And "Mind Over Mayhem" contains one of Peter Falk's favorite clues: the burned match. The actor remembers the clue with something closely related to rapture.

"Oh, yes," Falk said, savoring the memory. "Great clue. Really great clue. That's one of the few that really stands out."

By the third season, the *Columbo* writers were starting to reveal a penchant for in-jokes. In "Publish and Perish," for instance, we got the line about Universal buying the murdered author's book for Rock Hudson. In "Mind Over Mayhem," we're introduced to a boy-genius character named Steve Spelberg (one letter away from Steve Spielberg, the boy genius who had directed the first *Columbo* episode, "Murder by the Book"). The gag may have been left by Bochco, since he and Spielberg were the boy wonders of the Universal lot. However it occurred, the timing is interesting. Spielberg's first feature, *The Sugarland Express*, was released in 1974. *Jaws* followed in 1975, launching the director on the path to mogul status.

Columbo explains a matter of "Mind Over Mayhem" to Dr. Marshall Cahill (Jose Ferrer).

CASE #24: SWAN SONG

(originally aired March 3, 1974)

Written by DAVID RAYFIEL
   (from a story by Stanley Ralph Ross)
Directed by NICHOLAS COLASANTO
Produced by EDWARD K. DODDS
Executive producers: DEAN HARGROVE AND ROLAND KIBBEE
Music Score: DICK DE BENEDICTIS
Sunday Mystery Movie Theme: HENRY MANCINI
Director of photography: WILLIAM CRONJAGER
Art director: JOHN W. CORSO
Set decorations: WILLIAM MCLAUGHLIN
Assistant director: PHILLIP COOK
Unit manager: BRAD ARONSON
Film editor: BOB KAGEY
Sound: WALLACE BEARDEN
Editorial supervision: RICHARD BELDING
Music supervision: HAL MOONEY
Costumes by GRADY HUNT
Main title design: WAYNE FITZGERALD
Titles and optical effects by UNIVERSAL TITLE

CAST

LT. COLUMBO	PETER FALK
TOMMY BROWN	JOHNNY CASH
EDNA BROWN	IDA LUPINO
LUKE BASKET	WILLIAM MCKINNEY
J.J. STRINGER	SORRELL BOOKE
ROLAND PANGBORN	JOHN DEHNER
MARYANN	BONNIE VAN DYKE
TINA	JANIT BALDWIN
MR. GRINDELL	VITO SCOTTI
THE COLONEL	JOHN RANDOLPH
LADY	LUCILLE MEREDITH
BENNETT	RICHARD CAINE
PHIL	DONALD MANTOOTH
FRANK	JEFFERSON KIBBEE
JEFF	DOUG DIRKSON

TV REPORTER .... LARRY BURRELL

TV CAMERAMAN .... MIKE EDWARD LALLY

POLICE PILOT .... TOM MCFADDEN

MANAGER .... HARRY HARVEY, SR.

Synopsis—The star of the Lost Soul Crusades, country-western singer Tommy Brown regularly sells out auditoriums and stadiums. But he sees very little of the enormous profits. Those are controlled by his pious and fanatical wife, evangelist Edna Brown.

Edna is able to keep Tommy under thumb because she knows he frequented motels with crusade singer Maryann when she was just sixteen years old. If he quits singing before the Lost Soul tabernacle can be built, Edna will turn him in on charges of statutory rape. An ex-convict, Tommy can't afford to call her bluff. Yet he has swallowed all the blackmail he can stomach.

After a concert in Bakersfield, Tommy makes one final request for a larger share of the profits. When Edna refuses, the singer goes ahead with his intricate murder scheme. First he prepares a thermos of coffee laced with sleeping pills. Next he packs a homemade parachute into a case designed to carry navigational charts.

Tommy will fly his own small plane to their next engagement in Los Angeles. Edna and Maryann will go with him. Before leaving for the airport, Tommy gives his favorite guitar to Luke, Edna's brother, and tells him to make sure it's put in a safe spot on the bus. Once in the air, Tommy tells Edna and Maryann that the plane's heater isn't working. He gives them the coffee to drink. When they are unconscious, he throws the thermos out the window and straps on his home-made parachute.

The plane crashes and Tommy lands nearby. His chute, however, had to be smaller than regulation to fit in the navigation case, so his rate of descent is faster than usual. His landing is rough and he breaks his leg. Quickly hiding the chute in a hollow log, he drags himself near the burning plane and passes out.

The next day, aviation investigator Roland Pangborn tells Lieutenant Columbo that the crash was caused by pilot error. Tommy's electrical system failed. He was miraculously thrown from the plane. It's a rare occurrence, Pangborn says, but not unheard of in his experience. What's a homicide officer doing at the site of a plane crash? Well, Columbo answers, Edna's brother is certain that somehow Tommy planned the whole thing. He's sure it's a case of murder. Luke knows that Edna had something on Tommy, but he doesn't know what it could have been.

Columbo notices that there are no ashes in the navigation kit. Tommy says that suction forced all the charts out the window during the flight. Columbo notices that the passengers' seat belts stayed fastened in the crash, but the pilot's seat belt was unlatched. Tommy says he had to unbuckle the belt to perform some emergency procedures. Columbo notices that Tommy gave Luke his prized guitar to put on the bus. Tommy says he was worried about the effects of unpressurized flying on the instrument. Columbo is concerned because the medical examiner found evidence of barbiturates in Edna's and Maryann's systems. Tommy says they took sleeping pills to help fight air sickness.

They're all plausible answers. Still, Tommy can't answer Columbo's two most troubling questions. First, the level of drugs found in the victims' bodies was too high. Second, the thermos bottle wasn't found in the wreckage. It wouldn't have burned (metal and glass), so what happened to it?

Columbo says he's worried because maybe the coffee was spiked and meant for Tommy. Maybe somebody wanted him to drink the coffee and fall asleep at the controls. It's imperative that the thermos be found, Columbo says.

Tommy says that he was thrown from the plane, maybe the thermos was also thrown clear.

That's a good thought, Columbo answers. He's going to have rangers and boy scouts and volunteers comb the woods. They'll find that thermos.

Tommy isn't worried about them finding the thermos. He's afraid they'll stumble on the parachute. That's exactly what Columbo wants him to think. His investigation turned up that Tommy had been an expert parachute rigger in the Air Force. And forty-five yards of material is missing from the crusade's seamstress shop.

When Tommy goes to retrieve the chute, Columbo is waiting for him.

"I'm glad it's over," the singer tells Columbo. His conscience was getting the better of him. If the lieutenant hadn't trapped him, sooner or later he would have confessed.

For once, Columbo is matching wits with a murderer who is every bit as blue collar and down-to-earth as he is. And Columbo gets to like Tommy Brown and his music. Tommy, like Adrian Carsini in "Any Old Port in a Storm," is quite willing to confess when Columbo corners him. He feels relief. Columbo experiences some regret.

Country-western singer Tommy Brown (Johnny Cash) entertains guests at a party on the day of his wife's funeral ("Swan Song").

But "Swan Song" isn't quite as successful as "Any Old Port" at justifying its two-hour running time. Although hardly a bad episode, it is too long and slightly choppy. Once again, director Nicholas Colasanto ("Etude in Black") was faced with the problems of stretching a natural ninety-minute story to two hours.

Yet the episode does have a great deal to recommend it, not the least of which is the work of country-western giant Johnny Cash. Rather than cast an actor who could approximate Nashville, Hargrove and Kibbee opted for the genuine article. Country's Man in Black wasn't a newcomer to acting. He had already starred with Kirk Douglas in the film *A Gunfight.*

Although not in the same class as Donald Pleasence, Jose Ferrer and Jack Cassidy, Cash was the wisest choice to play a country singer who always dresses in black. As Tommy Brown, he is natural and likable. His down-home style mixes very well with Falk's New York tones. There might have been better actors available, but none could have brought the same level of authenticity to the role. The opening credits, for instance, cleverly blend studio shots with footage from an actual Cash concert.

Humor always was an integral part of the Columbo concept, all the way back to *Prescription: Murder*. In later episodes, though, there was a tendency to put a heavier emphasis on the comedy. It was a trend that bothered Dick Levinson.

"Peter tended to play broader comedy," Columbo's co-creator commented. "He also could make it too cute. They started using too many close-ups, which we disagreed with."

Entire scenes were being improvised or designed to showcase an elaborate joke that ostensibly moves the plot forward. One suspects that many such interludes were inserted to help the episode reach two hours. The results were hit and miss. "Swan Song" contains a good example of a hit and a miss.

The scene in which funeral parlor director Mr. Grindell (Vito Scotti, of course) tries to sell Columbo a burial plot is inspired lunacy. At the opposite extreme, there's the scene with the Colonel (veteran character actor John Randolph), which seems labored and heavy-handed. The talented Randolph is asked to play a caricature of a career military officer, and his bluff-and-bluster manner comes off as a contrivance to prolong the encounter by making it difficult for Columbo to extract information.

Not surprisingly, "Swan Song" features another in-joke.

"I talked to your arranger," Columbo tells Tommy.

"Nick Colasanto," Tommy says.

CASE #25: A FRIEND IN DEED

(originally aired May 5, 1974)

Written by PETER S. FISCHER
Directed by BEN GAZZARA
Produced by EDWARD K. DODDS
Executive producers: DEAN HARGROVE AND ROLAND KIBBEE
Music Score: BILLY GOLDENBERG AND DICK DE BENEDICTIS
Sunday Mystery Movie Theme: HENRY MANCINI
Director of photography: WILLIAM CRONJAGER
Art director: JOHN W. CORSO
Set decorations: WILLIAM MCLAUGHLIN
Assistant director: PHILLIP COOK
Unit manager: BRAD ARONSON
Film editor: ROBERT L. KIMBLE, A.C.E.
Sound: WALLACE BEARDEN
Editorial supervision: RICHARD BELDING
Music supervision: HAL MOONEY
Costumes by GRADY HUNT
Main title design: WAYNE FITZGERALD
Titles and optical effects by UNIVERSAL TITLE

CAST

LT. COLUMBO .... PETER FALK

DEPUTY COMMISSIONER MARK HALPERIN .... RICHARD KILEY

HUGH CALDWELL .... MICHAEL MCGUIRE

MARGARET HALPERIN .... ROSEMARY MURPHY

ARTIE JESSUP .... VAL AVERY

BRUNO WEXLER .... ERIC CHRISTMAS

THELMA .... ELEANOR ZEE

LT. ~~DRYER~~ *Duffy* .... JOHN FINNEGAN

SALESGIRL .... ARLENE MARTELL

DOYLE .... VICTOR CAMPOS

DR. MACMURRAY .... JOSHUA BRYANT

CHARLIE SHOUP .... JOHN CALVIN

AMOS LAWRENCE .... BYRON MORROW

SHARKEY .... JAMES V. CHRISTY

MRS. FERNANDEZ .... ALMA BELTRAN

AL COMO .... ALBERT POPWELL

SGT. NED RANDALL .... BEN MARINO

CHARLES .... JUDSON MORGAN

POLICEMAN .... TOM CASTRONOVA

POLICE PILOT .... PAUL SORENSEN

NATHAN FLOWERS .... BERNIE KUBY

SECOND BARTENDER .... MIKE LALLY

FIRST PATROLMAN .... RICHARD LANCE

PHOTOGRAPHER .... ELDON BURKE

LIMOUSINE DRIVER .... JACK KRUPNICK

Synopsis—Hugh Caldwell, who lives in the fashionable Bel Air section of Los Angeles, has just murdered his wife, Janice. In a panic, he calls his neighbor and best friend, Mark Halperin, who is gambling at their club. Mark tells Hugh to calm down and stay in plain sight at the club's bar. He'll take care of everything.

Mark goes to the Caldwell house and stages a break-in. To help establish his alibi, Hugh calls from the club's bar and fakes a conversation with Janice. Wearing gloves, Mark pulls out one of Janice's nightgowns so the police will think that she was surprised by a burglar while getting ready for bed. He also takes several of Janice's jewels so blame will fall on a thief who has been hitting the neighborhood lately.

Back at his own house, Mark ribs his philanthropic wife, Margaret, about giving away vast sums of her fortune to liberal causes. Strolling by their bedroom window, he pretends that he sees a man running from the Caldwell house. He calls the police.

Actually, Mark is the police. He is Deputy Police Commissioner Mark Halperin. And he is the boss of the man called in to investigate Janice Caldwell's murder, Lieutenant Columbo.

Columbo isn't so sure that Janice was killed by the jewel thief. As the robbery officers point out, the MO is the same, but the Bel Air burglar hasn't killed anybody before. Other things bother Columbo. Hugh says he talked to Janice before she started getting ready for bed. Yet her fingerprints aren't on the phone. A nightgown was taken from her closet, but her prints aren't on the closet, either. And Janice didn't even need to get a nightgown from the closet. It was her custom to keep one folded underneath her pillow.

The thief also left a huge ring that Janice was wearing. Why? That's easy, a robbery detective says. It's made of glass. It's a phony. A pro would have spotted it from a mile off, and this guy is a pro. But just about all of Janice's jewels were glass. She was seeing younger men and selling her precious gems to buy them expensive gifts. Why did this so-called pro steal a bunch of glass?

The next day, Mark tells reporters that the force will catch this thief-turned-murderer. He's already made one slip, the deputy commissioner explains: he ran from the Caldwell house while Mark and his wife could see him. Margaret, of course, didn't see any burglar. Anybody watching the televised press conference, though, would get the impression that she did.

While attending Janice's funeral, Mark tells Hugh that it's time to redeem his favor. Hugh murdered his wife and Mark helped him establish an alibi. Now Mark is going to murder his wife and Hugh must help him. Hugh has no choice.

Early that evening, Mark drowns Margaret while she is taking a bubble bath. He dresses the body and cleans the tub.

That night, Mark is riding in a police helicopter that's patrolling the neighborhood. The deputy commissioner tells the pilot that he sees something suspicious going on at his own house. Flying closer, they see a man (Hugh in disguise) carrying Margaret's body to the pool. He dumps the body in the water and runs away. Mark drags the body out and shams a desperate bid to revive his dead wife.

In the house, Mark tells Columbo that he blames himself. His "poor" choice of words at the press conference obviously made the murderer think that Margaret could identify him. There is no sign of forced entry, so the thief probably surprised her when she was leaving for a testimonial dinner.

There are just as many details about the second murder that bother Columbo. The clothes Margaret was found in were the same ones Columbo saw her wearing earlier that day. She had torn them while working in the garden. It isn't likely that she'd choose that outfit for a testimonial dinner. Somewhat more troubling is the coroner's report: the autopsy doesn't reveal any trace of chlorine in her lungs, but soap is found.

Columbo becomes more and more certain that Mark and Hugh killed their wives. How can he go after his boss?

The lieutenant shakes the deputy commissioner by bringing up the inconsistencies and suggesting that they should be looking for a murderer who made it look like the work of a robber. Mark firmly tells Columbo that he should abandon that route and concentrate on the burglary aspects of the case.

That gives Columbo an idea. Leave out the last two murders, he asks an officer in the robbery division, and who is your primary suspect? That's easy: veteran jewel thief Artie Jessup.

Columbo goes to see Artie and persuades him to call Hugh. Artie

Columbo in the process of tripping up his boss, deputy police commissioner Mark Halperin (Richard Kiley), in "A Friend in Deed."

tells Hugh he knows he killed his wife. He wants $5,000 as the first payment for his silence.

Hugh gets in touch with Mark, who tells him to go ahead and deliver the money and he'll do the rest.

Columbo is going over the files of the major suspects. He says the answer to the case must lie somewhere in these folders. Mark agrees and casually flips through some of the records. Maybe something will click, he says. What he's actually looking for is the address on Artie Jessup's file.

The deputy commissioner gets the jewels he took from the Caldwell house and plants them in the apartment listed on Artie's record. When Hugh goes to deliver the blackmail money, the police are there to arrest Artie. Hoping to complete the frame job, Mark leads a raid on Artie's apartment.

They find the jewels, of course, but Columbo has a curve for the deputy commissioner. Artie Jessup doesn't live in this apartment. Columbo lives there! He just signed the lease. Then he took the address and put it on Artie's folder. Only two people knew the address: Columbo and Mark Halperin. When Hugh understands the situation, he'll fill in the missing details.

The first of two episodes directed by Falk's close friend Ben Gazzara (who had starred in NBC's Run for Your Life), "A Friend in Deed" is a two-hour mystery that needs to be two hours.

"Both of the ones I did were originally supposed to be ninety minutes," Gazzara said, "and both spilled over to two hours."

Of all the episodes Peter Fischer had a hand in writing, this one remains his favorite.

"The premise came from Hargrove and Kibbee," Fischer related. "What would happen if Columbo had to go after the guy who was his boss? That one was done under tremendous pressure, but if I had to pick out one that I particularly like, it would be 'A Friend in Deed.'"

The episode certainly ended the third season on a strong note and solidified the possibility that Fischer would inherit the story editor's job once held by his friend Bochco.

Keeping up the tradition of classy guest murderers is Richard Kiley, best known for his portrayal of Don Quixote in the original Broadway production of Man of La Mancha.

"I loved the show," Kiley said, "so I was quite pleased to appear on it. It was a wonderful experience. It was doubly enjoyable because Ben Gazzara directed the episode. He was an old friend of Peter's, so it was an enormously enjoyable, easygoing set. Peter really set a tone of quality."

Indeed, the atmosphere may have been a little too easygoing for Universal's tastes. Gazzara was quite familiar with Falk's celebrated penchant for numerous takes. When studio executives were hovering around the set, the director would make a point of drawing attention to the precious time that was being consumed by the star's call for take after take.

"Peter can exhaust you," Gazzara laughed. "Peter can go on forever. He's warming up on take seventy. I enjoyed it. I'd beat him to it. I'd say, 'Let's do it again.' He'd say, 'Yeahhh!'"

It was not a pretty sight for budget-minded executives.

"We're gonna do it until we get it right," Gazzara would announce, knowing the effect it would have on the worried onlookers.

"Yeah, that's right," Falk would answer. "We're gonna do it until we get it right."

"I'd laugh my ass off," Gazzara recalled. "The studio guys are tearing their hair out. We're on take fifty and Peter is saying, 'I'm just warming up, Ben. I'm just warming up.'

"We had a lot of fun. The fact that we were friends certainly had something to do with the fact that I directed those episodes. I don't know that much about mystery. Peter is a stickler for the clues. He would say, 'The clues are the thing, Ben. That's what the audience wants—the logic of the clues.'"

Kiley also came away with stories to tell.

"My favorite story that came out of that show is that there was a scene in which I pretend to rescue my wife, played by Rosemary Murphy, from a swimming pool," he said. "I had to run, dive in the pool, drag her out and do mouth-to-mouth resuscitation. Well, I threw myself into the scene and I'm doing the mouth-to-mouth when I suddenly realize that I have never met Rosemary before. So, while the cameras are still rolling, I looked down and said, 'How do you do, Rosemary? We've never met before. I'm Richard Kiley.'"

Summing Up the Third Season

"I'm sure you'll find others to harass," Dr. Barry Mayfield (Leonard Nimoy) told Lieutenant Columbo during the second season's "A Stitch in Crime" episode. How right he was.

The excellence of the third season was justifiably recognized on the evening of May 28, 1974. That night, *Columbo* finally was named Outstanding Limited Series at the Emmy awards (Dean Hargrove and Roland Kibbee, executive producers; Douglas Benton, Robert F. O'Neill and Edward K. Dodds, producers).

Although it had been a mighty struggle to produce eight episodes (four two-hour shows), the season had included some of the series' best stories ("Any Old Port in a Storm," "Mind Over Mayhem," "Double Exposure," "Publish or Perish").

Falk was convinced that the series could not maintain its high level of quality at a rate of eight episodes a season. NBC wasn't pleased, but the actor pushed and got a six-episode schedule for the fourth season.

PART V

THE FOURTH SEASON (1974–75)

"Now we're talking about murder—pure and simple."
—LIEUTENANT COLUMBO
"By Dawn's Early Light" (1974)

Fourth and Six

The biggest philosophical change of the fourth season was the change from eight episodes to six.

"The fewer you make, the better they are," Falk reasoned at the time. It also would give him time to pursue movie projects.

Actually, though, *Columbo* was not a better series with fewer episodes to produce. The fourth season, while quite good, would not compare with the remarkably strong first and third seasons.

Perhaps the production team ran on all cylinders when driven by the frantic pace of a seven- or eight-episode season. Perhaps after twenty-five mysteries featuring the unkempt lieutenant, it was getting increasingly difficult to keep the format fresh.

Whatever the reason, the fourth season was a slight step back in quantity and quality. Still, several contributions did help maintain high standards.

First, Roland Kibbee and Dean Hargrove returned as executive producers. They brought with them a team of *Columbo* veterans: Edward K. Dodds, William Cronjager, Everett Chambers. In fact, Chambers, whose association with the series ran all the way back to "Dead Weight" (1971), was absorbing many of the day-to-day producing duties (probably in anticipation of his taking over the series in the fifth season).

And Falk, far from bored with the role, was exerting more and more control.

"It's no secret that, as the years went by, Peter became more and more the de facto producer of the show," Peter S. Fischer explained. "The proof of the pudding is that the character maintained his integrity."

Despite minor quibbles, Dick Levinson agreed with Fischer's assessment: "Falk wouldn't let anyone violate that character. And he understood the character better than anyone. Falk became the guardian of the show, and a good one. He could become too whimsical. We tried to stay away from schtick. But as he gained more control, Peter became the conscience of the show. Even if we had stayed, we would have given him more authority. Remember, Peter was the one continuing thread throughout the run of the show."

Certainly Universal was feeling the weight of Falk's growing power. At one point in 1974, the actor told reporters that he wanted out of his contract. Studio and network executives gagged as headlines blared: Peter Falk Quits *Columbo*—Charges Breach of Contract. When spotted back at work by reporters and asked about the walkout, Falk shrugged his shoulders and said, "Well, you know how it is." Which everyone took to mean his demands had been met.

They assumed correctly. During the third season, Falk's salary was reported to be $100,000 per episode. It was boosted to $132,000 for the fourth season. By 1976, it would jump to $300,000 per episode, the highest paycheck in the business.

Falk's salary wasn't the only thing going up. The shooting schedule was getting longer. During the first season, Levinson and Link had tried to shoot each episode in ten days. When Hargrove took over, the schedule was ten days for a ninety-minute episode and thirteen or fourteen for a two-hour show. The longer the series was on, the less rigid those guidelines became. In 1977, one episode had a twenty-two-day shooting schedule.

Budget overruns on an already expensive series were sure to make Universal executives nervous. There would come a day when the studio would tell NBC that it could not afford the overruns, and the Peacock Network, still desperate for the popular *Columbo* episodes, would say, "Okay, we'll pick up the excess tab." Richard Irving, by then a television executive at Universal, thought that was a terrible mistake.

"It was a quality show, but getting there was too expensive," Irving said. "It went so far overbudget that Universal refused to pay for it. That was the first time a network agreed to pay us. That didn't last long, but it set in motion a practice where the network might help the studio pay for an expensive show. It was a dangerous precedent set in motion by the studio's loss of control over tight budgets. Now production costs are so high that the network and the studio fight over who will pay for *Miami Vice.*"

But in 1974, NBC and Universal were overjoyed to have a tremendous hit to their credit. Falk's demands would be met.

The final reason for the strength of the fourth season was the addition of Peter Fischer as story editor (executive story consultant). Two of his scripts, "Publish or Perish" and "A Friend in Deed," had been produced during the third season, and Falk, always appreciative of good scripts, was very impressed.

"The next thing I knew, they were offering me a job as story editor on the show," Fischer recalled. "I didn't have a deal with the studio then, but I got a forty-five-minute sales pitch on why I should join the company and become a story editor and sign a long-term deal. When I got home, my agent called and said, 'Universal has just made you the most wonderful offer.' It was sort of a seven-year indentured servitude contract at minimum terms. I said, 'Did you know that Peter Falk was up in Sid Sheinberg's office about an hour ago, banging on the desk and saying that if I wasn't the story editor, he wouldn't do the show?' There was dead silence and then, 'Really?' I said, 'Now go see what they want to offer.' But we didn't hold them up. It was good all around."

Yes, it was good all around. Hargrove and Kibbee gained an invaluable story editor. Fischer gained an invaluable amount of experience. And Falk gained a writer he liked and trusted.

"Falk loved Peter Fischer," Levinson said. "And he came to trust him. Peter Fischer was the one guy who understood the show and could write it."

Hoping to knock off the NBC *Sunday Mystery Movie*, CBS moved a big gun, Telly Savalas as *Kojak*, against it in September 1975. Falk told reporters that he was confident *Columbo* would beat back the *Kojak* challenge. The actor pointed out that his contract called for a fifth season.

When the dust settled, all sides could claim victory. *Columbo* topped *Kojak* in head-to-head (or cigar-to-lollipop) meetings, but

Kojak ended up with a higher rating than the NBC *Sunday Mystery Movie* (in fact, so did *Mannix*, which was canceled after the 1974–75 season). Both *Kojak* and the *Mystery Movie* made the season's top twenty-five, so everyone went home happy.

After two seasons, Richard Boone's *Hec Ramsey* was dropped from the *Mystery Movie* wheel. It was replaced by a series that was ahead of its time. *Amy Prentiss* starred Jessica Walter (Margaret Nicholson in "Mind Over Mayhem") as San Francisco's first female chief of detectives. Viewers did not respond to a woman in command and the promising effort only lasted one season.

CASE #26: AN EXERCISE IN FATALITY

(originally aired September 15, 1974)

Written by PETER S. FISCHER
    (from a story by Larry Cohen)
Directed by BERNARD KOWALSKI
Produced by EDWARD K. DODDS
Executive producers: DEAN HARGROVE AND ROLAND KIBBEE
Music Score: DICK DE BENEDICTIS
Sunday Mystery Movie Theme: HENRY MANCINI
Director of photography: WILLIAM CRONJAGER
Art director: JOHN W. CORSO
Set decorations: WILLIAM MCLAUGHLIN
Assistant director: RAY TAYLOR
Unit manager: MAURIE M. SUESS
Film editor: BOB KAGEY
Sound: JOHN KEAN
Editorial supervision: RICHARD BELDING
Music supervision: HAL MOONEY
Costumes by GRADY HUNT
Main title design: WAYNE FITZGERALD
Titles and optical effects by UNIVERSAL TITLE

CAST

LT. COLUMBO	PETER FALK
MILO JANUS	ROBERT CONRAD
GENE STAFFORD	PHILIP BRUNS
BUDDY CASTLE	PAT HARRINGTON
JESSICA CONROY	GRETCHEN CORBETT
RUTH STAFFORD	COLLIN WILCOX
AL MURPHY	JUDE FARESE
LEWIS LACEY	DARRELL ZWERLING
JERRY	DENNIS ROBERTSON
SGT. RICKETS	RAYMOND O'KEEFE
MEDICAL EXAMINER	VICTOR IZAY
FRED	ERIC MASON
HARRY LASSITER	J.R. CLARK
DR. FREEMAN	MEL STEVENS
PHOTOGRAPHER	MANUEL DEPINA

NURSE .... KATHLEEN O'MALLEY
DOBERMAN .... DON NAGEL
WOMAN (ROSE) .... SUSAN JACOBY

Synopsis—Physical fitness expert Milo Janus, the owner of a string of successful health spas, looks much younger than his fifty-two years. His financial accounts, however, are not in such good shape. He has been skimming off profits and shipping them into European bank accounts.

A business associate, Gene Stafford, is close to uncovering the truth about Milo's creative accounting methods. Working in the office at one of the spas, Gene has promised to follow the trail of corruption to the end.

Milo puts up a brave front while he plans to murder Gene. He has thought out an ingenious alibi. Milo's secretary, Jessica Conroy, tapes all telephone calls that come into the office. Milo snips out a piece of tape from a call Gene recently made. The key passage is: "Hi, Jessica. Gene Stafford. Can I speak to him?" Milo takes this recording, puts it on a tape machine in his home office and hooks the machine to one of two phone lines in his house. He then unscrews the lightbulb for that line on the living room phone.

At about eight o'clock that night, Milo confronts Gene at the spa. They are alone. There is a scuffle and Gene pours hot coffee on Milo's arm. He runs but Milo catches him on the gym floor and strangles him. Milo's plan is to make Gene's death look like an accident. He dresses the body in sneakers and gym clothes. He puts the body on a bench and lowers a 180-pound barbell on Gene's neck. The police will think that the weight slipped while Gene was working out in the deserted building.

But Milo still has to establish an alibi. He drives to his home, where friends have gathered for a party. At nine, he slips into his study and uses the tape machine on one phone line to call the other home number. Of course, it rings in the living room, where Jessica picks it up. The other line should be lit, indicating that the phone in the study is being used, but Milo has unscrewed the bulb.

When Jessica picks up the phone, she hears Gene's voice: "Hi, Jessica. Gene Stafford. Can I speak to him." Milo emerges from the study and stages a conversation with the already-dead Gene. The guests at the party get the impression that Gene is alone at the spa and about to start a workout.

The body is found the next morning by the maintenance staff.

Several things don't seem right to Lieutenant Columbo. He notices the spilled coffee on the new rug in Gene's office. And he is intrigued by the brown scuff marks on the gym floor. Only police officers have walked on the surface since it was cleaned the night before, and they all wear black polish. The shoes in Gene's locker are brown.

These scuff marks can only be made by running and stopping short. Why would Gene be running back and forth on a gym floor in his street clothes? Columbo also is bothered by the fact that Gene ordered a large Chinese meal at 7:30. Why would he eat a heavy meal and immediately start working out?

Two things catch Columbo's eye when he goes to tell Milo the news. A lightbulb in his living room phone is out and the fitness guru has a nasty burn on his arm. "The last time that happened to me," Columbo says, it was spilled coffee.

Gene's estranged wife, Ruth, tells the persistent lieutenant that Milo and Gene didn't get along. Several entries in Gene's calendar refer to meetings with a Lewis Lacey, who, it turns out, was hired to investigate Milo's financial dealings.

During a visit to Milo's office, Columbo sees that Jessica records all incoming phone calls. Digging through the files, he finds a gap in a conversation Jessica had with Gene Stafford. The secretary tells him that the night of the party was the first time she was at Milo's house. If that's the case, Columbo wonders, why wasn't Gene surprised to hear her voice answer the phone? Instead, he said, "Hi, Jessica. Gene Stafford," just as if he were calling the office and expected her to pick up the phone.

After meeting with Lacey, Ruth tells Milo about her suspicions. He laughs at her. Gene couldn't prove anything, he says, and you can't, either. Hurt, bewildered and depressed, Ruth nearly kills herself with a combination of pills and liquor. Revived by doctors, she tells Columbo about her meeting with Milo.

Angry, Columbo informs Milo of his investigation. While the lieutenant is leaving the hospital, he sees a mother tying her son's shoes. That gives him an idea.

The knots in Gene's sneakers were reversed. The loop normally on top was on the bottom. Somebody else put those sneakers on Gene, somebody facing him. Columbo knows this for sure because the knots in the brown shoes found in Gene's lockers are normal.

"Okay," Milo says to Columbo, you've proved that someone else put on the sneakers, but "you can't prove that I did it."

It could only have been you, Columbo answers. At 7:30, Gene was last seen wearing his street clothes. He was supposed to have been alone. No one was supposed to have been in the spa until the next

The mentally sharp Columbo tries to keep pace with the physically fit Milo Janus (Robert Conrad), the perpetrator of "An Exercise in Fatality."

morning. Yet at nine o'clock, several hours before the body was discovered, Milo told everyone at the party that Gene was wearing his gym clothes. How could Milo know that Gene was in his gym clothes? How could he have known unless he put them on Gene?

"You try to contrive a perfect alibi, sir," Columbo says, "and it's your perfect alibi that's going to hang you."

The year before "An Exercise in Fatality" aired, Peter Fischer had submitted his introductory spec script. It wasn't used by Hargrove and Kibbee, but Fischer "cannibalized" (his word) six clues for other scripts. Well, why not? As Falk will tell you, good clues are hard to come by.

The lightbulb in the telephone was one of those cannibalized clues.

Still, even though the mystery is quite good, "An Exercise in Fatality" is one of the more bloated of the two-hour episodes. Even the talented director Bernard Kowalski ("Death Lends a Hand") couldn't do much to maintain the pacing. A scene in which Columbo tries to get information from a bureaucratic clerk is labored and unnecessary. It just ambles along, pushing and stretching the episode to two hours.

At least the episode provided Robert Conrad (*The Wild, Wild, West, Black Sheep Squadron, The Duke, A Man Called Sloane*) with a muscular role (pun intended).

"I was thrilled with it," Conrad said. "I wasn't thrilled with being cast as fifty-two when I was forty. There's one great memory I have of working on that show. Peter Falk, as you know, is a very meticulous actor. I can't speak for that style, although I am a great admirer of it. Well, my character was supposed to be drinking a particular juice because he was a health addict. And Columbo was supposed to just taste what I was drinking. Well, it started to create an uncomfortable acidity in my stomach, so I said, 'Now we have something that looks just like this juice, Peter. I'm up to here with this juice.' He just said, 'Well, I'm not.' His method, whatever it was, was to use the real juice. So I was stuck drinking something I had had more than enough of."

CASE #27: NEGATIVE REACTION

(originally aired October 6, 1974)

Written by PETER S. FISCHER
Directed by ALF KJELLIN
Produced by EVERETT CHAMBERS
Executive producers: DEAN HARGROVE and ROLAND KIBBEE
Associate producer: EDWARD K. DODDS
Executive story consultant: PETER S. FISCHER
Music Score: BERNARDO SEGALL
Sunday Mystery Movie Theme: HENRY MANCINI
Director of photography: WILLIAM CRONJAGER
Art director: JOHN W. CORSO
Set decorations: WILLIAM MCLAUGHLIN
Assistant director: PHILLIP COOK
Unit manager: RAY TAYLOR
Film editor: RONALD LAVINE
Sound: ROBERT MILLER
Editorial supervision: RICHARD BELDING
Music supervision: HAL MOONEY
Costumes by GRADY HUNT
Main title design: WAYNE FITZGERALD
Titles and optical effects by UNIVERSAL TITLE

CAST

LT. COLUMBO	PETER FALK
PAUL GALESKO	DICK VAN DYKE
FRANCES GALESKO	ANTOINETTE BOWER
ALVIN DESCHLER	DON GORDON
LORNA MCGRATH	JOANNA CAMERON
RAY (SERGE SAN MARTIN)	DAVID SHEINER
MR. WEEKLY	LARRY STORCH
SISTER OF MERCY	JOYCE VAN PATTEN
SGT. HOFFMAN	MICHAEL STRONG
THOMAS DOLAN	VITO SCOTTI
MRS. MAYLAND	ALICE BACKES
HARRY LEWIS	HARVEY GOLD
CAPT. SAMPSON	BILL ZUCKERT
DEPT. OF MOTOR VEHICLES CLERK	ADRIAN RICARD
MANAGER	THOM CARNEY

DOCTOR .... TOM SIGNORELLI
CALVIN MACGRUDER .... JOHN ASHTON
MINISTER .... EDWARD COLMANS
MRS. CHARLESWORT .... IRENE TEDROW
FIRST POLICEMAN .... MIKE SANTIAGO
SECOND POLICEMAN .... EDWARD CROSS

Synopsis—Brilliant photographer Paul Galesko plans to murder his domineering wife, Frances, and pin the crime on an ex-convict named Alvin Deschler. His plan is to make it look as if Alvin kidnapped his wife and killed her before picking up the ransom money.

Paul has been secretly giving the recently paroled Alvin several odd jobs to perform. Working out of a motel room, the ex-con visits possible photographic sites and takes pictures with an old Polaroid camera. He tells real estate agents that he's looking on his own behalf. Paul has ordered him to keep his name out of the business transactions. Otherwise, the price would go up.

Paul breaks into Alvin's motel room and takes the ancient camera. After sending himself a ransom note of letters cut from a newspaper, the photographer asks Frances to go see a ranch he wants to buy. Actually, this is isolated property he had Alvin lease.

Once at the ranch, he ties Frances to the chair near the fireplace. He puts a clock set for two on the mantel behind her and takes a picture. Paul discards the first picture and takes another. Then he shoots Frances.

He leaves the ranch and meets with Alvin. He asks Alvin to meet him at an abandoned junkyard the following day. What time? Paul says to call him the next day at ten o'clock and they'll set a time.

When Alvin calls in the morning, the Galeskos' maid, Mrs. Mayland, hears what sounds like a conversation with a kidnapper. After Alvin hangs up, Paul continues his clever ruse. He asks if he can talk to Frances. He says he'll keep a meeting at five that evening. He jots down the phrase "$20,000 in small bills" on a pad near the phone.

Paul gets the money from his publisher. He again stops by Alvin's motel room, this time to return the camera and plant the newspaper he used to make the ransom note.

The photographer arrives at the junkyard at 5:30. He apologizes to Alvin for being late. He shows the ransom note and the picture of the tied-up Frances to Alvin, making sure the ex-con's fingerprints are left on both.

The trap is complete. Paul shoots Alvin. He then puts the gun used to kill Frances in the dead man's hand and fires a shot through the fleshy part of his own leg. As Paul limps off to his car, he is surprised by a drunken derelict named Thomas Dolan.

The case looks open and shut. Alvin kidnapped Frances and took her to a ranch he leased. The real estate agent can identify Alvin.

The ex-con, who has a history of extortion, sent Paul a ransom note and a picture of his wife. The police have his fingerprints on the note, and motel records show he made a call at the exact time Paul says he got the ransom instructions. They also find the newspaper used to make the note in his motel room. And they find the camera that took the picture of Frances.

Alvin, the police think, shot Frances and intended to kill Paul when he delivered the ransom money. A scuffle occurred at the junkyard. After being shot in the leg, Paul killed Alvin in self-defense. The murder weapon is in Alvin's hand.

Yes, the evidence is overwhelming. But little things bother Lieutenant Columbo. First, kidnappers rarely kill their victims before getting the money. They may have to prove the captive is safe. And Alvin Deschler had no record of murder.

Second, Paul shot Alvin before learning the whereabouts of his wife.

Third, the motel manager says that Alvin claimed someone stole his camera. Why would he draw attention to himself like that?

Fourth, the real estate agent says that Alvin acted like a person who was scouting property for someone else. He's seen countless middlemen in his day.

Fifth, although drunk at the time, wino Thomas Dolan tells police that there was a gap between the first and second shots fired at the junkyard (Paul says it happened in a matter of seconds).

Sixth, Paul spent a long time at San Quentin while working on a book about the prison. He took several pictures of Alvin Deschler.

Seventh, Paul reached the junkyard at 5:30 when the phone message was for five o'clock. That's easily explained, the photographer tells Columbo, he was instructed to go to a phone booth at five o'clock and from there he was ordered to the junkyard. Gee, Columbo says, it's funny he didn't write down directions to the phone booth. He scribbled down "$20,000 in small bills," which is relatively easy to remember, but not directions to a phone booth he'd never been to before.

Eighth, there's the discarded picture found in the ranch's fireplace. It's a perfectly good picture, Columbo observes. Why would a murderous kidnapper throw it away and take another? It's not a good picture, Paul points out. The framing is off. The exposure is poor. But only a professional would be bothered by such things.

Weary of the lieutenant's constant questions, photographer Paul Galesko (Dick Van Dyke) has a negative reaction to Columbo.

Ninth, no newspaper scraps were found in Alvin's motel room. If he had cut up a paper to make the ransom note, there should be all sorts of little bits of paper. The maid probably cleaned up the room, Paul suggests. Then why didn't the newspaper get thrown out?

Finally, Columbo is troubled by the fact that Alvin rode around in cabs until the day of the murder. Why? It's cheaper to rent a car. In fact, he did rent a car on the day of the murder. Why did he wait so long? Then the lieutenant remembers that Alvin was an ex-con. Maybe he didn't have his driver's license. Sure enough, on the morning of the murder, he was taking the road test for his driver's license. Then he rented the car. Still, would he have cut everything so close? Suppose he had failed?

It all doesn't fit together. Columbo believes that Paul murdered Frances and framed Alvin. How to prove it?

In the basement of police headquarters, Columbo tells Paul that he's being charged with his wife's murder. His alibi doesn't wash. The police officer shows the photographer an enlarged copy of the picture of Frances at the ranch. The clock says ten o'clock. Alvin had an alibi. At ten o'clock, he was taking his road test. Paul, however, has no alibi.

Wait, Paul shouts, while enlarging the picture, you reversed the negative. The clock says two o'clock, not ten. Look at the original picture, Paul says, and the mistake will be obvious. There is no original picture, Columbo admits. It was mistakenly destroyed during the enlarging process. But there's been no mistake, the lieutenant insists. Paul is to be arrested.

Despite your clumsiness, Paul says, there is proof of my innocence. The original picture is unnecessary. The negative will serve the same purpose. He walks to a shelf full of cameras and removes the one found in Alvin's motel room. There, he says, look at the negative and it will confirm my alibi.

Not exactly, Columbo says. Paul has just incriminated himself. He's identified the camera that took the picture of Frances. But he would have no way of knowing which camera it was on a shelf full of cameras—unless he took the picture himself.

A cunningly crafted episode, "Negative Reaction" is entertaining proof of Peter Fischer's genius for clues. The murder does seem foolproof, yet Columbo turns up one inconsistency after another. As Falk has said, the best clues make us scratch our heads and say, "Why didn't I think of that?" "Negative Reaction" causes that reaction time and again.

The humor also is blended in at just the right moments. Columbo enters by driving his hacking wreck past a sign that reads, "We Buy Junk Cars." Columbo shows up at a mission and a sister of mercy (Joyce Van Patten) mistakes him for a derelict. "That coat," she murmurs while shaking her head. "I've had this coat for seven years," he answers. And best of all, there's the scene in which Columbo tells Paul Galesko that Dog is moping around because the cocker spaniel that lived next door has moved away. Might Paul have a picture of a cocker spaniel he could borrow?

"I wrote that line thinking, 'He's never going to do this,'" Fischer recalled. "He did it exactly as I wrote it."

Playing a murderer was a daring change of pace for Dick Van Dyke, the lovable, rubber-faced comedian who had established himself as a "nice-guy" performer in his long-running CBS situation comedy and the movies Mary Poppins, Bye Bye Birdie and Chitty Chitty Bang Bang. The same year as "Negative Reaction," he stunned critics with his shattering portrayal of an alcoholic in the TV movie The Morning After. His work as a Columbo villain also showed how effectively Van Dyke could play against type. It's a shame that more dramatic opportunities didn't come his way.

Adding a wonderful moment to the episode is veteran character actor Larry Storch (once Corporal Agarn on ABC's F Troop), who plays the fussy and nervous road test examiner, Mr. Weekly.

CASE #28: BY DAWN'S EARLY LIGHT

(originally aired October 27, 1974)

Written by HOWARD BERK
Directed by HARVEY HART
Produced by EVERETT CHAMBERS
Executive producers: DEAN HARGROVE and ROLAND KIBBEE
Executive story consultant: PETER S. FISCHER
Associate producer: EDWARD K. DODDS
Music Score: BERNARDO SEGALL
Sunday Mystery Movie Theme: HENRY MANCINI
Director of photography: JACK PRIESTLY
Art director: MICHAEL BAUGH
Assistant director: G. WARREN SMITH
Unit manager: RAY TAYLOR, JR.
Film editor: BOB KAGEY
Sound: DONALD F. JOHNSON
Editorial supervision: RICHARD BELDING
Music supervision: HAL MOONEY
Costumes by GRADY HUNT
Main title design: WAYNE FITZGERALD
Titles and optical effects by UNIVERSAL TITLE

CAST

LT. COLUMBO	PETER FALK
COLONEL LYLE C. RUMFORD	PATRICK MCGOOHAN
WILLIAM HAYNES	TOM SIMCOX
CADET ROY SPRINGER	MARK WHEELER
CAPTAIN LOOMIS	BURR DEBENNING
SUSAN GERARD	KAREN LAMM
MISS BRADY	MADELEINE THORNTON-SHERWOOD
SGT. KRAMER	BRUCE KIRBY, SR.
OFFICER CORSO	SIDNEY ARMUS
JONATHAN B. MILLER (BOODLE BOY)	ROBERT CLOTWORTHY
CADET MORGAN	B. KIRBY, JR.

Synopsis—Colonel Lyle C. Rumford, the strict commandant of the Haynes Military Academy, is appalled to learn that board chairman

William Haynes intends to turn the venerable old institution into a coed junior college. The idea is abhorrent to Rumford, who prizes tradition, discipline and duty.

He is not about to relinquish his command, even if enrollment is down. The country needs places where boys learn to become men. The impudent Haynes has become the enemy, and the enemy must be removed.

There are only three occasions during the year when Rumford fires Old Thunder, the cannon that proudly stands in the middle of the parade grounds. One is Founders Day: the following day.

As dawn is breaking on Founders Day, Rumford stuffs a cleaning rag down the barrel of Old Thunder. He's also doctored the shell with a powerful charge. The results will be explosive. While preparing the cannon for its murderous purpose, the iron-willed commandant spots a jug of hard cider hanging in a barracks window. Later that day, he orders Captain Loomis to conduct a painstaking search for the fermenting fluid, which he assumes the crafty cadets will have moved as a matter of always staying one step ahead of the officers.

During a morning meeting with William Haynes, Rumford goads the board chairman into insisting on presiding at the Founders Day ceremony. Those duties include firing Old Thunder.

Haynes' death looks like an accident. Roy Springer, a cadet with a sloppy record, apparently left a cleaning rag in the cannon. But Springer denies it and Lieutenant Columbo believes him. The policeman, however, gets the feeling that Springer is holding something back.

Slowly, Columbo starts to suspect Rumford. Why? Well, the explosion was heard by people who never complained before about the cannon's noise. Sure enough, lab reports turn up traces of a powerful explosive in the fragments found on the field. And Rumford is an explosives expert.

Only three people had a key to the storeroom containing the cannon supplies: Springer, Captain Loomis and Rumford. A blueprint found in Haynes' car supplies the motive. It is a redesign for the academy gym. The alterations are for a girls' locker room.

When Roy runs away, Columbo learns that the cadet had an alibi. The night before Founders Day, he was with his girlfriend, Susan Gerard.

Now Columbo is sure of Rumford's guilt, yet he needs proof. He gets it when the boys tell him about the cider. Rumford claims he saw the cider the day before the explosion.

But that's not possible. The cider was hung out for the very first time during the night before Founders Day. Rumford couldn't have

Columbo searches for clues the old-fashioned way in "By Dawn's Early Light."

seen it in the dark. The cadets put the cider in another hiding place at 6:25 on Founders Day morning. So, the jug was visible only from 6:10 until 6:25. That's the only time there was enough light. And it was only visible from one spot—directly behind the cannon. By launching his investigation, Rumford has placed himself at the scene of the murder a full thirty minutes before he claims to have left his bed for morning coffee.

Shot on location at a South Carolina military school, "By Dawn's Early Light" is a stylish and extremely satisfying departure for the series. Director Harvey Hart's opening is one of the most memorable since "Murder by the Book." The pacing is deliberately slow. There is no music. Step by step, we see Rumford prepare for murder. The camera plays on each detail, even the washing of hands. It is the calm of dawn. It is the quiet before the battle.

Much of the credit for the episode's high quality must go to Patrick McGoohan, the New York–born actor whose distinctive Irish-British tones were heard in the sixties series *Secret Agent* (an expanded version of England's *Danger Man*) and *The Prisoner* (the cult favorite he produced and created).

Usually associated with suave action roles, McGoohan must have seemed like an odd choice to play a blood-and-guts American colonel. But the versatile actor, like Falk, had a reputation as an uncompromising artist. His portrayal of Rumford is every bit as quirky and fascinating as Falk's detective. One gets the feeling of watching two performers working on the same level and wavelength.

McGoohan also says he contributed to the script, although exactly how much is unclear. The teleplay is credited to Howard Berk, who would work on several more *Columbo* scripts and author the final episode of the series. Falk remembers that the script needed polishing, but he doesn't recall how much.

"Peter would go crazy when the scripts didn't meet his standards," McGoohan explained. "Everett Chambers produced the first *Columbo* I did, and he was responsible for talking me into it. I think Ed Asner had been asked to do it. Then he couldn't do it, and Everett asked me. It was a rare privilege for me. It was a classy show. It was a pleasure to work on them [he'd end up working on three]. How many TV series in the United States are done with that much care? M*A*S*H is the only one I can think of that's comparable. But the script was in lousy shape. I got on the plane for South Carolina and was going over the script when Peter, looking all the world like Columbo, got on board. There was a stopover. He finally walked over to me with his head down and asked, 'What do you think of the script?'"

According to McGoohan, before he could really answer, Falk was telling him what he thought of the script. Knowing that his guest star was a talented writer, Falk asked him to polish the story.

McGoohan says he did a fair amount of rewriting on "By Dawn's Early Light." "It needed fixing," he claimed.

Berk dismisses McGoohan's claims, calmly pointing out that the Writers Guild decides who is entitled to credit.

"As a matter of fact," Berk said, "there were very few changes made. There's little difference between the original script and what ended up on the screen. I have no idea of what McGoohan says he did. He couldn't have done all that much. There's no way he could. There's no question about that. Patrick is a very flamboyant character—period, end of story."

Both Hargrove and Fischer say some rewriting was necessary, yet neither man remembers it being that extensive.

"All of the scripts needed some rewriting," Fischer said. "The job of story editor requires, by necessity, a lot of rewriting. A lot of it is to protect the character. Freelancers write terrific plots, but they get lost because they don't understand the character. You have to have Columbo, not semi-Columbo. I'd sit at my typewriter and do the character as I was writing—to make sure it sounded right. My children would look at me like I was nuts. I wouldn't even realize I was doing it."

The question of who did what on "By Dawn's Early Light" was further muddled by the appearance of MCA Publishing's British edition of the Columbo novel *The Dean's Death*. The American Popular Library edition, one of six tie-in paperbacks issued in a series, says that it's an original novel by Alfred Lawrence. This seems entirely plausible. Lawrence wrote the first book in the series, and it was an original novel. The other four books were written by different authors and were based on episodes. Yet the British copy says that *The Dean's Death* is adapted from the episode "By Dawn's Early Light," written by Howard Berk.

What makes the reference all the more strange is the fact that *The Dean's Death* bears almost no relation to "By Dawn's Early Light." The murder is different. The characters are all completely different. About the only similarity is the academic setting. Placed on the campus of fictional Meredith College, Lawrence's novel deals with a school president, Franklin Torrance, who kills Dean Arnold Borchardt (with a lead pipe) to cover up an affair with Linda Kittredge, a beautiful coed. The story is unfamiliar to Berk, so it's hardly likely that Lawrence based his novel on any draft of the script.

"I have several copies [of *The Dean's Death*]," Berk said, "but I must confess that I've never read it. It does sound like a bit of a stretch."

What we do know is that the Writers Guild was sufficiently convinced that Berk's name belonged on the episode as the author. McGoohan may or may not have fine-tuned his strong concept at Falk's request. We also know that, whatever the process was, the results were brilliant.

"That's probably my favorite [of the three *Columbo* episodes]," McGoohan said. "It might be my favorite role in the United States. It took a bit of work, but I thought it was excellent. It was on the basis of that experience that I agreed to do the others."

The excellence of McGoohan's characterization was recognized the following May when he was awarded the Emmy for Outstanding Single Performance by a Supporting Actor in a Series.

"It was a terrific part," he commented. "I made him somewhat more neurotic. I didn't see the commandant as a villain. Not at all. He thought he was doing the right thing. He committed a murder because of his ideals. He would live and die a soldier."

And you could say that Falk and McGoohan hit it off in a big way.

"Patrick McGoohan was great for the series," said Richard Levinson, who was still keeping close tabs on the show. "I just loved him. And so did Falk. They had a real love affair going on the set. Their acting styles clicked. They both were very caring and dedicated, so those episodes took forever."

"It was a very happy experience," McGoohan agreed. "With Everett producing, the decision-making was quite simple. Peter has extraordinary concentration, which, of course, is the essence of Columbo. There's two marvelous things about Columbo: You know who the murderer is and Columbo is always up against an able protagonist. How is he going to catch him this time?"

Again, the humor was used wisely. When Rumford starts to take a liking to Columbo, he asks, "Do you have a first name?"

"I do," the lieutenant answers. "My wife is the only one who uses it."

Since we never see Mrs. Columbo, the odds against learning his first name are prohibitive. By now, viewers were demanding to know Columbo's first name. It was never given, but columnists have mistakenly said it's Frank and Joseph. Falk had a stock answer. Whenever anybody asked him Columbo's first name, he would say it's "Lieutenant." About ten years after "By Dawn's Early Light" aired, a popular trivia-minded board game incorrectly gave Columbo's first name as Phillip.

"By Dawn's Early Light" is the first episode to feature character actor Bruce Kirby as Sergeant Kramer. Kirby had already appeared in the third season's "Lovely but Lethal" as a lab attendant. Kramer, though, became a recurring character during the fourth and fifth seasons. Kirby would appear in six episodes. Only Falk and Dog appeared in more.

CASE #29: TROUBLED WATERS

(originally aired February 9, 1975)

Written by WILLIAM DRISKILL
  (from a story by Jackson Gillis)
Directed by BEN GAZZARA
Produced by EVERETT CHAMBERS
Executive producers: DEAN HARGROVE and ROLAND KIBBEE
Executive story consultant: PETER S. FISCHER
Associate producer: EDWARD K. DODDS
Music Score: DICK DE BENEDICTIS
Sunday Mystery Movie Theme: HENRY MANCINI
Director of photography: WILLIAM CRONJAGER, A.S.C.
Art director: MICHAEL BAUGH
Assistant director: KEVIN DONNELLY
Unit manager: RAY TAYLOR
Film editor: ROBERT L. KIMBLE, A.C.E.
Sound: JERRY E. SMITH
Editorial supervision: RICHARD BELDING
Music supervision: HAL MOONEY
Costumes by GRADY HUNT
Main title design: WAYNE FITZGERALD
Titles and optical effects by UNIVERSAL TITLE

CAST

LT. COLUMBO	PETER FALK
HAYDEN DANZIGER	ROBERT VAUGHN
SHIP'S CAPTAIN GIBBON	PATRICK MACNEE
SHIP'S PURSER PRESTON WATKINS	BERNARD FOX
ROSANNA WELLES	POUPÉE BOCAR
LLOYD HARRINGTON	DEAN STOCKWELL
SYLVIA DANZIGER	JANE GREER
SHIP'S DOCTOR FRANK PIERCE	ROBERT DOUGLAS
MELISSA	SUSAN DAMANTE
ARTIE PODELL	PETER MALONEY
THE MAGICIAN	CURTIS CREDEL

Synopsis—Lieutenant Columbo and his wife are taking a cruise to Mexico. Mrs. Columbo won the trip in a raffle for the Holy Name

Society. Also aboard is auto executive Hayden Danziger, a man cruising in a murderous direction.

Hayden is being blackmailed by Rosanna Welles, the featured vocalist on the cruise. If her demands aren't met, she'll reveal the details of their affair to his wife, Sylvia. Hayden plans to shoot Rosanna and frame Lloyd Harrington, the band pianist she recently dumped. Lloyd even helps matters by getting into a fight with the singer.

Before setting up his alibi, Hayden plants the receipt for a British .38 pistol in Lloyd's cabin and hides the gun in Rosanna's cabin. Standing by the pool, Hayden breaks a capsule under his nose and inhales a chemical that will bring on the symptoms of a heart attack.

The "stricken" man is taken to the ship's infirmary, where Dr. Pierce diagnoses a mild coronary incident. The doctor orders the attending nurse to take Hayden's pulse and blood pressure every thirty minutes.

That night, when the band is on break and just after the nurse has checked his vital signs, Hayden slips out of the infirmary and into the ship's service stairwell. He has thirty minutes before the nurse will return. Having taken this same cruise before, he knows the band's schedule and the ship's routine.

Dressing as a steward, Hayden puts on a pair of surgical gloves he took from the infirmary. He goes to Rosanna's cabin, knowing the singer will be there for her costume change. He sneaks in, gets the gun and shoots her, using a pillow to muffle the noise. He uses her lipstick to put an L on the mirror.

He puts the steward's outfit and the gun in a bin in the laundry. When the nurse comes back to take his blood pressure, Hayden is in bed, pretending to be asleep.

Captain Gibbon asks Lieutenant Columbo to investigate the shocking murder. Suspicion immediately falls upon Lloyd. There were several witnesses to his argument with Rosanna. The band was on break and people saw the musician running after the singer. There's the L on the mirror. A pair of surgical gloves is missing and Lloyd, a diabetic, had access to the cabinet where they are stored. And the receipt for the .38 is found in the pianist's cabin. It says that the gun was purchased in Las Vegas at a time when the band was performing there.

While Captain Gibbon is satisfied with obvious conclusions, several details bother Columbo.

Why would someone keep the receipt for a gun when he planned to use it to murder a former lover? The only other receipts Lloyd saved were ones that represented tax deductions. He couldn't deduct the gun. So why was it stuck in with all these other receipts?

Then there's that lipstick *L* on the mirror. Rosanna was shot through the heart. Dr. Pierce says death would have been instantaneous. She couldn't have left the mysterious letter. It looks as if someone is going to an awful lot of trouble to pin this crime on Lloyd Harrington.

Columbo's suspicions are diverted in another direction when he spots a feather outside Hayden Danziger's infirmary room. Hospitals only use foam pillows, and this feather matches the pillow remains found in Rosanna's cabin.

The gun is discovered in the laundry bin, but that only raises another question in Columbo's mind. Why didn't Lloyd merely throw the gun overboard? Hayden suggests that the musician didn't have time before he was due back on the bandstand. Okay, Columbo says, then where are the gloves? Why, Hayden asks, did he have to use gloves? A pair of surgical gloves is missing, Columbo tells him, and there was no powder residue on Lloyd's hands. He either wore gloves or he didn't fire the gun.

Perhaps, the auto executive replies, Lloyd threw the gloves overboard (which, of course, is exactly what Hayden did after being released from the infirmary). Yes, Columbo answers, but if he had time to throw the gloves overboard, he had time to get rid of the gun.

The persistent lieutenant slowly builds his case against Hayden. He finds the capsule stuck in the pool's filter, a possibility Hayden hadn't considered. He learns that Hayden has taken this cruise before. Talking to Sylvia, he finds out that her husband was in Las Vegas when the murder weapon was purchased. Looking at Hayden's medical chart, Columbo sees that his pulse and blood pressure jumped way up shortly after the murder.

Still, the policeman needs some hard evidence. Columbo tells Hayden that he must find the surgical gloves with the powder marks. Without them, it will be difficult to obtain a conviction against Lloyd.

Hoping to secure the case against Lloyd, Hayden steals another pair of surgical gloves and borrows the cruise magician's stage pistol. He goes to the engine room and, wearing the gloves, he fires a shot. He then hides the gloves in a fire hose, knowing they'll be discovered during the next day's emergency drill.

When they're found, Columbo asks that Hayden be brought to the bridge. Here, the lieutenant says, are the gloves, and they have powder marks. There's something else, though. Surgical gloves, unlike the leather or fur-lined varieties, are made of rubber. They retain

Lieutenant Columbo bounces some ideas off a confident Hayden Danziger (Robert Vaughn) in "Troubled Waters."

fingerprints. And there are fingerprints in these gloves. They don't belong to Lloyd. Hayden is trapped by his own rigged evidence.

And a good time was had by all. Filmed aboard the Princess Cruises' *Sun Princess* during an actual voyage to Mexico, "Troubled Waters" was completed under a full sail of high spirits. Real tourists gladly cooperated as director Ben Gazzara ("A Friend in Deed") guided his cast and crew around the luxury ship.

"Of the two episodes I directed," Gazzara said, "'Troubled Waters' was an especially good time. It was great watching the actual customers mix with the show folk. We sailed from San Francisco to Puerto Vallarta, and about the only thing that wasn't fun was the vomiting. We had a storm. The sound man would say 'action,' and you got it."

Although the mystery isn't one of the series' best, "Troubled Waters" remains tremendous fun through repeated viewings. The delightful cast includes two leading men from popular spy series of the sixties—Robert Vaughn (*The Man from U.N.C.L.E.*) and Patrick Macnee (*The Avengers*)—and two actors who have played Dr. Watson (Macnee and Bernard Fox).

Repeating a twist used in "Candidate for Crime," the episode opens with a shot of Columbo's face. The references to Mrs. Columbo are

Patrick Macnee, also known as John Steed of The Avengers, *tries to calm "Troubled Waters" as Captain Gibbon.*

hilarious ("My wife likes to have a good time. Sometimes she gets carried away."), as are the lieutenant's constant battles to distinguish between a ship and a boat.

"That episode was Everett Chambers' idea," Falk said. "It was great fun. Benny was directing. It was wonderful."

Columbo even (finally) forsakes his traditional costume (suit and raincoat) for slacks and a casual shirt. He seems to truly enjoy resorting to old-fashioned detective tricks, because the ship has no forensics equipment. How natural he looks peering through the basic tool of the sleuthing trade—the magnifying glass.

Best of all is the notion that Mrs. Columbo is right there on the ship. Surely we'll finally get a glimpse of the woman. She's waiting around the next corner. The teasing is beautifully sustained until the final credits.

CASE #30: PLAYBACK

(originally aired March 2, 1975)

Written by DAVID P. LEWIS AND BOOKER T. BRADSHAW
Directed by BERNARD KOWALSKI
Produced by EVERETT CHAMBERS
Executive producers: DEAN HARGROVE AND ROLAND KIBBEE
Associate producer: EDWARD K. DODDS
Executive story consultant: PETER S. FISCHER
Music Score: BERNARDO SEGALL
Sunday Mystery Movie Theme: HENRY MANCINI
Director of photography: RICHARD C. GLOUNER, A.S.C.
Art director: MICHAEL BAUGH
Set decorations: JERRY ADAMS
Assistant director: KEVIN DONNELLY
Unit manager: CARTER DeHAVEN, JR.
Film editor: RONALD LaVINE
Sound: FRANK H. WILKINSON
Editorial supervision: RICHARD BELDING
Music supervision: HAL MOONEY
Costumes by GRADY HUNT
Main title design: WAYNE FITZGERALD
Titles and optical effects by UNIVERSAL TITLE

CAST

LT. COLUMBO	PETER FALK
HAROLD VAN WYCK	OSKAR WERNER
MARGARET MIDAS	MARTHA SCOTT
ELIZABETH VAN WYCK	GENA ROWLANDS
ARTHUR MIDAS	ROBERT BROWN
FRANCINE	PATRICIA BARRY
BAXTER	HERB JEFFERSON, JR.
MARCY	TRISHA NOBLE
THOMPSON	BART BURNS
POLICEMAN	STEVEN MARLO
ATTENDANT	JOE O'HAR

Synopsis—Electronics genius Harold Van Wyck married into wealth and power. But the high-living inventor has wasted hundreds of thousands of dollars pursuing extravagant experiments, and he's about to be ousted as head of the family-owned Midas Electronics. The only thing that has kept Harold's iron-willed mother-in-law, Margaret Midas, from firing him before is her devotion to Elizabeth, her sheltered invalid daughter. Elizabeth refuses to think or hear ill of her husband, Harold. He knows this and is perfectly willing to manipulate Elizabeth as a weapon against her mother.

This time, however, Margaret is holding a trump card. She hired a private detective who discovered and documented the details of Harold's philandering ways. Margaret intends to replace Harold with her son, Arthur, a nice man with little business sense.

Knowing he's trapped, Harold has devised an elaborate scheme to prevent the imminent purge.

The Midas estate is guarded by the most sophisticated electronic devices—an infrared electric eye, wired cyclone fences, window alarms and a closed-circuit TV system that allows the guard constant views of the entrance hall, study and drawing room. Since Harold designed the safety features, he has the knowledge of how to defeat them. After planting the evidence of a forced entry, Harold returns to his car and drives into the estate.

Secreted in the small control room that contains the surveillance equipment, Harold makes a videotape of the empty study. He then feeds this tape into the monitor that shows the guard a view of the study. While the guard is observing this peaceful scene, Harold makes certain that the surveillance camera in the study records what happens next—the shooting of his mother-in-law. Harold, of course, makes certain that he's out of camera range.

Elizabeth, who is in her bedroom, thinks she's heard something, but Harold assures her that everything is all right. Harold tells Elizabeth that he's promised their friend Francine he'll attend the opening of a special show at her art gallery. After he leaves, a timer on the recorder plays the tape of Margaret's murder on the guard's monitor. The guard sees the shooting and rushes into the mansion. Harold's technical know-how has provided him with a seemingly perfect alibi. The guard establishes the time of death as 9:30, the exact time several witnesses were with Harold at Francine's gallery.

Lieutenant Columbo arrives on the scene with a bad cold. Watching the videotape of the murder, the detective comments on how frustrating it is that the killer always stayed out of the camera's range. It's almost as if he knew about them, Columbo observes.

The camera doesn't cover the whole room, Harold tells him, just the safe. "We were expecting a thief, not a murderer."

The early theory is that a thief broke into the back of the house and

Harold Van Wyck (Oskar Werner) shows Lieutenant Columbo his state-of-the-art watch, unaware that a "Playback" will cause his undoing.

Margaret surprised him. The theory doesn't satisfy Columbo. Why would a robber choose to break into such a heavily guarded house? And if he did gain entrance through the back, he would have had to cross the hall. Why didn't the hall camera pick him up? Why, after all that bother, didn't the thief take anything?

Columbo presses his investigation and finds out something even more troubling when he talks to the unsuspecting Elizabeth. Because Elizabeth is confined to a wheelchair, the doors to her rooms open with a hand clap or a loud noise. She remembers her bedroom door opened for no reason at nine o'clock, a half hour before the killing supposedly took place. Harold blames this on a glitch in the system. The detective needs harder evidence to place Harold in the house at the time of the murder.

The answer occurs to Columbo when he sees an instant-replay device used during a televised football game. Columbo shows Harold the tape of the shooting. Something is there that shouldn't be. On the table behind Margaret's body is a distinctive envelope. It is his engraved invitation to the art gallery. There's only one like it, and Harold turned it in at the gallery. To get the invitation, he would have had to step right over his mother-in-law's body. The conclusion is inescapable: Margaret Midas was shot before Harold left the house and Harold shot her. The rigging of the home security system, which Harold counted on to establish his perfect alibi, contains the evidence that has trapped him.

In desperation, Harold turns to his pliant wife for an alibi. She refuses him. Harold has not seen what Columbo had been counting on—that the ordeal has brought out a strength that's always been in Elizabeth.

Although a ninety-minute episode with a terrific final clue, "Playback" seems a bit sluggish at times. The pacing is a bit too deliberate, and the abrupt nature of the conclusion gives us little chance to savor the ultimate clue or consider the shattering blow dealt to Elizabeth. The poignant last look at Elizabeth's tear-streaked face loses some of its emotional impact in the hasty nature of the ending. Yet the mystery is extremely cunning and the acting is very strong. One of four episodes directed by Bernard Kowalski, it is given an electrifying jolt by the presence of Falk's close friend Gena Rowlands. The year before, they had co-starred in A Woman Under the Influence, a film directed by Rowlands' husband, John Cassavetes (who had played Alex Benedict in "Etude in Black").

The year after "Playback," Cassavetes and Falk co-starred in director Elaine May's Mickey and Nicky. In 1970, the two pals had shared star billing in Husbands with another close friend, Ben Gazzara (director of "A Friend in Deed" and "Troubled Waters").

Giving a far less moody performance than the ones for which film audiences best know him (Ship of Fools and Fahrenheit 451), Oskar Werner is rigid and aloof as the meticulous Harold Van Wyck. Because we come to like and admire Rowlands' Elizabeth so much, Harold's sham of affection and coldhearted manipulation of her feelings make him one of the most despicable of the Columbo murderers.

Considering the level of the performances in "Playback," it is not surprising that Falk singles it out as one of his very favorites.

CASE #31: A DEADLY STATE OF MIND

(originally aired April 27, 1975)

Written by PETER S. FISCHER
Directed by HARVEY HART
Produced by EVERETT CHAMBERS
Executive story consultant: PETER S. FISCHER
Associate producer: EDWARD K. DODDS
Music Score: BERNARDO SEGALL
Sunday Mystery Movie Theme: HENRY MANCINI
Director of photography: EARL RATH, A.S.C.
Art director: MICHAEL BAUGH
Set decorations: JERRY ADAMS
Assistant director: KEVIN DONNELLY
Unit manager: RAY TAYLOR
Film editor: RONALD LAVINE
Sound: JERRY E. SMITH
Editorial supervision: RICHARD BELDING
Music supervision: HAL MOONEY
Costumes by GRADY HUNT
Main title design: WAYNE FITZGERALD
Titles and optical effects by UNIVERSAL TITLE

CAST

LT. COLUMBO	PETER FALK
DR. MARCUS COLLIER	GEORGE HAMILTON
NADIA DONNER	LESLEY ANN WARREN
KARL DONNER	STEPHEN ELLIOTT
DR. ANITA BORDEN	KAREN MACHON
SERGEANT KRAMER	BRUCE KIRBY
DR. HUNT	WILLIAM WINTERSOLE
CHARLES WHELAN	RYAN MACDONALD
DANIEL MORRIS	JACK MANNING
DAVID MORRIS	FRED DRAPER
BRENDA	GLORIE KAUFMAN
ARNOLD	REDMOND GLEESON
OFFICER HENDRYX	VANCE DAVIS
GARY KEPPLER	DANNY WELLS
LAB MAN	MORRIS BUCHANAN
SECOND RECEPTIONIST	KATHY SPEIRS

* * *

Synopsis—The head of the Institute of Behavioral Studies, a university research project, dashing psychiatrist Dr. Marcus Collier is romancing his very beautiful, very wealthy and very married patient, Nadia Donner. He's also regularly hypnotizing her and using the revelations for a book that he hopes will be a successful follow-up to his first bestseller.

But Nadia's husband, powerful and imperious businessman Karl Donner, has learned about the affair. A trustee of the university, he's threatening to expose and ruin Mark.

If Karl cuts him off from Nadia, the book Mark's publisher is screaming for won't materialize. If Karl lets it be known that Mark is sleeping with a patient, the psychiatrist's reputation will be ruined.

Mark drives out to the Donners' beach house, hoping to reason with Karl. A fight breaks out and Mark strikes Karl with the fireplace poker. The businessman is dead.

Knowing how much Nadia depends on him, Mark instructs her to tell the police that men broke into the house and robbed them. Karl resisted and they killed him. She waits to call the police so Mark can drive back to the institute and establish an alibi.

Speeding away from the house, Mark almost hits a blind man walking with his seeing-eye dog.

When the police arrive, Lieutenant Columbo finds a tiny piece of metal under the living room coffee table. And he notices the tracks left in the mud by the killer's car. It's a foreign model.

Nadia is so distraught that the doctor in attendance decides to summon her psychiatrist, Marcus Collier.

Columbo tells Marcus that he doesn't really believe Nadia's story. If the robbers did drive to the beach house door, she and Karl would have been warned. They were sitting in the living room and headlights coming down the driveway shine right into that window. And Nadia says the men had guns. When Karl resisted, why didn't they just shoot him? Why chance things with the poker?

The lieutenant wants Nadia to take a lie detector test. Mark realizes that it's only a matter of time before this emotionally unstable woman cracks and spills the truth. He can't let her take that lie detector test. She must be eliminated.

Mark tells Nadia that hypnosis will help her pass the lie detector test. When she's under, however, the psychiatrist provides a posthypnotic suggestion that will cause Nadia to inadvertently take her own life. Later that night, he says, she will be alone, the door locked from

Psychiatrist Marcus Collier (George Hamilton) is amused by Columbo's efforts to figure out "A Deadly State of Mind."

the inside. At ten o'clock the phone will ring and she'll hear a man's name: Charles Whelan. She'll become very hot. She'll have an overwhelming desire to go swimming. She'll *have* to swim. She'll have to jump in the cool, refreshing water of the pool below her balcony. But the pool is empty and she will kill herself. Her father, Mark continues, will be watching her dive—just like when she was a little girl.

That night, Mark is having a party. Columbo shows up and captivates the guests with details of his investigation. The detective has deduced that someone else was in the beach house on the night of the murder. Nadia said that the robbers wore stocking masks, so they couldn't smoke. Yet the little piece of metal he found was a flint from a lighter. The lieutenant also notices that Mark uses a lighter, but, on the night of the murder, he lit his cigarette with a match. Further fueling Columbo's suspicions is the fact that Mark's car is a foreign make with tires that match the tread in the Donners' driveway.

At ten o'clock, with Columbo sitting with his guests, Mark makes his murderous call to Nadia. Summoned to the scene, the lieutenant wonders why Nadia would interrupt a conversation (the phone was found off the hook), take her clothes off, neatly fold them, stack them on a chair and then jump to her death. Her valuables were wrapped in a scarf and tucked in a shoe, as if Nadia thought she was going for a swim.

The autopsy reveals traces of amobarbital and xylothin, drugs that can deepen a hypnotic state. Mark's associate, Dr. Anita Borden, explains to Columbo that you can't hypnotize someone to do something against their will. Can you hypnotize someone to think they're doing one thing when they're actually doing another, especially when using these drugs?

After talking with Anita, who confirms that Mark uses the drugs in his research, Columbo has a good idea of how the psychiatrist worked the two murders. He needs proof. The policeman finally realizes that he had a witness.

The suspect is brought to the Donner house. Columbo says that he can't prove how Mark killed Mrs. Donner, but he can prove Mark killed Mr. Donner. There is a witness.

A Mr. Morris is brought in. He was walking by the Donner house on the night of the murder. Mark nearly ran him down.

Mark laughs at Columbo. This man is blind, the psychiatrist says.

What makes you think this man is blind? On the night of the murder, Columbo says, did you see a blind man at the driveway entrance?

Realizing he almost incriminated himself, Mark answers that anyone with medical training could see that this man is blind. You can tell by the way he moves. You can tell by the cast of his eyes. Have him read something.

To Mark's utter horror, Mr. Morris starts to read. He isn't blind. This is David Morris. He can see.

Columbo then calls in Daniel Morris, a brother who looks very much like David. He is blind. This is the man Mark nearly hit. But there is no way Mark should have assumed that David Morris was blind. David had entered the room and done everything like a person with sight—because he has sight. Why would Mark think he was blind unless he saw someone who looked just like him—someone who is blind?

Yes, Columbo says, there is an eyewitness that places Mark at the driveway on the night of the murder. But it isn't David Morris and it isn't Daniel Morris. The lieutenant looks at the psychiatrist and says, "It's you."

Peter Fischer's association with *Columbo* didn't completely end with "A Deadly State of Mind," but his involvement would gradually taper off. During the fifth season, he would share story editing duties with Bill Driskill.

In fact, he was working less than part-time on *Columbo* by mid-

1975. Writing for the series had brought him the respect and friendship of Dick Levinson and Bill Link. They were so impressed with Fischer that he was chosen to produce their new series, *The Adventures of Ellery Queen.* So, the bulk of his energies were diverted away from *Columbo.*

Ellery Queen, by the way, lasted only one season. It may have been too clever for its own good (too much a mystery fan's mystery series). Brighter things were on the horizon for the Levinson/Link/Fischer connection.

Fischer's contributions to *Columbo* were intense and immense. From the middle of the third season until the conclusion of the fourth, he wrote (incredibly) five out of ten episodes, several while acting as story editor.

"I don't think the writing could have been sustained if we were doing one a week," Fischer said. "I think it helped that it wasn't on every week. The formula was so rich that if you got it every week, it wouldn't have been so special. We were only doing six a year, but we were doing ninety-minute or two-hour movies. And it's a lot easier to sustain a mystery in an hour. Sustaining a mystery over ninety minutes is really hard. And it's not even a whodunit. It's a cat-and-mouse. So you have to keep the story going basically by talking—talk and talk and talk.

"What made it rewarding was Peter Falk. Peter is a consummate professional. Some actors can butcher what you write. But talents like Peter Falk and Angela Lansbury read your lines and you get a warm feeling all over when you watch the dailies. Oh, sometimes Peter could make a mountain out of a molehill. Mostly, though, his input was terrific. The show could have worked with a couple of other actors in the part, but it wouldn't have become a classic without Peter Falk. It was the right part for the right actor. He was a one-of-a-kind actor in a one-of-a-kind role."

An episode that teamed the sloppy Falk with an actor known for his sartorial splendor, George Hamilton, "A Deadly State of Mind" is a grand ninety-minute mystery. The second of four episodes directed by Harvey Hart, it contains a memorable climax—a payoff not designed by Fischer.

"That was Dick Levinson's idea," Fischer explained. "It was a clue he could never work into a story. Well, I had written the plot of the psychiatrist, but I didn't know how to end it. One day, Dick said, 'I've always had this clue I wanted to use. A blind man at the driveway when the murderer escapes.' I said, 'Oh, yeah? Watch this.' I took my story and put it together with his clue."

And it worked. Once in a great while, a *Columbo* writer would give the murderer a profession already represented in an earlier episode. Gene Barry played a psychiatrist in the very first Columbo mystery, *Prescription: Murder*. Thirty outings later, here's George Hamilton as a psychiatrist (although a very different character). When the series ended and the rogues gallery was complete, there would be two writers, three actors, three actresses and two gourmet chefs among the *Columbo* murderers. It supports Dick Levinson's contention that it was difficult to continually come up with interesting occupations for the killers.

Bruce Kirby is back as Sergeant Kramer, and Columbo has grown fond enough of the character to call him "Sarge."

Summing Up the Fourth Season

While not as strong as the previous three seasons, the *Columbo* fourth proved the format could sustain repetition and emerge fresh and entertaining. Capping off the season was a *Rolling Stone* magazine cover story on Falk.

On the evening of May 19, 1975, Peter Falk won his second Emmy for *Columbo*. His delight was compounded by Patrick McGoohan's victory in a category with a rather bulky title: Outstanding Single Performance by a Supporting Actor in a Comedy or Drama Series (For a One-time Appearance in a Regular or Limited Series). In simpler terms, he won for "By Dawn's Early Light."

PART VI

THE FIFTH SEASON (1975–76)

"*A light goes on up here, and sometimes I can't turn it off.*"

—LIEUTENANT COLUMBO
"**Forgotten Lady**" (1975)

A Fifth of Columbo

By the end of the fourth season, Dean Hargrove and Roland Kibbee had relinquished their producing chores to Everett Chambers.

After three seasons with the show, Hargrove was ready to move on to other projects.

"I had done it long enough," he said. "Everett Chambers knew the show as well as anybody, so he was an obvious choice to take over. We felt totally comfortable turning production over to Everett Chambers."

Twenty-two episodes, almost half of all the *Columbo* mysteries, had been produced during the three seasons of Hargrove's tenure. His significance can't be overstated. He had kept the series running on a quality track.

Hargrove's association with the mystery genre was far from over. He and Kibbee immediately set about fashioning a fourth *Mystery Movie* entry for the 1975–76 season. This was the spot on the wheel unsuccessfully filled by *Hec Ramsey* and *Amy Prentiss*. Their answer was *McCoy*, which starred Tony Curtis as a high-living Robin Hoodish con man. It lasted a season.

The fall of 1975 saw the premiere of another Hargrove/Kibbee series, *The Family Holvak*, a *Waltons*-like Depression-era drama with Glenn Ford as a preacher. It was gone by January.

In 1979, Kibbee and Hargrove presented *Dear Detective*, a four-part mystery miniseries. Kibbee, a veteran writer with a long list of film (The Marx Brothers' *A Night in Casablanca*, *The Crimson Pirate*, *Vera Cruz*, *The Devil's Disciple*) and television (*The Virginian*, *The Alfred Hitchock Hour*, *The Deputy*) credits, would win a second Emmy as Danny Arnold's co-executive producer on *Barney Miller* (1981–82 season). His work with another situation comedy, *Newhart*, would bring him a third Emmy for a series with a third network: NBC (*Columbo*), ABC (*Barney Miller*), CBS (*Newhart*).

In 1985, Hargrove started producing NBC's series of highly rated *Perry Mason* TV movies. Reuniting Raymond Burr and Barbara Hale, these popular ventures whetted the network's appetite for a weekly program that would combine the mystery and the lawyer show— something in the tradition of, well, *Perry Mason*.

Hargrove responded with *Matlock*, which featured Andy Griffith as folksy Atlanta attorney Benjamin Matlock. His partner in these ventures was Fred Silverman, the former NBC president who launched Mrs. Columbo on her lamentable sleuthing career (more about that in a later chapter).

But in 1975, Silverman was still at ABC (where he was plotting the network's rise to the top with such cultural landmarks as *Charlie's Angels* and *Three's Company*). NBC was still hungry for more *Columbo* and Hargrove was quite willing to leave the show in the capable hands of Everett Chambers.

"Everett Chambers also was Peter Falk's close personal friend," Fischer said. "He had produced several episodes, so it only made sense that he would step in."

Chambers and Falk again went with a six-episode schedule. Fischer, who was producing Levinson and Link's *Ellery Queen* series, shared the executive story consultant credit with William Driskill ("Troubled Waters"). All deals were off in 1976, so there was a feeling that the fifth season might be the last.

CASE #32: FORGOTTEN LADY

(originally aired September 14, 1975)

Written by WILLIAM DRISKILL
Directed by HARVEY HART
Produced by EVERETT CHAMBERS
Executive story consultants: PETER S. FISCHER AND BILL DRISKILL
Music Score: JEFF ALEXANDER
Sunday Mystery Movie Theme: HENRY MANCINI
Director of photography: CHARLES CORRELL
Art director: JOHN W. CORSO
Set decorations: JERRY ADAMS
Assistant director: SAM FREEDLE
Unit manager: FRANK LOSEE
Film editor: JAMIE CAYLOR, A.C.E.
Sound: JERRY E. SMITH
Choreographer: MIRIAM NELSON MEYERS
Editorial supervision: RICHARD BELDING
Music supervision: HAL MOONEY
Costumes by BURTON MILLER
Main title design: WAYNE FITZGERALD
Titles and optical effects by UNIVERSAL TITLE

CAST

LT. COLUMBO	PETER FALK
GRACE WHEELER WILLIS	JANET LEIGH
DR. HENRY WILLIS	SAM JAFFE
NED DIAMOND	JOHN PAYNE
RAYMOND	MAURICE EVANS
DR. LANSBERG	ROSS ELLIOTT
DR. WESTRUM	ROBERT F. SIMON
ARMY ARCHERD	HIMSELF
ALMA	LINDA SCOTT
SERGEANT LEFTKOWITZ	FRANCINE YORK
HARRIS	JEROME GUARDINO
BOOKSTORE CLERK	DANNY WELLS
DEPUTY CORONER HENDERSON	HARVEY GOLD

Synopsis—The big news in Hollywood is the gala opening of *Song and Dance*, a *That's Entertainment!* type of compilation of memorable numbers from classic musical films. The grand reception has stirred the comeback hopes of onetime screen queen Grace Wheeler. With former co-star Ned Diamond on her arm, Grace tells Tinseltown reporter Army Archerd that she plans to star in a Broadway revival of *One Touch of Venus*. Ned will direct and choreograph.

But Grace's husband, eminent diagnostician Dr. Henry Willis, refuses to finance the show. Having tasted some of the glory of her days as a star, Grace will not be denied a return to the spotlight.

She spikes his evening milk with a heavy dose of sleeping pills. At eleven o'clock, the butler, Raymond, leaves her in the house's screening room. Grace is watching one of her old musicals, *Walking My Baby*. Raymond returns to the kitchen, where he and the maid, Alma, settle down to watch their favorite program, *The Tonight Show*.

After Raymond makes a reel change in the screening room, Grace goes up to her husband's room and locks the door behind her. She has the gun Henry kept in the glove compartment of his car.

The sleeping pills have taken effect. Henry is unconscious. Grace removes the book he was reading and replaces it with a medical report. She puts the gun in his hand and wraps his finger around the trigger. She puts the gun to his head and fires. The agile dancer leaves the room by dropping from a tree limb near the balcony.

When she gets back to the screening room, however, Grace sees that the film has broken. She quickly splices the movie. She is again sitting comfortably just as Raymond returns.

The immediate conclusion, of course, is suicide. The door was locked from the inside. The gun is found in Henry's hand. And the medical report on his chest is a recommendation for prostate surgery. The assumption is that Henry was feeling aimless because of his recent retirement and depressed over his health problems. In this state, he took his own life.

Lieutenant Columbo isn't satisfied with a verdict of suicide. Raymond noticed no signs of despondency. And the book Henry was reading is a light, humorous fantasy—not exactly the material someone about to commit suicide would be reading.

Other things bother Columbo. Why would a man about to take his own life take sleeping pills? There's no reason for it. Maybe he decided on suicide after taking the sleeping pills. That would account for such an absurd action. But if that's true, why did Henry bring the gun in from the car? If he hadn't decided on suicide until after taking the sleeping pills, how did he know to bring the gun inside?

The book was found on the table next to the bed. Henry had a habit of concluding each night's reading with a dog-eared page. Yet there is no dog-ear for the night of his death. This disruption of a lifetime habit becomes more troubling when the autopsy reveals how much sedative Henry had in his system. It was enough to knock him out. It was enough for someone to put a gun in his hand without him knowing what was happening.

Ned, who has always been in love with Grace, tells Columbo to stop hounding the actress. Columbo tells Ned about his most damaging piece of evidence.

On the night of Henry's death, Grace was watching the movie *Walking My Baby*. The running time is an hour and forty-five minutes. Raymond started the film at eleven o'clock. It was still running after Johnny Carson went off the air at one. Why did the film take more than two hours that night? What accounts for all that extra time? Splicing a film only takes minutes. The only answer is that the film broke and Grace wasn't there to see it happen. She was upstairs murdering Henry.

The idea that Henry was upset about his health is ridiculous. Prostate surgery is common and usually successful. Being a doctor, Henry would know that.

What possible motive would Grace have for killing Henry? He was going to finance her comeback, Ned says. No, Columbo answers, he would never do that. Going through the doctor's files, the lieutenant found a medical report labeled "Rosie." It's the name of Grace's character in *Walking My Baby*. And it was Henry's code name for his wife.

The report says that Grace has an inoperable aneurism of the brain. It is causing progressive memory loss. She has a month, maybe two months.

Columbo has a problem. Grace probably doesn't even remember killing Henry. She is now deep in the past.

Just when Columbo must act, Ned confesses to killing Henry. The policeman is bewildered.

"It won't take long to break your story," Columbo tells him.

"It might take a couple of months," Ned says.

Columbo understands. Yes, he agrees, it might take a couple of months. "Yes, yes, it might."

"Forgotten Lady" is the only time that Columbo (technically) didn't bring in the murderer. And we're very glad that he doesn't. The ending is the most touching since "Any Old Port in a Storm."

Bill Driskill's script cleverly drops clues about Grace Wheeler's condition (she repeatedly forgets appointments and Columbo's name), yet the conclusion still comes as a surprise. When Columbo reveals the big secret to Ned, we wonder why we didn't suspect something all along. It helps, of course, that Janet Leigh was once a musical star (Rosie, in fact, had been her name in *Bye Bye Birdie*, a movie that featured another *Columbo* murderer, Dick Van Dyke). Director Harvey Hart makes effective use of song-and-dance clips from her old films (she made her film debut in 1947's *The Romance of Rosy Ridge* and one of her musicals was actually titled *Walking My Baby Back Home*). Hardly strangers, Leigh and Falk had co-starred in a November 1966 *Bob Hope Presents* presentation titled "Dear Deductible."

Like Anne Baxter in "Requiem for a Falling Star," Leigh plays a fading screen queen who's murdered her husband. But her Grace Wheeler has a vulnerability that is refreshingly different for the series. Adding to the fun is Maurice Evans, cast as Grace's devoted English butler.

Nearly stealing the proceedings is John Payne (best known as the lawyer who defends Santa Claus in the classic *Miracle on 34th Street*). He plays Ned with believable doses of sympathy and nobility.

And the humor is nicely balanced (Internal Affairs notices that the gun-shy Columbo hasn't been to the pistol range in ten years). Viewers are also treated to the sight of Columbo in a tuxedo.

Yet, for all this, "Forgotten Lady" is something of a disappointment. The complaint against it is a familiar one. The sensitive storyline is damaged by the excessive running time (ironic, considering that a movie running too long is one of the story's major clues).

"We had all kinds of problems getting that one to two hours," Peter Falk recalled.

And it shows. The padding is all the more frustrating because "Forgotten Lady" could have been one of the very best *Columbo* episodes. It joins "Etude in Black" at the top of a list of two-hour shows that are very good but should have been great.

CASE #33: A CASE OF IMMUNITY

(originally aired October 12, 1975)

Written by LOU SHAW
   (from a story by James Menzies)
Directed by TED POST
Produced by EVERETT CHAMBERS
Executive story consultant: PETER S. FISCHER
Associate producer: EDWARD K. DODDS
Music Score: BERNARDO SEGALL
Sunday Mystery Movie Theme: HENRY MANCINI
Director of photography: RICHARD C. GLOUNER, A.S.C.
Art director: JOHN W. CORSO
Set decorations: JERRY ADAMS
Assistant director: KEVIN DONNELLY
Unit manager: FRED R. SIMPSON
Film editor: RONALD LAVINE
Sound: JERRY E. SMITH
Editorial supervision: RICHARD BELDING
Music supervision: HAL MOONEY
Costumes by BURTON MILLER
Main title design: WAYNE FITZGERALD
Titles and optical effects by UNIVERSAL TITLE

CAST

LT. COLUMBO	PETER FALK
FIRST SECRETARY HASSAN SALAH	HECTOR ELIZONDO
RAHMIN HABIB	SAL MINEO
THE KING	BARRY ROBINS
YOUSEFF ALAFA	ANDRE LAWRENCE
POLICE COMMISSIONER	KENNETH TOBEY
ZENA	XENIA GRATSOS
KERMIT MORGAN	DICK DINMAN
KURA	GEORGE SKAFF
HAKIM	NATE ESFORMES
CAPTAIN AUGUST	BILL ZUCKERT
SECOND PICKETER	BART BRAVERMAN
CORONER	HARVEY GOLD
CAPTAIN ORTEGA	JAY VARELA

*   *   *

Synopsis—Hassan Salah, first secretary of the Surian legation in Los Angeles, wants to see his country hold to traditional ways. The young King of Suria, however, seems quite open to Western influences and ideas.

The ruthless Hassan sees a way to get rid of a dangerous opponent, legation chief of security Youseff Alafa, and blame it on the protesting Surian students who support the King. He secures the cooperation of Rahmin Habib, an idealistic legation employee who works in the code room. After Hassan opens an office safe and burns several documents, Rahmin spray-paints student protest slogans on the oak walls. Hassan then calls Youseff to the scene.

While the security chief is inspecting the damage, Hassan hits him from behind with a tire iron. Youseff is dead and the scene is staged. It will look as if students broke into the office and Youseff surprised them in the act of burning papers. But Hassan still has to establish an alibi, and what better place than police headquarters? When Hassan is in the police commissioner's office discussing security arrangements for the King's upcoming visit, Rahmin calls him and pretends to be Youseff. So, a dozen high-ranking Los Angeles law enforcement officials listen as Hassan talks to a man he's already killed.

With the ruse complete, Rahmin sets off a charge that blows open the safe Hassan emptied. Dressed as a student, he makes his escape by crashing a car through the legation gate. Youseff's assistant, Kura, has a clear shot at the car, but his gun jams. Hassan made sure of that.

Lieutenant Columbo is certain that the murder was an inside job. What first troubled the detective was the fact that Youseff never pulled his gun. It was found in his holster. If Youseff did enter the room and surprised looting students, why didn't he pull his revolver? And how does an experienced security guard allow himself to get hit on the back of the head, especially when there's no sign of a struggle? The only conclusion is that Youseff wasn't alarmed when he entered the room. The security chief must have been summoned to the room by someone he knew.

There's another reason Columbo thinks it was an inside job. The papers from the safe were burned before the explosion that blew it open. How in the world, Hassan asks, do you know that? The ashes of the documents were found in a pile on the floor. The explosion caused some plaster to fall from the ceiling. The plaster settled on the ashes. There's no question: the documents were removed and burned before the safe was blown open. And that means the murder was committed by someone who knew the combination.

Immediate suspicion falls on Rahmin, the only legation employee not accounted for. Rough descriptions of the fleeing student match Rahmin. The code room employee made a hotel reservation for the day of the murder, yet he didn't keep it. Hassan is all too eager to be impressed by Columbo's findings.

Sneaking away from the legation grounds, Hassan goes to meet Rahmin. He gives him $10,000 and praises his heroism. The compliments last until Hassan can knock out Rahmin. He puts the unconscious Rahmin behind the wheel of his car and is about to push the vehicle over a cliff. He stops. He remembers that Rahmin always wore glasses. He checks the young man's driver's license. Sure enough, it says that Rahmin must wear glasses. Hassan takes the glasses out of a breast pocket, puts them on Rahmin and sends the car over.

To Hassan's disgust, Columbo and the King hit it off famously. To Hassan's horror, Columbo now believes he killed both Youseff and Rahmin. Why? Kura's gun had never misfired before, and only Youseff and Hassan had keys to the arsenal. Hassan knew the combination to the safe.

And Rahmin's death was no accident. He was wearing glasses, but he was also wearing contact lenses. He would have been almost blind. Someone else put those glasses on him. Columbo knows it was Hassan because the $10,000 found in Rahmin's car was not from the legation safe. A bank wrapper indicates that this money was withdrawn from the bank on the day after the murder—withdrawn by the first secretary.

Hassan lodges a complaint against Columbo. He threatens to have the lieutenant thrown off the police force.

An apologetic Columbo shows up at the legation. He asks Hassan for a chance to apologize.

"You beat me," the lieutenant says. The case was largely circumstantial and, even if the evidence was stronger, Hassan is protected by diplomatic immunity. He can't be touched.

Feeling expansive, Hassan admires the detective's determination and fills in the missing details. Of course, he wouldn't be admitting all of this if it wasn't for the diplomatic immunity. Suddenly, the King emerges from the next room. He's overheard everything. Surian justice will be swift and harsh.

Even though he knows this trap was arranged by Columbo, Hassan has no choice. Rather than face a horrible fate in Suria, he renounces his diplomatic immunity and signs a confession.

The mystery aspects of "A Case of Immunity" are fine. It's a good story.

"I liked that one," said *Columbo* contributor Howard Berk ("By Dawn's Early Light"). "I wrote a draft with Lou Shaw, but he ended up with the on-screen credit. Well, that happens. There have been times that I got credit when I thought another writer deserved it, and there were times I thought I should get credit and I didn't."

What hurts "A Case of Immunity" is its regrettably simplistic treatment of complex and sensitive issues in Arab nations. The episode has been singled out by the American-Arab Anti-Discrimination Committee, and one can understand why. Hassan becomes the obvious villain because he values traditional Arab ways. The young King is wonderful because he embraces Western ideas and ideals. Hassan dresses in traditional garb. The King wears a uniform. There's a painfully offensive message that emerges from this contrast of stereotyped characters: Arabs aren't such bad guys as long as they're willing to act more American. Suria (a fictional country) will be just fine if it merely accepts "civilized" Western standards.

While the episode tries to move beyond the all-Arabs-are-contemptible-beings thinking that American entertainment usually panders to, "A Case of Immunity" substitutes understanding with platitudinous dialogue. This black-and-white representation of complicated tensions would look all the more shallow in light of subsequent events in Iran and other nations. Unfortunately, Hollywood's stereotyping of Arabs grew worse. In fact, the flaws in "A Case of Immunity" seem mild compared to the parade of Arab terrorists, thugs and oil barons that Tinseltown has thrown at us. Positive Arab images are almost nonexistent. At least *Columbo* made an attempt at balance.

Lifting the episode is the chemistry between Falk and Hector Elizondo, the actor who replaced him in the Broadway production of Neil Simon's *The Prisoner of Second Avenue*.

"Peter and I compared notes about *Prisoner* on the set of *Columbo*," Elizondo said. "I went to see him in *The Prisoner of Second Avenue*. We shared our experiences while filming that episode. It was a complete coincidence.

"You know what I remember? I remember laughing a lot. We had a great time."

A versatile actor, Elizondo has played Jews, Arabs, Hispanics and a melting pot of other ethnic types.

"I'm the American Express kind of actor," he joked. "Do you know me? People stop me on the street and say, 'Weren't you? Didn't you?' There's a nice anonymity. I have a neutral puss. If anything, I look like a Russian border guard."

CASE #34: IDENTITY CRISIS

(originally aired November 2, 1975)

Written by WILLIAM DRISKILL
Directed by PATRICK MCGOOHAN
Produced by EVERETT CHAMBERS
Executive story consultants: PETER S. FISCHER AND BILL DRISKILL
Music Score: BERNARDO SEGALL
Sunday Mystery Movie Theme: HENRY MANCINI
Director of photography: RICHARD C. GLOUNER, A.S.C.
Art director: JOHN W. CORSO
Set decorations: JERRY ADAMS
Assistant director: REUBEN WATT
Unit manager: FRANK LOSEE
Film editor: RONALD LAVINE
Sound: JERRY E. SMITH
Editorial supervision: RICHARD BELDING
Music supervision: HAL MOONEY
Costumes by BURTON MILLER
Main title design: WAYNE FITZGERALD
Titles and optical effects by UNIVERSAL TITLE

CAST

LT. COLUMBO .... PETER FALK
NELSON BRENNER .... PATRICK MCGOOHAN
"GERONIMO"/A.J. HENDERSON .... LESLIE NIELSEN
LAWRENCE MELVILLE .... OTIS YOUNG
SERGEANT KRAMER .... BRUCE KIRBY
SALVATORE DEFONTE .... VITO SCOTTI
LOUIE THE BARTENDER .... VAL AVERY
PHIL CORRIGAN (THE DIRECTOR) .... DAVID WHITE
JOYCE .... BARBARA RHOADES
GALLERY ATTENDANT .... WILLIAM MIMS
CORONER CLIFF ANDERSON .... CARMEN ARGENZIANO
DON (PHOTO SHOP MAN) .... CLIFF CARNELL
EXECUTIVE .... EDWARD BACH
PARSONS .... PAUL GLEASON
RUTH .... ANGELA MAY
DELLA .... BETTY MCGUIRE

BELLBOY .... KELLY FLYNN

KID .... ALICIA CHAMBERS

Synopsis—Top government operative Nelson Brenner is surprised to learn that an old partner, code name Geronimo, is still alive. Geronimo, who is using the cover identity of businessman A.J. Henderson, suspects that Nelson is a double agent—using vital information to improve his bank account.

Fearing that Geronimo is too close to the truth, Nelson arranges a meeting at an amusement park. He tells Geronimo that the agency is dealing with a spy selling microfilm—a crafty old fellow named Steinmetz. He arranges a meeting between Geronimo and Lawrence Melville, a go-between for Steinmetz.

That night, Geronimo makes contact with Melville at the Sinbad Club, a bar near the Santa Monica Pier. The agent follows Melville to an isolated spot under the pier. It's known as Muggers' Haven.

When Melville leaves, Nelson emerges from the shadows. He strikes Geronimo with a tire iron, first on the side of the head and then a more lethal blow to the back of the skull. The police will assume that he was killed by muggers.

Nelson, who is known as a powerful business consultant, goes to his office to establish an alibi. At six o'clock the following morning, he starts dictating a speech he's writing for winemaker Salvatore De-Fonte. He has set his clock so it will chime eleven while the tape recorder is running. When his secretary reports to work at nine, the tape is waiting for her. She assumes her boss stayed late at the office and worked into the night.

Arriving at the scene of the murder, Lieutenant Columbo is disturbed by one troubling fact. The murderer removed the victim's jacket. Why? You don't need to remove a jacket to get at money, credit cards and valuables.

Matches in the dead man's jacket lead the police to the Sinbad Club. The bartender, a former policeman, remembers that the victim left with a black man. He later identifies that man from a file of mug shots. It's Lawrence Melville.

No identification is found on the dead man, but there is something from the hotel where he was staying. He checked in under the name of A.J. Henderson. They trace A.J. Henderson to a Los Angeles firm. There's only one problem. Their A.J. Henderson is very much alive. So who is the dead man? Columbo not only doesn't know whodunit, he doesn't know whogotit.

Yet a cab driver remembers that Henderson asked to be taken to an amusement park. Nosing around the park, Columbo finds a photo booth with a woman taking pictures of customers as they go by. Going through the previous day's stack of shots, they find two views of the man who called himself Henderson. With him, clear as day, is Nelson Brenner.

Nelson at first denies knowing Henderson. When Columbo says there are pictures, Nelson claims that Henderson had asked about working with his company. Since the meeting had been secret, Nelson naturally denied any acquaintance with him. But the real Henderson is alive. This man was using his name. Nelson says he doesn't know why that would be.

Meanwhile, Columbo has found Lawrence Melville. Scared, Melville asks the advice of his boss, Steinmetz, who is actually Nelson in disguise.

After calming the young man's fears, "Steinmetz" leaves behind a bomb. The explosion is not enough to kill Melville. It's just enough to divert suspicion toward the fictional Steinmetz.

Columbo, though, is not so easily shaken. The bomb squad tells him that the explosion wasn't the type you'd use to kill a man. And it was placed in the door, not the engine, where it would have a greater chance of killing a passenger.

Nelson wants to get Columbo off his trail, so the director of the agency meets with the police lieutenant. He tells Columbo that Nelson is one of his most valuable operatives. The man known as Henderson also was an agent. They are after a spy called Steinmetz. That should answer all of the detective's questions.

During a visit to Nelson's house, however, Columbo's suspicions are refueled. He sees a picture of Nelson taken several years ago. Something about it is familiar. Although younger, Nelson's hairline is higher. Yes, he does wear a piece. Working with this old picture, police artists add a beard, glasses and a few age lines. The result is a match with Melville's description of the mysterious Steinmetz.

Listening to the tape Nelson says he made on the night of the murder, Columbo finds the evidence that shatters the agent's alibi. First, there's the sound of venetian blinds being closed. At six o'clock in the morning, Columbo says, the sun hits Nelson's desk. That's why he got up and closed the blinds.

Nelson claims he just wanted privacy. Columbo will have to do better than that. Okay, secondly, the speech contains a reference to the Chinese pulling out of the Olympics. That news wasn't announced until the morning after the murder. Yet Nelson claims to have dictated this speech seven hours before the event occurred.

The agent is impressed. How did Columbo know?

It was that jacket, the lieutenant answers. There was no reason for a mugger to remove it. That didn't make sense until Columbo was told about Henderson being an agent. He would have been carrying a gun in a shoulder holster. The jacket would have been removed if someone wanted to remove the holster and keep people from discovering that Henderson was an agent.

"Identity Crisis" is similar in many ways to "The Most Crucial Game." Both episodes present Columbo listening to a tape of the murderer's voice, searching for a sound that will destroy the alibi. Both have weak conclusions.

At the end of "The Most Crucial Game," Columbo has broken Paul Hanlon's alibi. Still, he hasn't done much more than that. There's no weapon. There's no evidence that puts Paul at the scene of the murder. The same things can be said of the lieutenant's case against Nelson Brenner. There's certainly proof that he lied about when he dictated the speech. There's no evidence that puts him under that pier at the time of the murder. There's no weapon with his fingerprints. And the motive isn't clear.

Almost too complex for its own good, "Identity Crisis" is rescued by the delight of again seeing Falk teamed with McGoohan. The combination worked so well in the previous season's "By Dawn's Early Light" that Chambers and Falk invited McGoohan to direct and star in "Identity Crisis" (having starred in *Secret Agent*, he was ideal for the role).

The actor makes Nelson even more eccentric than Colonel Rumford. Rare is the performer who can direct himself and not weaken his characterization. McGoohan pulled off the feat, never allowing the distractions of directing to interfere with a delightfully offbeat portrayal.

Indeed, his unusual clipped delivery offers an enchanting array of surprises for the ear. He'll suddenly shift to a high pitch or an unpredictable inflection.

"McGoohan had the best line reading in the history of the show," Richard Levinson said.

Faced with an extremely eccentric adversary, Columbo seems to become more eccentric in "Identity Crisis." The episode was particularly delightful for Falk. In addition to McGoohan, the two-hour outing (yes, it's padded) features three of his favorite character actors: Vito Scotti, Bruce Kirby and Val Avery. One or more of this trio appeared in thirteen of the forty-five *Columbo* mysteries.

"Peter wanted a director he could rely on," McGoohan commented.

"I had been spoiled in England. I was given total control of the projects I directed. So I was wary about directing an American television show, but I was given total control by Peter and Everett Chambers. They had a classy story. It needed some work, but Peter was a wonderful actor for a director. Peter is a meticulous man. He is a very careful actor. My association with *Columbo* continued because Peter liked me and I liked him. If he said, 'I want you to do this,' I would try to do it."

CASE #35: A MATTER OF HONOR

(originally aired February 1, 1976)

Written by BRAD RADNITZ
  (from a story by Larry Cohen and Brad Radnitz)
Directed by TED POST
Produced by EVERETT CHAMBERS
Executive story consultants: PETER S. FISCHER AND WILLIAM DRISKILL
Music Score: BERNARDO SEGALL
Sunday Mystery Movie Theme: HENRY MANCINI
Director of photography: GABRIEL TORRES
Art director: JOHN W. CORSO
Set decorations: RAPHAEL SUAREZ
Assistant director: KEVIN DONNELLY
Unit manager: FREDERICO SERRANO
Film editor: RONALD LAVINE
Sound: JERRY E. SMITH
Editorial supervision: RICHARD BELDING
Music supervision: HAL MOONEY
Costumes by RUDY NAVA LUNA
Main title design: WAYNE FITZGERALD
Titles and optical effects by UNIVERSAL TITLE

CAST

LT. COLUMBO .... PETER FALK
LUIS MONTOYA .... RICARDO MONTALBAN
LIEUTENANT SANCHEZ .... PEDRO ARMENDARIZ, JR.
CURRO RANGEL .... A. MARTINEZ
HECTOR RANGEL .... ROBERT CARRICART
NINA MONTOYA .... MARIA GRIMM

Synopsis—Legendary Mexican bullfighter Luis Montoya is a national hero respected for his great courage and daring. Only his longtime friend and assistant Hector Rangel knows that the retired matador exhibited paralyzing fear when faced with a ferocious bull on his ranch. The proud Luis must get rid of the only witness to his shame.

Knowing this terrible secret, Hector plans to leave the Montoya ranch. "Everything is different," Hector tells Luis. "I must leave." His bags are all packed. Before he can depart, however, Luis puts on a show of bravado. Together they will kill the animal that wounded Hector's tempestuous son, promising young toreador Curro Rangel. "Why?" the surprised Hector asks, "he would make a good seed bull." Luis tells his old friend it's because he's afraid Curro will try to again face the killer bull, Marinaro.

Once Luis has lured Hector into the ring, he uses an air pistol to shoot his old friend with a dart dipped in a strong tranquilizer. With Hector helpless and only barely conscious, Luis releases Marinaro.

Meanwhile, vacationing Lieutenant Columbo is involved in a fender-bender on the streets of the small town near the Montoya ranch.

"I need the car," Columbo tells local police chief Emilio Sanchez. "It's very special."

Sanchez, who has heard about Columbo's brilliant investigation into the murder of a singer on a cruise ship, jokingly holds the beloved car hostage while the American detective helps with the report on Hector's death. Several details bother the policeman from north of the border.

Why are Hector's bags packed? Where was he going?

Luis says he doesn't know. He claims to have been on his way to a speaking engagement when Hector was killed.

What is the strange needle mark found on Hector's body? The dead man wasn't on any type of medication.

And why would a loyal employee like Hector try to destroy a bull—valuable property—without asking? In way of an explanation, Luis tells Sanchez and Columbo about Curro's encounter with Marinaro. In the version Luis tells, Curro was wounded by the bull. Hector dragged his son to safety while Luis bravely kept the bull at bay. Luis says that Hector must have rashly decided to fight the bull to avenge and protect his son. There was no one to help when the bull gored the elderly man and killed him.

Two other clues prove that this story is a lie. First, Columbo finds a piece of wood in the ring. It's from Hector's lance, which is used for herding cattle. It is not from his pick, which is used to wound a bull. So how could Hector's lance have been broken in the ring? Curro tells Columbo that his father had the lance moments before Marinaro knocked the younger Rangel unconscious. Hector must have broken his lance while he, not Luis, fought the bull to save Curro.

The second clue breaks the story Luis told. There are no water stains on the cape found in the ring with Hector's body. Even a novice knows that you put water on the cape so it won't move unexpectedly in the wind. Since the winds didn't die down until after dark, Hector must have entered the ring when Luis was still on the ranch.

With Curro's help, Columbo tricks Luis into again displaying his cowardice in the presence of Marinaro. Curro can see that Hector was leaving because he knew of this cowardice. Luis killed to cover it up.

In tribute to his adversary, Luis presents Columbo with the cape and sword.

"Well, it was obvious," Ricardo Montalban said of his being cast in "A Matter of Honor." "If you want a Spanish bullfighter, how many actors were around to play the role? That was one of the few times my accent was in my favor. Hollywood has never written anything for me. This time out, the competition was very narrow."

Yet there's nothing obvious about Montalban's performance. A hero of enormous dignity, his Luis Montoya has learned fear after leaving the professional bull ring. Confident and poised, the matador is certain he can elude the clumsy rushes of the slouching Columbo.

"The contrast worked very well," Montalban commented. "He was the fumbling, bumbling guy who was, as we all know, really very bright. And the character I played had a certain amount of stature and tradition. You pit one against the other and it makes for very interesting casting. I loved it. I have very fond memories of that show. I did so many guest shots. Very few of them stand out. That one stands out."

Adding to the overall mood is the camaraderie between police officers Columbo and Sanchez. They respect each other. They like each other. They enjoy each other's sly ways. Armendariz, thankfully, isn't asked to play the stereotyped crooked, small-town Mexican cop. His Sanchez is a caring, responsible official who appreciates the chance to talk shop with another policeman.

CASE #36: NOW YOU SEE HIM

(originally aired February 29, 1976)

Written by MICHAEL SLOAN
Directed by HARVEY HART
Produced by EVERETT CHAMBERS
Executive story consultants: PETER S. FISCHER AND
    WILLIAM DRISKILL
Associate producer: EDWARD K. DODDS
Music Score: BERNARDO SEGALL
Sunday Mystery Movie Theme: HENRY MANCINI
Director of photography: RICHARD C. GLOUNER, A.S.C.
Art director: JOHN W. CORSO
Set decorations: JERRY ADAMS
Assistant director: SAM C. FREEDLE
Unit manager: FRED R. SIMPSON
Film editor: JAMIE CAYLOR, A.C.E.
Sound: JERRY E. SMITH
Magic sequences staged by MARK J. WILSON
Editorial supervision: RICHARD BELDING
Music supervision: HAL MOONEY
Costumes by BURTON MILLER
Main title design: WAYNE FITZGERALD
Titles and optical effects by UNIVERSAL TITLE

CAST

LT. COLUMBO	PETER FALK
THE GREAT SANTINI	JACK CASSIDY
SERGEANT JOHN J. WILSON	BOB DISHY
HARRY BLANDFORD	ROBERT LOGGIA
JESSE T. JEROME	NEHEMIAH PERSOFF
DELLA SANTINI	CYNTHIA SIKES
DANNY GREEN	PATRICK CULLITON
THACKERY	GEORGE SPERDAKOS
CLERK	THAYER DAVID
GEORGE THOMAS	REDMOND GLEESON
LASSITER	VICTOR IZAY
ROGERS	ROBERT GIBBONS
JEFFERSON	MICHAEL PAYNE

*   *   *

Synopsis—Master magician the Great Santini is amazing audiences at the Cabaret of Magic. What they don't know is that Santini hopes to pull off the grandest illusion of his career—making club owner Jesse T. Jerome disappear.

The crude Jerome is the only person who knows that Santini was once a Nazi death camp guard named Stefan Mueller. He has been blackmailing the magician since learning his dark secret.

Santini has told Jerome that he will no longer hand over extortion money. That night, while Santini is performing on stage, Jerome is typing a letter to the Department of Immigration in Washington, D.C.

Santini's act builds to his famous water tank escape. The magician is locked into a metal cube that is lowered into a glass water tank. He has ten minutes to get out.

What the audience doesn't realize is that the airtight cube has a false bottom. By the time the cube is put in the water, Santini has let himself out through a trapdoor in the stage. A ladder beneath this escape hatch leads into his dressing room.

Moving quickly, Santini disguises himself as a waiter and glides through the chaotic kitchen. Every night, the magician has a brandy sent to his dressing room. This night, using a remote-controlled microphone hooked to a speaker in his dressing room, the clever illusionist is able to talk to the waiter outside his dressing room, making it seem like he's never left his quarters beneath the stage.

The door to Jerome's office is locked. That's no problem for a master escape artist. Jerome hears the door open. As he approaches the outer office, Santini shoots him. He then returns to the stage and completes his act.

Jerome's body is discovered by an employee just as the audience is applauding Santini. The police are summoned.

The first thing that bothers Columbo is the position of the body. Actually, the first thing that bothers him is the new raincoat his wife bought for him. He looks distinctly uncomfortable in the garment.

They know the door was locked, Columbo tells his eager assistant, Sergeant John J. Wilson. If the murderer knocked and Jerome opened the door for him, the body would be closer to the door. If he had opened the door and wasn't alarmed by the person he saw, Jerome would have been walking back to his inner office. That puts the body in the right place, but then he would have been shot in the back. Columbo also wonders why the back of Jerome's shirt is damp.

Maybe the lock was picked. Impossible, Columbo is told. It's a new lock that was just installed. Yet the police lab finds scratch marks. The lock was picked. How many people at the club that night had the ability to open this lock? Columbo suspects Santini, even though his alibi is seemingly as airtight as the cube he escapes from.

But Columbo has to be certain. He has a locksmith make a set of handcuffs with the lock from Jerome's office. That night, he challenges Santini to escape from them. As the crowd showers the magician with applause, Columbo gives his primary suspect a knowing smile. "I knew you could do it," he says.

A clerk at a local magic store tells Columbo how mind readers will wire roving assistants with portable microphones. Standing on stage with a tiny receiver behind their ears, they can hear the secrets being exchanged at a great distance. And Santini used to be part of such an act. It means he could have staged his alibi.

Still, Columbo and Wilson have to discover the motive. Why

would Santini murder Jesse Jerome? If anybody had a motive it was Jerome's junior partner, Harry Blandford.

Comparing notes at police headquarters, Columbo and Wilson see how working in a leather chair will cause someone to sweat. That's why Jerome's back was damp. They know he was working at his desk before the murderer entered.

What was he doing? He hadn't started counting the money. Maybe he was typing. Wilson admires the IBM Selectric that Jerome used. It's the same kind they use in the academy typing classes. Why doesn't the carriage move? Wilson explains that all the letters are on a ball that moves from left to right. It strikes a carbon ribbon that's fed from one side of a disposable cartridge to another. It isn't reused.

It sets Columbo to thinking. If space on the plastic typing ribbon is only used once, that means whatever Jerome was writing is recorded on a portion of the ribbon.

You only made one mistake, Columbo informs Santini. You didn't look close enough at that typewriter. He unwinds the used portion of the ribbon and we see that Jerome was typing a letter to the Department of Immigration. He was trying to tell them that Santini is an ex-Gestapo sergeant named Stefan Mueller. The magician smiles and admits that he thought this had been the perfect murder.

"Perfect murder, sir?" Columbo says. "Oh, I'm sorry. There is no such thing as a perfect murder. That's just an illusion."

Considering Richard Levinson and William Link's fascination with murder and magic, it's odd that the team didn't write a *Columbo* with an illusionist as the killer. That seemingly inevitable plot fell to Michael Sloan, and he did a magical job with the concept. Columbo's creators must have been pleased.

The episode is given added boosts by the expertise of top illusionist Mark Wilson, the hauntingly appropriate strains of Henry Mancini's "Charade" (the composer, after all, was the author of the *Mystery Movie Theme*) and the stylish performance of Jack Cassidy, making the last of his three stellar appearances as a *Columbo* murderer.

Cast in the relatively small role of Della Santini is young Cynthia Sikes (later to star on NBC's *St. Elsewhere*). And Bob Dishy is back as the eager but ineffectual Sergeant Wilson, although somehow his first name got changed from Freddy (in "The Greenhouse Jungle") to John. It was another of the series' rare continuity problems.

In a scene that recalls Columbo's great joy at being summoned before the television cameras by Dexter Paris ("Double Shock"), the lieutenant is tickled as can be when he hops on stage with Santini.

There's also a great running joke with Columbo trying to lose his

The Great Santini with his daughter, Della (Cynthia Sikes, later a star of NBC's St. Elsewhere).

new raincoat. Again and again, he hopes the offending garment will just disappear.

"That new raincoat made him very uncomfortable and self-conscious," Falk said. "It was a brilliant idea."

At one point, he leaves the coat in his car and tells Dog that if anyone tries to steal it, he's to look the other way.

CASE #37: LAST SALUTE TO THE COMMODORE

(originally aired May 2, 1976)

Written by JACKSON GILLIS
Directed by PATRICK McGOOHAN
Produced by EVERETT CHAMBERS
Executive story consultants: PETER S. FISCHER AND BILL DRISKILL
Music Score: BERNARDO SEGALL
Sunday Mystery Movie Theme: HENRY MANCINI
Director of photography: WILLIAM CRONJAGER, A.S.C.
Art director: SEYMOUR KLATE
Set decorations: JOSEPH J. STONE
Assistant director: KEVIN DONNELLY
Unit manager: RALPH SARIEGO
Film editor: ROBERT L. KIMBLE, A.C.E.
Sound: JERRY E. SMITH
Women's costumes by BURTON MILLER
Titles and optical effects by UNIVERSAL TITLE

CAST

LT. COLUMBO	PETER FALK
CHARLES CLAY	ROBERT VAUGHN
SWANNY SWANSON	FRED DRAPER
JOANNA CLAY	DIANE BAKER
KITTERING	WILFRID HYDE-WHITE
COMMODORE OTIS SWANSON	JOHN DEHNER
THEODORE "MAC" ALBINSKY	DENNIS DUGAN
SERGEANT GEORGE KRAMER	BRUCE KIRBY
WAYNE TAYLOR	JOSHUA BRYANT
LISA	SUSAN FOSTER
COAST GUARD OFFICER	ROD McCARY
GUARD	J.P. FINNEGAN
SHOP FOREMAN	JOSEPH ROMAN
WOMAN	HANNA HERTELENDY
WATCHMAN	JERRY CREWS
SAILOR	FRED PORTER
HANDWRITING EXPERT	JIMMY JOYCE
BARTENDER	TOM WILLIAMS

* * *

Synopsis—The family and friends of brilliant naval architect Commodore Otis Swanson have gathered for the company's annual party. The Commodore, however, has become increasingly discontented with the way his son-in-law, Charles Clay, has developed the shipbuilding firm into a vast, impersonal corporation. He is tired of being surrounded by freeloaders like his alcoholic daughter, Joanna, his irresponsible nephew, Swanny, and, of course, Charles. The only man he respects is Wayne Taylor, the head of the boatyard. In fact, the Commodore intends to sell the company.

That night, Charles is wiping clean the belaying pin used to bash the Commodore's skull. While cleaning up the signs of struggle in the Commodore's study, Charles is surprised by a knock on the door. It is Wayne. He is dropping off the self-steering mechanism for the Commodore's ship. The Commodore had mentioned that he would be going for a sail in the evening.

Charles tells Wayne that he's just leaving. He makes sure that the guard notices him driving out of the estate.

Dressing in scuba gear, Charles swims back to the Commodore's harbor-front home. He dons one of the Commodore's familiar outfits and takes his father-in-law's ship out from the dock. From the distance, no one is able to tell the difference.

Once at sea, Charles throws the Commodore's body overboard. Putting the scuba gear on again, he swims back to shore. The police will assume that the ship's boom made an abrupt swing, striking the Commodore and knocking him into the water.

But the autopsy reveals that the Commodore was dead before he entered the water. Assisted by Sergeant Kramer and the promising young Sergeant Mac Albinsky, Lieutenant Columbo searches the Commodore's house. The study yields the most clues: a tube of lipstick, a broken watch and the rack of belaying pins.

Columbo notices that all the belaying pins have dust on them—all but one. Tests prove that it was the murder weapon. Charles is the primary suspect. He had the most to lose. He was at the house on the night of the murder.

Columbo builds an impressive case against Charles. Everything seems to be heading toward a logical conclusion until the chief suspect turns up quite dead.

There are now four suspects for the two murders: Joanna, who says she passed out drunk on the night the Commodore was killed; Swanny, who was at the Yacht Club at the time indicated by the

Commodore's smashed watch; Wayne, who admits to being at the house; and Kittering, who claims he was with a young woman.

Columbo gathers all of the suspects and explains what happened. Charles found the Commodore's body. He also found a broach and assumed Joanna had done the evil deed. He staged the boating accident to protect his wife and his interests. But Joanna didn't kill the Commodore, even though she has no memory of that night.

The scene was staged by someone else—someone who also left the lipstick to incriminate her.

The lieutenant holds in his hands a watch. He goes to each of the four suspects and lets them hear it tick. To each he says, "The Commodore's watch."

"T'isn't," replies Swanny.

"So what?" asks Wayne.

"Big deal," Kittering remarks.

"Daddy's watch?" says Joanna.

You see, Columbo continues, this watch was found at the scene of the murder. It was smashed. It did not tick. The police had it fixed, so now it ticks. They all heard it tick, but none of them actually saw it as the lieutenant took it around. Only Swanny's reply revealed something. He said, "T'isn't."

Only Swanny knew the watch shouldn't tick. He knew because he smashed it at the scene of his crime. He set the watch ahead to give himself an alibi, then he made sure it would no longer tick. The rest of the things he left behind would lead the police to Joanna.

The motive? Joanna inherits everything, but not if she was convicted of murdering the Commodore. With the Commodore dead and Joanna in jail for his murder, the estate would go to Swanny.

Columbo has been trying to give up cigars. After the case is solved, he lights up a cheroot and heads for a rowboat.

"I thought you were going to quit," Kramer says.

"Not yet," Columbo chuckles. "No, not yet, Sergeant. Not yet."

Whistling "This Old Man," he joyfully rows to the Yacht Club, where his wife is waiting.

The second episode directed by Patrick McGoohan is easily the show's greatest departure. "Double Shock" flirted with the idea of slipping from the open mystery to the whodunit, yet "Last Salute to the Commodore," after drawing you into the traditional *Columbo* formula, completely embraces the English drawing room style of Christie and Sayers.

"You thought you were following the usual *Columbo*," Falk chuckled. "You're following Robert Vaughn."

Yes, they even hired an actor already associated with the series.

"Let's do the one where we see the guy with the murder weapon in his hand and the audience swears they're seeing the same old thing," was how executive story consultant Peter S. Fischer explained the thinking behind the episode written by Jackson Gillis. "Then the guy ends up dead and we flip it around to a whodunit. Your villain has to be Robert Vaughn, Robert Culp or Jack Cassidy."

"Last Salute to the Commodore" is as much a departure in style as formula. Under McGoohan's guidance, Columbo is at his most eccentric. He seems more absorbed and quirky than ever before.

"When we did that episode," McGoohan explained, "the series had been on for a while. We discussed it and said, 'The Columbo character is fairly well defined. Let's take the character a step farther.' That made Peter apprehensive, but he was willing to try it."

The results are unusual and enchanting. In addition to getting his crack at a classic Christie-like denouement (the suspects gathered as the great detective unravels a complex web of clues), Falk's Columbo has two sidekicks—Kramer (we finally learn his name is George) and the young Mac (played by Dennis Dugan, later Captain Freedom on Bochco's *Hill Street Blues*).

"I wanted the young guy," McGoohan said. "That character wasn't in the original script. It was a special relationship that helped to add a little dimension to Columbo. It's a tiny other area—an association he hasn't had before."

Amused that the young sergeant should have a nickname like Mac when his last name is Albinsky, Columbo keeps asking him if he is Irish. By the end of the episode, Mac has a new hero. The sergeant has taken to carrying around a raincoat.

"Are you expecting rain, Mac?" Columbo asks with an impish grin.

"You never can tell," answers Mac.

"Patrick was fantastic as the head of the military school [in 'By Dawn's Early Light']," Falk said. "When he returned to direct two shows, he moved *Columbo* into all sorts of exciting and new directions. That's particularly true of 'Last Salute to the Commodore.' That really had a different tone to it. Patrick put his stamp on it. There was a slightly different sense of humor to it. He had other wonderful ideas about where to take *Columbo*. I'm sorry we didn't get him back to do more."

Richard Levinson didn't catch up with the episode until 1985. He was delighted. Columbo's co-creator particularly liked the scene in which a young woman named Lisa (guest star Susan Foster) tries to get the detective into a cross-legged position on the deck of Charles Clay's yacht.

"A station was running it out here [Los Angeles] the other night," Levinson said. "There's Columbo trying to do transcendental meditation. I thought it was hilarious."

Indeed, everyone seems to be having a good time, particularly the extraordinarily bemused Columbo. He never enjoyed a case more. He was never more whimsical in his pursuit of a murderer.

The final scene of "Last Salute to the Commodore" has the feel of a series finale. Falk was making rumblings about quitting after five seasons. Universal was making grumblings about the show's ballooning budget. It's almost as if Chambers and McGoohan wanted to give the old boy a proper send-off. If the thirty-seventh case had become the last, this would at least have given the series a sense of completeness. We leave Columbo blissfully rowing away, whistling his favorite tune and enjoying a cigar (which he gave up at the end of the first season).

Then again, Columbo leaves the door open to future escapades. When Kramer says he thought Columbo was going to quit (smoking), the detective mirthfully responds, "Not yet."

Summing Up the Fifth Season

The fifth season also ended on a note of personal triumph for Peter Falk. On the night of May 17, 1976, he was named Outstanding Lead Actor in a Drama Series by the National Academy of Television Arts and Sciences. His portrayal of Lieutenant Columbo had brought him three Emmys in five years.

If the series was truly going to leave on top, this would have been the time to call it quits. *The NBC Mystery Movie* was no longer the ratings winner that gave the network the power to hold Sunday nights, and Universal was growing less tolerant of budget excesses.

During production of "Last Salute to the Commodore," the gossip around the Universal lot was that the episode had gone two million dollars over budget. Falk's reaction to the rumors could hardly have pleased Universal executives.

"Ridiculous!" the actor said. "I doubt it will cost much over one million."

Claiming that it was impossible to maintain the quality of the scripts, he hinted that there would be no more *Columbos*. His business agent, attorney Bert Fields, confirmed that Falk was hanging up his raincoat after five hit seasons. "Peter is through with *Columbo*," Fields told reporters. "He is definitely not going back."

Falk also told the Associated Press that there were too many movies he wanted to make (which turned out to be all too true). Headlines blared the news. Falk and *Columbo* wouldn't be back for a sixth season.

Still, while the *Mystery Movie* was sagging, *Columbo* remained a formidable programming weapon. NBC wouldn't hear of discontinuing the series. The *Mystery Movie* would be back for a sixth season, and *Columbo* had to be a part of it.

Falk was lured back with a salary increase (boosted to a reported $300,000 an episode), which cynical columnists suggested was all he wanted in the first place.

Yet there were several film commitments, and these would reduce Lieutenant Columbo's presence in prime time.

PART VII

THE SIXTH SEASON (1976–77)

"I can't think of a time when I wasn't working."

—Lieutenant Columbo
"The Bye-Bye Sky High I.Q. Murder Case" (1977)

A Season of Sorts

When *The NBC Mystery Movie* returned for a sixth season, *Columbo* was still a part of the wheel—barely.

The network realized that the presence of *Columbo* (no matter how small) was crucial if the *Mystery Movie* had any hope of surviving. But between a change in production teams and Falk's outside projects, only three episodes aired during the 1976–77 season. It was by far the fewest number of shows produced during a single season. In fact, it hardly qualifies as a true season.

Everett Chambers produced the first two *Columbo* mysteries of this short season—one aired in October, the other in November. Another original episode didn't appear until May, and by then the series had a new producer, Richard Alan Simmons.

The addition of Simmons was added incentive for Falk to stick around. Levinson, Link, Bochco, Hargrove, Gillis, Kibbee, Fischer and Chambers had moved on to other projects. Falk needed someone he liked and trusted.

Simmons was not only a friend, he had produced and written Falk's earlier series, *The Trials of O'Brien*. The remainder of Columbo's prime-time career would be played out under the Simmons regime.

Practically from the start, NBC knew it would be receiving *Columbo* episodes on a greatly reduced basis. Falk told one reporter that he'd do two episodes back-to-back with Chambers, then a third much later in the season and maybe even a fourth. There would be no more than that.

Ironically, in its final season, *The NBC Mystery Movie* at last found a workable fourth element for the wheel. After failing with *Hec Ramsey*, *Amy Prentiss* and *McCoy*, Universal fielded a sleuthing Los Angeles County coroner played by Emmy-winner Jack Klugman (Oscar Madison on ABC's sitcom version of *The Odd Couple*). *Quincy, M.E.* proved so successful that NBC pulled it out of the rotation in January and made the monthly feature a weekly series. It ran for several seasons.

Quincy was replaced on the wheel by *Lanigan's Rabbi*, a series version of Harry Kemelman's novels about a police chief helped in his investigations by a local rabbi named David Small. Art Carney and Bruce Solomon starred.

CASE #38: FADE IN TO MURDER

(originally aired October 10, 1976)

Written by LOU SHAW AND PETER FEIBLEMAN
   (from a story by Henry Garson)
Directed by BERNARD L. KOWALSKI
Produced by EVERETT CHAMBERS
Associated producer: JOSEPH D'AGOSTA
Executive story consultant: BILL DRISKILL
Music Score: BERNARDO SEGALL
Sunday Mystery Movie Theme: HENRY MANCINI
Director of photography: MILTON R. KRASNER, A.S.C.
Art director: MICHAEL BAUGH
Set decorations: PEG CUMMINGS
Assistant director: MARK SANDRICH, JR.
Unit manager: ROBERT ANDERSON
Film editor: RONALD LAVINE
Sound: JERRY E. SMITH
Sound effects editor: BRIAN COURCIER
Music editor: ROBERT MAYER
Women's costumes by GEORGE R. WHITTAKER
Titles and optical effects by UNIVERSAL TITLE

CAST

LT. COLUMBO	PETER FALK
WARD FOWLER	WILLIAM SHATNER
CLAIRE DALEY	LOLA ALBRIGHT
SID DALEY	ALAN MANSON
MARK DAVIS	BERT REMSEN
SERGEANT JOHNSON	WALTER KOENIG
DIRECTOR	DANNY DAYTON
TONY	TIMOTHY AGOGLIA CAREY
ASSISTANT DIRECTOR	J.P. FINNEGAN
CONROY	VICTOR IZAY
MOLLY	SHERA DANESE
CAMERA OPERATOR	JIMMY JOYCE
WALTER GRAY	FRANK EMMETT BAXTER
JOSEPH	FRED DRAPER

* * *

Synopsis—Ward Fowler, who plays debonair television detective Lieutenant Lucerne, has a reputation for being a difficult actor. His series is a hit, however, so the network and studio executives again and again capitulate to his demands.

Although separated, husband-and-wife team Sid and Claire Daley continue to produce the *Inspector Lucerne* program. Claire continually advises everyone else to go along with their star's demands. Not even Sid knows that Claire is blackmailing Ward.

Claire discovered Ward in Canada. She knows that he deserted from the United States Army during the Korean War. If that information got out, it would ruin Ward's career.

When Claire takes a phone call in Ward's trailer, the actor overhears her saying that she'll be getting a sandwich at Tony's Deli.

To establish an alibi, Ward invites his gofer, Mark, to watch a baseball game on television. He gives Mark a drink laced with a powerful sedative. The actor then turns on his videocassette recorder to tape the action his assistant will miss. Ward dresses in a ski mask and a bulky parka he took from the studio's wardrobe department. He also has a pistol he took from the prop department.

Ward gets to Tony's Deli just after Claire. Disguising his voice, he pretends to be a holdup man. After knocking out Tony, he drops the charade. Ward tells Claire to walk toward the door with her hands over her head. She keeps going, sure that he hasn't the nerve to pull the trigger. He does.

Returning home, Ward sets Mark's watch back and starts the tape, just after the point Mark fell asleep. The ruse works. Mark assumes that he was only out for a few seconds. Later, when Mark again dozes off, Ward sets his watch for the correct time.

Immediate suspicion falls on Sid. He gets everything, including a stash of silver certificates and more than $500,000 in IOUs from Ward Fowler.

Assigned to investigate the murder, Lieutenant Columbo wonders why the highest-paid actor in television would owe his producer so much money. There are other details that bother the detective.

The first assumption was that Claire was shot while running away from a holdup man. But the bullet hole in her dress is considerably higher than the actual wound. That means her hands were in the air, and nobody runs away in such an attitude.

And she was hit in the heart at a distance of thirty feet. That indicates an expert marksman. When Columbo digs deep enough into Ward's past, he discovers that the actor deserted from an artillery outfit. His sole distinction as a soldier was marksmanship.

The police find the jacket and the ski mask in a garbage dumpster. They trace them to the studio wardrobe. Searching the prop department, they locate the pistol. Ward has wrapped a thread from one of Sid's sweaters around the trigger. Surely this will convince Columbo that his suspicions are unfounded.

Yet Lieutenant Columbo is closing in on Lieutenant Lucerne. Tony had described the holdup man as below average height. Columbo notices that Ward wears shoes with lifts. During a visit to Ward's home, Columbo sees his videocassette equipment.

He needs one piece of hard evidence. The gun supplies it. There are no fingerprints on the barrel, handle or trigger. But the pistol has always been used as a prop. It usually contains blanks. That means Ward had to remove the blanks and replace them with real bullets. While he remembered to clean the gun, he forgot to wipe off the blanks when he put them back in. They have his fingerprints. It's an example of detective work that Inspector Lucerne would have to admire.

Once again, show business provides the backdrop for a *Columbo* mystery. Like "Requiem For a Falling Star," "Fade in to Murder" gives the cameras a chance to roam around the Universal lot. Bernard Kowalski, directing his fourth and final *Columbo* episode, again and again finds the most natural and inexpensive sets in the studio's backyard.

A meeting between network and studio executives is staged in the Universal commissary. Columbo wanders by the *Jaws* exhibit on the Universal tour and asks if that's the shark used in the movie (directed, of course, by Steven Spielberg).

And if Kowalski went "Requiem for a Falling Star" one better in using the studio, writers Lou Shaw and Peter Feibleman took the in-joke humor to new heights.

William Shatner, best known as Captain James T. Kirk on *Star Trek*, is cast as a demanding actor who stars in a hit series about a brilliant detective. Sound familiar? Yes, when representatives of the studio and the network meet with Claire and Sid Daley, their gripes about Ward Fowler could easily have been inspired by Peter Falk.

"Who does Ward Fowler think he is?" the studio boss demands.

"Ward Fowler is not the first actor on this network to win an Emmy," adds the network executive. "And he's already one of the highest-paid performers in television. If we give into him now . . ."

They're having great fun with Falk's reputation, yet somehow it doesn't hurt the illusion. Despite the fact that "Fade in to Murder" hits

The in-jokes flew when William Shatner appeared in "Fade in to Murder," playing a difficult actor who stars in a TV series about a brilliant detective.

terribly close to home, we still believe that Columbo is real and Lieutenant Lucerne is fictional.

Shatner's portrayal helps a good deal here. The glimpses of his Inspector Lucerne remind us how phony most television detectives are. His Ward Fowler, though, is a character with several intriguing shadings.

An interesting footnote is the presence of Walter Koenig, who played Ensign Chekov to Shatner's Captain Kirk on NBC's *Star Trek* (of course, another Enterprise regular, Leonard Nimoy, had already played a *Columbo* murderer).

Today, with VCRs hooked to a healthy share of the nation's televisions, Ward's alibi scheme seems a little thin. In 1976, though, videocassette recorders were out of the reach of most Americans. Not yet a household item, they were still something of a novelty.

And with a final clue worthy of Jackson Gillis, "Fade in to Murder" proved that after five seasons there was still life in the *Columbo* format.

CASE #39: OLD FASHIONED MURDER

(originally aired November 28, 1976)

Written by PETER S. FEIBLEMAN
  (from a story by Lawrence Vail)
Directed by ROBERT DOUGLAS
Produced by EVERETT CHAMBERS
Associate producer: JOSEPH D'AGOSTA
Executive story consultant: BILL DRISKILL
Music Score: DICK DE BENEDICTIS
Sunday Mystery Movie Theme: HENRY MANCINI
Director of photography: IRVING I. LIPPMAN
Art director: MICHAEL BAUGH
Set decorations: PEG CUMMINGS
Assistant director: CHARLES WALKER
Unit manager: ROBERT ANDERSON
Film editor: STANLEY FRAZEN
Sound: JERRY E. SMITH
Sound effects editor: BRIAN COURCIER
Music editor: JAMES D. YOUNG
Costume designer: GEORGE R. WHITTAKER
Titles and optical effects by UNIVERSAL TITLE

CAST

LT. COLUMBO	PETER FALK
RUTH LYTTON	JOYCE VAN PATTEN
PHYLLIS BRANDT	CELESTE HOLM
JANIE BRANDT	JEANNIE BERLIN
EDWARD LYTTON	TIM O'CONNOR
DR. TIM SCHAEFFER	JESS OSUNA
MILTON SCHAEFFER	PETER S. FEIBLEMAN
SERGEANT MILLER	JON MILLER
DARRYL	ANTHONY HOLLAND
ELISE	LUCY SAROYAN
WATCH SALESMAN	GARY KRAWFORD
MAID	ELOISE HARDT
SECOND DETECTIVE	MORRIS BUCHANAN
PHOTOGRAPHER	GILES DOUGLAS

* * *

Synopsis—Ruth Lytton is the curator of the Lytton Museum, a family-owned collection of medieval artifacts and art. She's sharp, efficient, old fashioned and proud of it. She tries to instill a sense of these virtues in her devoted niece, Janie.

The museum is controlled by Ruth, her brother, Edward (who is the trustee), and their fragile sister, Phyllis. Ruth is horrified when Edward tells her that he intends to shut down the museum. It is losing too much money. He is certain that Phyllis will go along with his wishes.

Rather than leave it to a vote, Ruth moves with Machiavellian swiftness. She arranges for the shifty security guard Janie had hired to break into the museum that night and steal several pieces. Everything is insured, she tells the trusting Milton Schaeffer, so everyone will prosper by his actions. In return, she'll pay him $100,000. She gives him a sizable advance to guarantee his cooperation.

Milton is worried that the police will suspect him. Don't worry about that, Ruth tells him. She's arranged to get him a new passport and identity. He can start over and forget about gambling debts. To keep everyone off his tail, Milton will call his brother, Dr. Tim Schaeffer, and pretend to be in danger. He'll plead for his life and then fire a shot.

What Milton doesn't know is that Edward will be upstairs taking inventory. When Milton breaks in, Ruth is waiting for him. She shoots him by the museum pay phone. Edward hears the shot and heads downstairs. Ruth takes Milton's gun and shoots her brother. She puts a gun in Milton's dead hand and the other in Edward's. Any rookie officer will figure out what happened. Milton broke in and Edward surprised him. They fired simultaneously, each bullet finding its mark. Surveying the bloody tableau, Ruth turns out the lights and leaves.

The next morning, a horrified Janie discovers the bodies and the police are called.

The first thing that bothers Lieutenant Columbo is the condition of Milton's body. It's incredibly well groomed for a thief. His clothes are new and suited more for a tropical vacation than a robbery. His hair has just been cut and he's had a manicure. Even his shoes are new. What kind of burglar breaks into a museum wearing stiff, uncomfortable new shoes? There's also a vaccination mark on his arm. Milton was leaving the country.

The police think the shooting took place before midnight. The time

All in the line of duty, Lieutenant Columbo agrees to have his unruly mop styled while solving an "Old Fashioned Murder."

is established by the call Milton made to his brother. But Columbo notices that the dead man's calendar watch already indicates May 1. To make sure the date reads correctly after a month with only thirty days, you have to turn the watch ahead past midnight again. That puts the shootings after midnight.

One other thing makes Columbo think the scene was staged. The lights were off when the bodies were discovered. The two men couldn't have hit each other in the dark. Obviously, neither of them could have turned off the lights. So who did?

Ruth sees that she must shift suspicion to someone else. She plants a belt buckle from the museum in Janie's room. When the police search the house, they find the piece and arrest Janie for murder. After all, she was the one who hired Milton.

Columbo is certain of Janie's innocence, especially after she fails to recognize the belt buckle when he visits her jail cell. She uses it as an ashtray.

The lieutenant has Janie released. He takes her home and tells Ruth about his suspicions. He thinks she killed Milton, Edward and Janie's father, Peter Brandt. Ruth had been engaged to Peter, but he eloped with Phyllis. Ruth ended up an old maid. Janie is the daughter she never had. Or is she the daughter Ruth could never claim?

When Peter was ill, Ruth was his nurse. She could easily have slipped him drugs that could have aggravated his heart condition.

As final proof of Janie's innocence, Columbo plays the tape Edward made while taking inventory. The belt buckle is among the items he counts. Janie couldn't have taken it.

It's not much. It's not enough for a conviction. But if Ruth stands trial, everything will come out—all of the questions about Edward's death, Janie's false arrest and Peter's "heart attack." Ruth can't stand to see Janie shattered by the idea that she murdered her father. If Columbo will tell Janie that there's really nothing to those suspicions, she'll confess to killing Edward and Milton.

Although Joyce Van Pattern is both strong and sympathetic as Ruth Lytton, "Old Fashioned Murder" is one of the series' weakest episodes. It is poorly paced and poorly plotted.

Ruth is perfectly willing to frame Janie for murder, but she ultimately confesses so her niece won't think badly of her. Further hurting the episode is the heavy-handed nature of the humor. Columbo enters by slamming into the back of a police car. Celeste Holm's Phyllis Brandt faints in the finest vaudeville tradition whenever someone mentions homicide or police.

The episode's strength should have been drawn from its atmospheric setting, yet such broad, almost comic opera touches destroy the mood. This time, they went too far.

The earliest glimmer of this episode started with Peter S. Fischer, who had a far different (and tantalizing) vision.

"I had an idea to do an updated version of *Richard III* and his two nephews as a *Columbo*," Fischer explained. "My idea was to have Burgess Meredith as a Richard III character who ran a medieval museum with his two nephews. He wants to get rid of both of them, so he kills one and frames the other. That was my vision of the show. It got all turned around. It was out of my hands and all turned around."

Fischer's concept sounds a good deal more promising than the story eventually developed by Lawrence Vail and turned into a teleplay by

Janie Brandt (Jeannie Berlin) ministers to her fragile mother (Celeste Holm) as Columbo ponders his next move in "Old Fashioned Murder."

Peter S. Feibleman (who also appears as Milton). By television mystery standards, "Old Fashioned Murder" manages to stand up quite well, largely due to the quiet strength of Joyce Van Patten's performance. By *Columbo* standards, however, the episode ranks fairly low.

CASE #40: THE BYE-BYE SKY HIGH I.Q. MURDER CASE

(originally aired May 22, 1977)

Written by ROBERT MALCOLM YOUNG
Directed by SAM WANAMAKER
Produced by RICHARD ALAN SIMMONS
Director of photography: TED VOIGTLANDER, A.S.C.
Music Score: BOB PRINCE
Sunday Mystery Movie Theme: HENRY MANCINI
Art director: HOWARD E. JOHNSON
Film editor: JERRY DRONSKY
Set decorations: RICHARD B. GODDARD
Assistant director: RAY TAYLOR
Unit manager: D. JACK STUBBS
Sound: EDWIN J. SOMERS, JR.
Sound effects editor: BRIAN COURCIER
Music editor: AL TEETER
Costume designer: GEORGE R. WHITTAKER
Titles and optical effects by UNIVERSAL TITLE

CAST

LT. COLUMBO .... PETER FALK
OLIVER BRANDT .... THEODORE BIKEL
VIVIAN BRANDT .... SAMANTHA EGGAR
BERTIE HASTINGS .... SORRELL BOOKE
MIKE MARKS .... KENNETH MARS
SERGEANT BURKE .... TODD MARTIN
MR. DANZIGER .... BASIL HOFFMAN
GEORGE CAMPONELLA .... HOWARD MCGILLIN
MR. WAGNER .... GEORGE SPERDAKOS
MISS ELSENBACK .... DORRIE THOMSON
CAROLINE TREYNOR .... CAROL JONES
WAITRESS .... JAMIE LEE CURTIS
AMY .... CARLENE WATKINS
ANGELA .... FAY DEWITT
SUZY .... KATHLEEN KING
RECEPTIONIST .... MITZI ROGERS

*   *   *

Synopsis—Friends since college, Oliver Brandt and Bertie Hastings are partners in a powerful accounting firm. And both are members of the Sigma Society, a club for geniuses.

Bertie has discovered that the flamboyant Oliver has embezzled funds to support his wife's expensive tastes. Bertie has threatened to expose his partner to the wealthy clients he is cheating.

When they are alone in the upstairs room of the Sigma Club, Oliver uses a gun with a silencer to kill Bertie—two shots fired at close range. He then sets up the elaborate scheme that will provide his alibi.

The gun goes into an umbrella that is stuffed up the chimney. Alligator clamps attached to two small charges are clipped to the umbrella's metal frame. A small electrical wire runs from the chimney to the club's computerized record turntable. And a marker is set in the path of the needle arm, poised over a dictionary that has been balanced on the edge of its stand. Oliver also knows that the opening of the front door of the room can cause the back door to swing shut.

This is how the alibi scheme works: a) Oliver sets the record player so the needle will come down near the end of an LP, leaving only four minutes until the arm rejects; b) Oliver leaves the room and joins the other club members downstairs; c) the arm rejects and makes contact with the first clamp, setting off the first charge; d) the people downstairs think they have heard a shot; e) the arm continues on its path, knocking over the marker, which tumbles onto the dictionary and causes the thick book to fall to the floor; f) the people downstairs hear a "body" hit the floor directly after the first shot; g) the arm makes contact with the second clamp, setting off the other charge; h) the people downstairs think they've heard a second shot; i) everyone rushes upstairs, bursting through the front door and causing the back door to slam shut; j) everyone assumes that the murderer has just escaped out the back way.

Oliver seems to have manufactured the perfect alibi. He was downstairs when everyone heard what they thought were shots and Bertie's body falling to the floor. The next day, Oliver returns to the club and removes the gun.

But even a genius can't anticipate a detective with the skills of Lieutenant Columbo. The policeman is bothered by the record player. Why would someone program it to start near the end? That leads him to the funny scratch marks on the right side of the turntable. The police lab concludes that they could have been made by alligator clamps.

Somewhat more troubling is the fact that everyone heard the body fall between the two shots. Yet the coroner says the two bullets entered at almost the same angle. Bertie was standing when both shots were fired. By accident, Columbo discovers how the back door has a habit of swinging shut when the front door is opened. He's sure the scene was staged, and after pressuring Oliver's secretary, the lieutenant uncovers a motive.

A trip to Oliver's home confirms his suspicions. Oliver has the same model turntable in his home and the accountant's umbrella has scorch marks on the inside.

Columbo summons Oliver to the club and demonstrates how he thinks Bertie was killed. He runs through the scenario at a fever pitch. The only thing this man left to chance, Columbo says, is the dictionary falling between the two explosions. Oliver is insulted. Such a genius wouldn't leave anything to chance. He would make sure the dictionary fell at the right time. That's not possible, Columbo challenges. Just as the arm is rejecting, Oliver grabs the marker and proves it is possible. See?

That's what a genius would have done. Yes, Columbo does see. Oliver has just supplied the missing piece of the puzzle.

Resigned and impressed, Oliver suggests that Columbo's brilliant mind might be put to better use in another field. He asks the detective if he has ever considered another line of work.

"No, never," the lieutenant says. "I couldn't do that."

"The Bye-Bye Sky High I.Q. Murder Case" (easily the longest *Columbo* title) is the first and least successful of the six episodes produced by Richard Alan Simmons.

The mystery is unsatisfying on two counts. First, it's highly unlikely that a man of Oliver's great intelligence would knowingly face such a formidable adversary and incriminate himself in such a stupid manner. Although effectively staged, the climax is not at all convincing.

Secondly, in trying to make Oliver one of the more sympathetic *Columbo* murderers, writer Robert Malcolm Young made him too weak. The fun is always in wondering how in the world Columbo will catch his suspect. Oliver isn't any challenge at all. We know our hero has got this guy nailed. Almost never dealing from an attitude of haughty superiority (odd since he's a genius), Oliver is on the run from the moment Columbo sees him. There's no challenge to this cat-and-mouse game. It's all too one-sided. You want Columbo to close the case and put this poor sweating guy out of his misery.

The script also contains a few contrivances that are hard to swallow. The club members, for instance, are all too conveniently talking about installing a burglar alarm just minutes before Oliver (surprise, surprise) makes it appear that a burglar killed Bertie.

Still, like all of the weaker episodes, "The Bye-Bye Sky High I.Q. Murder Case" has plenty to recommend it, not the least of which is the robust likability and charm of Theodore Bikel. The Viennese-born actor/singer/guitarist was better suited for the role than anyone knew.

"I got involved with it through [actor] Sam Wanamaker," Bikel explained. "He directed it. I was close to that character. At one point or another in my checkered past, I was a member of that type of society—Mensa. The members were drawn from the top two percent of tested intelligence. So I had something to draw on."

"I always thought Mensa was the silliest organization on earth," Simmons said.

By the time Bikel got involved with *Columbo*, the ten- and fourteen-day shooting schedules of the early seasons had been expanded to accommodate Falk's perfectionism.

"I remember we had twenty-two shooting days for a ninety-minute episode," Bikel recalled. "That was wonderful. The whole experience was a lot of fun. I read mysteries and like them, so it was a pleasure to do a *Columbo*. Peter is not what he plays. He's much more cultured. He had a lot of artistic control and he used it to make other artists comfortable. He'd tell me he would go for as many takes until I was pleased with it. That's very rare in television."

Look closely and you'll spot a brief but funny appearance by Jamie Lee Curtis—a year away from her starring role in John Carpenter's *Halloween* and six years away from her portrayal of a good-hearted hooker in the John Landis comedy *Trading Places*. The daughter of a *Columbo* murderer (Janet Leigh in "Forgotten Lady") plays a stern waitress who forces Columbo to give up a doughnut he brought into her restaurant.

The episode is also significant because it introduces departures that Simmons would make better use of in his five remaining episodes.

Columbo's entrance usually was underplayed. People would dismiss the bedraggled figure in a raincoat.

"Dick Simmons had a slightly different approach," Falk said. "Dick tried to create a lot more tension between Columbo and the murderers. So he made the entrances a little more formidable. Columbo was no longer looking for his pen. In the first shows, the adversaries were totally confident and Columbo represented some minor annoyance. I don't think Dick quite believed that. Dick wanted more tension. It was another way of looking at it. On reflection, the entrances in Dick's shows aren't all that dissimilar to what Levinson and Link wrote for *Prescription: Murder*. There is a certain amount of tension when he first meets the murderer."

There's a scene in "The Bye-Bye Sky High I.Q. Murder Case" in which Columbo runs through a torrential downpour. For once it is raining in sunny California and the lieutenant doesn't have his raincoat. Mrs. Columbo picked that night to use her new spot remover.

The scene comes very close to the series finale concocted by Levinson and Link.

"We always wanted the last show to be a story in which he doesn't wear his raincoat during the entire case," Dick Levinson related. "It's being dry-cleaned. At the very end, with the case solved, he walks outside and it's starting to rain. He puts his hands in the air and we have a freeze-frame. That's how we wanted the series to end."

Summing Up the Sixth Season

Bad enough that the quantity dropped in the sixth season, the quality also took a noticeable dip. Two of the episodes were below average (again, by *Columbo* standards). Granted, most seasons contained two lackluster mysteries, but this time there were two disappointments out of only three shows.

For the first time, the ratio between good and fair was tilted in favor of fair. The major accomplishment of the sixth season was to keep the series alive for a seventh and final and better season.

PART **VIII**

THE SEVENTH SEASON (1977–78)

"This far and no farther."

—LIEUTENANT COLUMBO
"The Conspirators" (1978)

Seventh Summit

NBC canceled its *Mystery Movie* in 1977. While *Quincy* had been spun off into a successful weekly series, *McCloud* and *McMillan* had come to the end of their prime-time careers. The day of the character cop was passing. *Cannon*, *Banacek* and *Hec Ramsey* had come and gone. *Kojak* and *Baretta* would be gone by the end of the following season.

Prime time belonged to the sitcom and jiggle mania of ABC. Four of the top five series during the 1977–78 season were *Laverne & Shirley*, *Happy Days*, *Three's Company* and *Charlie's Angels*. This was not Lieutenant Columbo's audience.

Still, even with the *Mystery Movie* gone after six seasons, NBC was desperate for more *Columbos*. By now deep in third place, the Peacock Network was willing to put up with long shooting schedules and zooming budget overruns if the lieutenant would just stick around.

Universal didn't feel quite so kindly. The *Columbo* price tag was becoming less and less tolerable to studio executives. This was the moment when NBC offered to pick up the excess expenses.

Columbo wasn't a regularly scheduled series during the 1977–78 season. Instead, NBC presented five *Columbo* mysteries as occasional specials. Under this arrangement, however, more episodes were produced than during the sixth season, when *Columbo* supposedly was a series in the *Mystery Movie* wheel.

The producer for this seventh season was Richard Alan Simmons. Falk's friendship with the writer/producer went back to *The Price of Tomatoes*, a 1962 *Dick Powell Show* drama that fetched the actor his only non-*Columbo* Emmy. Simmons was everything Falk wanted in a *Columbo* comrade: a friend who could be trusted, a gifted writer who could polish scripts and an experienced producer who was dedicated to quality.

But the candid Simmons was not one to reverently follow everything that had been done in the previous six seasons. He believed that the *Columbo* formula could be shaken up and improved.

"I wasn't a big fan of the show," Simmons said ten years after the seventh season. "I found it synthetic. What was interesting about the show was Peter's character. Peter and Columbo—it was like a hand going into a glove. Only Peter could have made it work. He deeply respects and enjoys this role. But I found *Columbo* profoundly dissatisfying entertainment because the villains weren't as interesting as Columbo. The show becomes interesting when you probe beneath the motives for murder. There are only a few motives anyway. You have to realize that *Columbo* is a relationship show: Columbo and the murderer. That's what makes it interesting."

Pursuing his vision of what *Columbo* should be, Simmons concentrated on variations he had experimented with in "The Bye-Bye Sky High I.Q. Murder Case." It is not difficult to spot an episode produced by Simmons. Although in large part they do adhere to the established *Columbo* ground rules, they are distinguished by three stylistic departures:

1) Columbo's more formidable entrance. "Columbo has to be a threat and not a threat at the same time," Simmons said. "Right away, the murderer should think, 'Oh, oh, I'm in trouble. I'll have to be careful, but I can handle this guy.' Columbo's entrance should be entertaining and interesting—a little theatrical."

2) The murderer's story. In an episode produced by Simmons, we get more of an examination of the murderer's background and emotional makeup. The producer thought we should understand the forces that drove this individual to kill. The seventh season's murderers might tell us about their childhoods, their hobbies, their motivations or their emotional attachment to an individual.

3) Columbo's background. And the detective gets very specific about himself in the seventh season. He talks about his childhood, people from his past and feelings concerning his job.

"I'm pretty good at what I do," Simmons said. "And there's a natural sync between Peter and me. I guess that's why I ended up doing *Columbo*. I want to entertain myself when I make a TV show. If I like it, maybe other people will like it, too."

Although not always in complete agreement with his new directions, Levinson and Link were impressed by Simmons' efforts. They complimented him on the high caliber of the seventh season's five mysteries. He told them about the constant battle for good scripts, about the long hours away from his family, about the never-ending rewrites, about the "intense physical and psychological pounding." Columbo's creators offered their sympathies. To paraphrase Mark Twain's Huckleberry Finn, they'd been there before.

CASE #41: TRY AND CATCH ME

(originally aired November 21, 1977)

Written by GENE THOMPSON and PAUL TUCKAHOE
  (from a story by Gene Thompson)
Directed by JAMES FRAWLEY
Produced by RICHARD ALAN SIMMONS
Director of photography: TED VOIGTLANDER, A.S.C.
Music: PAT WILLIAMS
Art director: HOWARD E. JOHNSON
Film editor: HOWARD S. DEANE
Set decorations: RICHARD B. GODDARD
Assistant director: DODIE FOSTER
Unit manager: D. JACK STUBBS
Sound: HAROLD LEWIS
Sound effects editor: WILLIAM WISTROM
Music editor: JAMES D. YOUNG
Costume designer: GEORGE R. WHITTAKER
Titles and optical effects by UNIVERSAL TITLE

CAST

LT. COLUMBO	PETER FALK
ABIGAIL MITCHELL	RUTH GORDON
VERONICA	MARIETTE HARTLEY
MARTIN HAMMOND	G.D. SPRADLIN
EDMUND GALVIN	CHARLES FRANK
ANNIE	MARY JACKSON
SERGEANT BURKE	JEROME GUARDINO
DANCE INSTRUCTOR	MARIE SILVA-ALEXANDER

Synopsis—Acclaimed mystery writer Abigail Mitchell, author of thirty-two bestselling books about murder, is certain that Edmund Galvin killed his wife, her beloved niece Phyllis. The police ruled that the young woman died in a boating accident four months ago. Rather than reveal her suspicions, however, Abigail has been playing up to the fortune-hunting nephew by marriage.

She has even altered her will in his favor. After all, the celebrated author tells Edmund, he is her only living relative.

After signing the proper documents in the presence of her attorney, Martin Hammond, and her secretary, Veronica, Abigail prepares to leave for a flight to New York City, where her mystery play *Murder of the Year* is closing after a nineteen-year run. Taking Edmund aside, she tells him to leave and sneak back by the service road. She wants to give him the combination to her walk-in vault, and Martin wouldn't approve.

Edmund is all too eager to cooperate, especially since the vault contains jewels, important documents, manuscripts and vast reserves of cash. Only three people know the combination: Abigail, Martin and Veronica.

When Edmund returns, Abigail has him open the vault for practice. She asks him to get something from inside. She shuts the door on him just as Martin arrives to take her to the airport.

The vault is soundproof. The one overhead light bulb is burned out and there is no ventilation. Edmund will die of suffocation—slowly and in darkness.

Before leaving the room, Abigail switches on the vault alarm and picks up the keys Edmund threw on the coffee table. While going out to the car, she hides the keys in the sand of a standing ashtray.

The body is discovered the next morning by Veronica. Abigail flies back from New York in time to see Lieutenant Columbo inspecting the vault. The clues are few: six burnt matches, black paint under the dead man's fingernails and one of the author's manuscripts with the title page torn off.

These clues are puzzling, and so are several other details. The alarm was on when Veronica came in to open the vault. If Edmund opened the vault and then accidentally locked himself in to avoid detection, how did the alarm get switched back into the on position?

There are two pieces of torn paper. Are they from the missing title page? What happened to the missing title part?

And what happened to Edmund's car keys? The house and grounds are being searched.

Veronica finds the keys in the ashtray. The opportunistic secretary gives them to Abigail and asks for certain rewards in return. The first is to accompany her boss on an ocean cruise.

Abigail tells Columbo that she found the keys near a lawn sprinkler. That's not possible, the lieutenant answers. The sections of the grounds where Edmund left footprints were photographed. There are pictures of the sprinkler. There are no keys.

The writer pleads the frailties of old age. She'll soon be leaving the country. Columbo has to work fast.

Just before the ship sails, Columbo informs Abigail that he has put

Columbo tries to point out an important clue to mystery writer Abigail Mitchell (Ruth Gordon), who's playing a game of "Try and Catch Me."

together the mysterious clues. Locked in the vault and waiting for death, Edmund was trying to leave behind a message that would identify his murderer.

He had black paint under his fingernails. The only black paint in the vault is on a filing cabinet. By arranging the drawers in the proper order, Columbo and Abigail see that he scratched an arrow pointing straight up.

The only thing up is the burnt-out lightbulb. Unscrewing the lightbulb, Columbo finds the missing piece of the manuscript's title page. Using the burned matches, Edmund had smudged out two words. The remaining words tell what happened: "I was Murdered by Abigail Mitchell."

Columbo knows why she did it. Abigail ruefully observes that none of this would have happened if the lieutenant had only investigated her niece's death.

Easily the oldest of the *Columbo* murderers, octogenarian Ruth Gordon was an ideal choice to play a kind of American Agatha Christie. Cute and charming, her Abigail Mitchell hardly seems to be a likely murder suspect—and she knows it.

Abigail's mind, trained by years of writing murder mysteries, is as sharp as ever, and that makes her more than a worthy adversary for Lieutenant Columbo. Riding high from her appearances in *Rosemary's Baby*, *Where's Poppa?* and *Harold and Maude*, Gordon brought tremendous energy and sparkle to her performance in "Try and Catch Me."

It certainly didn't hurt to have a script full of clever twists and rich dialogue. Writers Gene Thompson and Paul Tuckahoe had a tremendous amount of fun with both the locked-room mystery and the *Columbo* format.

For instance, several characters use Columbo's favorite phrase, "Oh, one more thing." It's not done in a cheap way. It's not obvious. Yet it's there to find if you're listening closely. The episode also has more two-edged dialogue than any other *Columbo* outing. A character says one thing when you know he or she means another.

"Oh, yes, the belly dancing outfit!" exclaimed Mariette Hartley after being reminded of her involvement with "Try and Catch Me." The scene she remembered best was the one in which an amused Columbo tries to question Veronica during a belly dancing class.

"That was great fun," the actress said. "And it was wonderful getting to play opposite Ruth Gordon, although she knew she was the queen on the set. Of the two *Columbos* I did, that was the one I enjoyed more. The role was a little better."

Veronica (Mariette Hartley) is surprised and amused when Columbo wanders into her belly dancing class.

CASE #42: MURDER UNDER GLASS

(originally aired January 30, 1978)

Written by ROBERT VAN SCOYK
Directed by JONATHAN DEMME
Produced by RICHARD ALAN SIMMONS
Director of photography: DUKE CALLAGHAN
Associate producer: ANTHONY KISER
Music: JONATHAN TUNICK
Art director: HOWARD E. JOHNSON
Film editor: GENE RANNEY
Set decorations: RICHARD B. GODDARD
Assistant director: DAVID O. SOSNA
Unit manager: JACK P. CUNNINGHAM
Sound: JAMES PILCHER
Sound effects editor: WILLIAM WISTROM
Music editor: JAMES D. YOUNG
Technical consultants: JEAN BRADY and CONNIE BURDICK
Costume designer: GEORGE R. WHITTAKER
Titles and sound effects by UNIVERSAL TITLE

CAST

LT. COLUMBO	PETER FALK
PAUL GERARD	LOUIS JOURDAN
EVE PLUMMER	SHERA DANESE
MAX DUVALL	RICHARD DYSART
MR. OZU	MAKO
MARY CHOY	FRANCE NUYEN
VITTORIO ROSSI	MICHAEL V. GAZZO
ALBERT	LARRY D. MANN
MARIO DELUCA	ANTONY ALDA
SERGEANT BURKE	TODD MARTIN
CRAWFORD	FRED HOLLIDAY
CHEF LOUIS	ALBERTO MORIN
CHARLIE	JIM MURPHY
LADY CASHIER	CAROLYN MARTIN
FIRST GEISHA	MIYAKO KURATA
SECOND GEISHA	MIEKO KOBAVASHI

*   *   *

Synopsis—Members of the Restaurant Developers Association routinely hand over twenty-five percent of their profits to powerful food critic Paul Gerard. In return, he praises their restaurants in his television show, radio program, newspaper column and magazine pieces.

Vittorio Rossi, however, is tired of paying blackmail money to the mercenary Gerard. At a private eight o'clock dinner in the kitchen of Vittorio's restaurant, the critic calmly listens as the volatile Italian repeats an earlier threat to expose the extortion scheme.

Seemingly unconcerned, Paul leaves before Vittorio opens the bottle of wine he's had his nephew Mario bring up from the cellar. With only Mario present, Vittorio drinks some wine and starts searching through drawers. He stops suddenly, doubles over in pain. Screaming in agony, he falls to the floor—poisoned.

Lieutenant Columbo immediately suspects Paul Gerard. Why? Well, after learning that a man with whom he shared a meal had been poisoned, the food critic didn't ask for a doctor or go to a hospital where he could have his stomach pumped. Instead, he headed directly for the restaurant to answer policemen's questions. It's the damndest piece of good citizenship Columbo has ever seen.

Reconstructing Vittorio's actions, Columbo finds a drawer loaded with canceled checks. They are all made out to the Restaurant Developers Association. By pressuring the organization's other major officers, restaurant owners Max Duvall and Mary Choy, the lieutenant discovers the blackmail scheme. He has established opportunity and motive for Paul. He needs to prove means.

How did the poison get into the wine? The vintage was chosen by Vittorio, so Paul couldn't know which bottle to spike in advance. Paul wasn't even around when the wine was opened. How did he do it? And what is the mysterious poison that was used? The police lab can't trace it.

Columbo happens to visit Paul's apartment when the critic is entertaining a Japanese colleague named Ozu. Paul is anxious for the lieutenant to leave before the food is served, but his assistant, Eve Plummer, invites the detective to stay for dinner.

While Paul tries to change the subject, Ozu explains that they are eating a rare delicacy—Japanese blowfish. Unless prepared by a master, like Paul, it is a deadly poison.

The lab confirms the poison. A fish market confirms that Paul buys Japanese blowfish. Yet Columbo still hasn't figured out how the poison got into the wine.

At a food writers' banquet, Columbo announces that he has the answer. He vows that Vittorio's killer will be in custody within twenty-four hours. Since the case is so near completion, Columbo invites Paul for a cooking session in the kitchen of Vittorio's restaurant.

The next day, Columbo tells Paul how the poison got into the wine. Vittorio used an automatic wine opener—a hollow needle attached to a cartridge of compressed air. The chef, Albert, changes the cartridges regularly. He put a full one in the opener the day after Vittorio's death. Later that same day, though, the cartridge was empty. Somebody had switched openers.

The poison wasn't in the wine. It was in the needle of the opener Paul left for Vittorio to use. Knowing Columbo is too near the truth, the critic has doctored another wine opener. Columbo uses it to uncork a bottle. Paul toasts his ingenuity.

Columbo drinks. Paul is about to, but Columbo stops him. You switched openers, the detective says. "I switched glasses." You see, there was no real proof of any of this—until now. When the boys in the lab analyze this glass of wine, there will be all the necessary evidence to convict Paul.

"You're a very able man, Lieutenant," Paul says. "I respect that. But I really don't care for you very much."

Columbo admits that he feels the same way about Paul: "I respect your talent, but I don't like anything else about you."

"Murder Under Glass" certainly ranks as the tastiest (literally) of Columbo's investigations. Once they learn he's trying to solve Vittorio's murder, every chef in Los Angeles is pushing food at the detective.

"As long as you're on this case," Albert (Larry D. Mann) announces at the funeral, "you'll never go hungry."

And he doesn't. While Columbo may never give up his beloved chili and hot dogs, he does appreciate good food.

In the first series episode, "Murder by the Book," Columbo showed that he was at home in the kitchen by fixing Joanna Ferris an omelet. His culinary knowledge became a recurring theme, and it's given full rein in "Murder Under Glass."

Columbo gets to wear a tuxedo for the third time in the series, but we suspect that it's more important to him that he gets to wear a chef's hat.

To use Columbo's expression, there's just one thing bothering me about "Murder Under Glass." How can Paul be absolutely sure that Vittorio will drink wine after he leaves the restaurant? Vittorio is in enough of a rage to forget the wine. Otherwise, this is a delicious mystery, a choice blend of humor and murder.

"Robert Van Scoyk is everything a writer should be," Simmons said. "He's a writer filled with knowledge."

Flavorfully directed by Jonathan Demme, the episode sizzles with the chemistry of Falk and Jourdan.

Speaking of chemistry, the actress playing Eve Plummer is former model and Miss Pennsylvania Shera Danese (cast in a much smaller role in 1976's "Fade in to Murder"). In December 1977, she had become Peter Falk's second wife.

CASE #43: MAKE ME A PERFECT MURDER

(originally aired February 28, 1978)

Written by ROBERT BLEES
Directed by JAMES FRAWLEY
Produced by RICHARD ALAN SIMMONS
Director of photography: DUKE CALLAGHAN
Associate producer: ANTHONY KISER
Music: PATRICK WILLIAMS
Art director: HOWARD E. JOHNSON
Film editor: HOWARD S. DEANE
Set decorations: RICHARD B. GODDARD
Assistant director: MARK SANDRICH
Unit manager: JACK P. CUNNINGHAM
Sound: LEROY JOSEPH
Sound effects editor: WILLIAM WISTROM
Music editor: JAMES D. YOUNG
Costume designer: GEORGE R. WHITTAKER
Titles and optical effects by UNIVERSAL TITLE

CAST

LT. COLUMBO	PETER FALK
KAY FREESTONE	TRISH VAN DEVERE
MARK MCANDREWS	LAURENCE LUCKINBILL
FRANK FLANAGAN	PATRICK O'NEAL
VALERIE KIRK	LAINIE KAZAN
WALTER MEARHEAD	JAMES MCEACHIN
LUTHER	RON RIFKIN
TV REPAIRMAN	BRUCE KIRBY
JONATHAN	KENNETH GILMAN
DUBBING CHIEF	MILT KOGAN
MADGE	DEE TIMBERLAKE
PETE COCKRUM	DON EITNER
AMES	MORGAN UPTON
AL STALEY	JOE WARFIELD
THE PRODUCER	GEORGE SKAFF
SERGEANT BURKE	JEROME GUARDINO
WENDY	SUSAN KREBS
ANGELA	SUSAN BREDHOFF

MASSEUR .... H.B. HAGGERTY
GUARD .... BUCK YOUNG
ROARK .... JAMES FRAWLEY
NANCY .... SOCORRO SWAN

Synopsis—When top network programmer Mark McAndrews gets promoted to a New York position, his chief assistant, ambitious Kay Freestone, expects to get his job—especially since they're lovers. But Mark doesn't think she's ready to handle the West Coast entertainment division. While Kay is good at developing series, she hasn't had enough programming experience. Finding strong shows is one thing, knowing where to schedule them is another.

Feeling abandoned and betrayed, Kay decides to murder her boss and lover. In addition to sweet revenge, she'll probably get the job he's leaving much sooner than expected.

Network president Frank Flanagan has flown in from New York to screen *The Professional*, a violent but stylish series pilot that Kay has developed. While Mark works in an office several floors above the screening room, Kay is in the projection booth with technician Walter Mearhead. Walter is making the changeovers between the two projectors.

Just four minutes before the end of a reel, Kay sends Walter out for another film. Knowing exactly how much time she has, Kay goes up several flights and finds Mark reading a script in his office. She shoots him and hides the pistol in the light fixtures of an elevator. She makes it back in time to make the changeover, setting a digital counter on the projector ahead so Walter will think she was in the booth at the exact moment the murder took place. Unable to get rid of the editor's glove she wore during the shooting, Kay throws it on the floor near the projector.

The first thing Lieutenant Columbo deduces is that Mark knew his killer. The murderer had come into the office at least eighteen feet before firing and Mark wasn't alarmed enough to get up from his sofa. Although alone at night, he didn't even bother to adjust his glasses so he could get a good look at the person entering the room. There's only one conclusion: Mark knew and trusted the person who shot him.

The discarded editor's glove in the projection booth bothers Columbo. He has Walter explain the changeover process to him. Toward the end of a reel, a flash appears in the upper right-hand corner of the screen. A second flash tells the projectionist he should switch from one machine to another.

Kay Freestone (Trish Van Devere) tries to run a network while avoiding the questions of a certain Lieutenant Columbo.

Walter keeps his booth immaculate and he didn't need an editor's glove on the night of the murder. This puts Columbo on the trail of the only other person in the booth—Kay Freestone.

Kay claims that her relationship with Mark was only professional. Columbo knows she's lying when a dry cleaner drops off one of her suits at Mark's beach house.

When *The Professional* airs, Columbo notices flashes right before a suicide scene. Yet that's what Walter saw when he returned to the booth. It means that Kay made the changeover just seconds before Walter got back. It means she's lying about when she made the changeover.

Columbo gets his big break when officers finally find the murder weapon. Kay doesn't know it. The lieutenant has a duplicate gun put on the elevator, but it's positioned so a shadow is visible on the plastic shade covering the lights. It looks as if the movement of the elevator has jarred the gun loose from its hiding place.

Kay gets on the elevator with Columbo. She sees the gun and pretends to have forgotten something in her office. On the trip back up, she removes the gun.

The lieutenant shows up a little later with videotape. It was taken on an elevator. It shows the shadow of a gun before Kay got on. It shows that the pistol has been removed when Kay got off.

Columbo explains to television executive Kay Freestone (Trish Van Devere) why murdered Mark McAndrews knew his killer.

"I see," Kay says resignedly.
"I'm sure you do, ma'am," Columbo answers.
"I'll fight," she promises. "I'll survive. I might even win."

A bit plodding at times, like most of the two-hour episodes, "Make Me a Perfect Murder" is the poorest of the five shows produced for the seventh season. The mystery is not only uneven, it is too reminiscent of previous *Columbo* outings ("Double Exposure," "Fade in to Murder," "Forgotten Lady").

The show business world is the setting yet again, although this time it's commercial television that suffers a few satiric swipes. There are blasts at the much-abused family hour concept (humor that seems a bit dated now) and violence on TV (appropriate since *Columbo* prided itself on being such a nonviolent series).

Even some of the clues are a bit thin. Columbo finds the glove Kay wore while shooting Mark, and he doesn't bother to find out if there are powder burns on it. That would have immediately narrowed the suspects to the two people in the booth.

While the middle is lackluster, the opening and closing sequences are terrific. The finale is a grandly edited ballet of imaginative video techniques. The manic music and the quick cuts effectively capture

Kay's growing panic. The walls of her electronic world are closing in on her.

The opening is a humorous highlight. For the third time, Columbo makes a surprise appearance during the initial credits. He's driving along, merrily singing a medley of favorite tunes: "Swing Low, Sweet Chariot," "Yankee Doodle," "My Darling Clementine." Suddenly, he finds himself in the middle of a high-speed police chase. His rear-view mirror falls off. We hear uniformed police complaining about a reckless driver getting in the way of their pursuit. Columbo is sandwiched by two police cars. There's a crash. The lieutenant is whiplashed. He's quickly surrounded by officers waiting for him to say something. Slowly, awkwardly, he looks from one to another and says, "I think I hurt my neck."

This hilarious touch was added when the network complained to Simmons that Columbo's entrance seemed to occur later in the episode than usual. Another of the episode's memorable scenes came about because of Falk's problem with the script.

"Peter came to me and said he was concerned because something seemed to be missing from the script," Simmons recalled. "Peter thought there was no nexus between the two characters (Columbo and Kay Freestone). Nothing in the script brought them together."

Falk told Simmons about an incident that happened during the filming of "Candidate for Crime." Guest murderer Jackie Cooper had taken Falk to the shack in Venice where he lived as a child. This served as the inspiration for the scene where Columbo finds Kay in the tiny, run-down home of her childhood. They share memories of youth, and we see how similar conditions shaped them in different ways.

CASE #44: HOW TO DIAL A MURDER

(originally aired April 15, 1978)

Written by TOM LAZARUS
  (from a story by Anthony Lawrence)
Directed by JAMES FRAWLEY
Produced by RICHARD ALAN SIMMONS
Director of photography: ISIDORE MANKOFSKY
Associate producer: ANTHONY KISER
Music: PATRICK WILLIAMS
Art director: HOWARD E. JOHNSON
Film editor: ROBERT WATTS, A.C.E.
Set decorations: RICHARD B. GODDARD
Assistant director: DAVID O. SOSNA
Unit manager: JACK P. CUNNINGHAM
Sound: JAMES PILCHER
Sound effects editor: WILLIAM WISTROM
Music editor: JAMES D. YOUNG
Costume designer: GEORGE R. WHITTAKER
Titles and optical effects by UNIVERSAL TITLE

CAST

LT. COLUMBO	PETER FALK
DR. ERIC MASON	NICOL WILLIAMSON
MISS COCHRANE	TRICIA O'NEIL
JOANNE NICHOLS	KIM CATTRALL
DR. CHARLES HUNTER	JOEL FABIANI
DR. GARRISON	FRANK ALETTER
OFFICER STEIN	ED BEGLEY, JR.
TECHNICIAN	FRED J. GORDON

Synopsis—Mind control guru Dr. Eric Mason knows that his colleague and best friend, Dr. Charles Hunter, was having an affair with his late wife. A rabid movie fan with a houseful of priceless Hollywood memorabilia, the noted psychologist has staged an ingenious scenario for murder.

Eric has conditioned his two pet Doberman pinschers, Laurel and Hardy, to attack when they hear a two-part command. The ring of a telephone readies them for the attack. After, they will kill anyone who says the word "Rosebud" (the dying gasp of Charles Foster Kane in the Orson Welles masterpiece *Citizen Kane.*)

Eric asks Charles to take Laurel and Hardy out to the house. He has a physical to take, and they'll play tennis afterward. When the doctor leaves Eric alone for a few minutes, the psychologist picks up the nearby telephone and calls his house. The ringing summons both Charles and the dogs.

Charles answers and is surprised to find Laurel and Hardy growling in front of him. Eric asks Charles to settle a bet. What was Charles Foster Kane's final word? "Rosebud," he answers. In an instant, the Dobermans are on their targeted victim.

When Eric gets home, he is surprised to see that Lieutenant Columbo is happily playing catch with the dogs. They aren't at all vicious and violent. He can't understand why Laurel and Hardy would suddenly turn and kill Charles.

Columbo is enchanted by the Mason house. It was once owned by Theda Bara, Eric tells him, and the pool table belonged to W.C. Fields. The detective is honored to hold the comedian's famous cue stick.

Between conversations about old movies, Columbo tells Eric what he has discovered. Charles was talking on the kitchen telephone when he died. The phone was found off the hook and the type of signal being made indicated that someone had called the house. It means that someone heard the victim's screams and didn't call the police.

Other details bother the lieutenant. There is straw in the corner of the kitchen (Eric says it's from a case of wine he unpacked) and a hook over the phone. Joanne Nichols, a young psychology student who lives on the grounds, tells Columbo that Eric often went away with the dogs on weekends. Where? He gets a clue when Eric shows him a baby spotlight that he picked up at a deserted ranch once used as a Hollywood Western set.

Out at the ranch, Columbo finds a hook just like the one in Eric's kitchen. He also discovers remains of a loudspeaker, shreds of a jacket that belonged to Charles and straw that matches the type in Eric's house.

It would seem that Eric had trained the dogs to attack by hanging up a straw dummy dressed in Charles' clothes and rigged with a loudspeaker.

A trainer informs Columbo that dogs can turn vicious, but it's unlikely that they'll turn nice again. She shows him how dogs can be conditioned with an attack word.

Trying to figure out "How to Dial a Murder," Columbo consults with dog trainer Miss Cochrane (Tricia O'Neil).

Snapshots of Charles with Eric's wife give Columbo the motive. To prove his case, he needs the attack word.

Hoping the egotistical Eric will betray himself, Columbo secretly tapes an evening of conversation with the psychologist. As the policeman is leaving, he remarks on the imposing gate with the letter *K* emblazoned on it. That looks so familiar, the lieutenant says. You can see it in the opening shots of *Citizen Kane*, Eric tells him.

"That's where it all begins," Columbo remembers.

Charles Foster Kane dies and says . . . Eric can't resist a chance to dangle the word in front of his adversary—"Rosebud."

When Columbo plays the tape for Laurel and Hardy, who are being held at police headquarters, the phone happens to ring. They respond. When the dogs hear Eric say "Rosebud," they go crazy.

Columbo takes Laurel and Hardy back to Eric's house and outlines all of the evidence he has against the psychologist. Actually Columbo says, for a supposedly smart man, Eric made lots of stupid mistakes. This wasn't all that difficult a case, the lieutenant continues, goading his adversary. The genius of mind control even forgot that he was hooked to an electrocardiogram machine when he called Charles. The chart shows an unaccountable jump at the exact time of the murder.

Pushed to the limit, Eric summons Laurel and Hardy. He points toward Columbo and shouts, "Rosebud!" But instead of attacking, the two Dobermans start playfully licking the detective. When he had learned the attack command, Columbo asked a dog trainer to replace one conditioned response with another. Now, instead of killing when they hear the word, they start kissing.

Originally titled "The Laurel and Hardy W.C. Fields Citizen Kane Murder Case," "How to Dial a Murder" is a sharply paced mystery that makes clever use of Hollywood nostalgia (Falk even indulges in a brief W.C. Fields impression).

The episode might have been subtitled "Columbo meets Sherlock Holmes." In 1976, Nicol Williamson had made an intriguing Holmes in the screen adaptation of *The Seven-Per-Cent Solution*. The same year as "How to Dial a Murder" aired, Williamson had a supporting role in the Neil Simon movie *The Cheap Detective*, a spoof starring Peter Falk.

Playing a *Columbo* murderer usually is a cherished memory for an actor. Williamson, who starred in the films *Hamlet* (1969) and *Excalibur* (1981), is the rare exception. The experience left almost no impression at all on him. Even after being refreshed with plot particulars, Williamson couldn't recall much about his involvement.

"I don't really remember that much about it," he said. "I was getting divorced and I had to have the money. It was one of those things. It was okay. You remember much more about it than I do. That was about ten years ago. I'm sorry."

It's a shame he doesn't remember more, because he was quite good as Eric Mason. For most of the episode, he is the typically urbane and genial *Columbo* murderer. With little warning, however, his face might suddenly contort into a snarl that chillingly testifies to the malignant force of his emotions.

Experimenting with the *Columbo* formula, Simmons introduced another new element during the seventh season—danger. In both "Murder Under Glass" and "How to Dial a Murder," we are made to worry about Columbo's welfare. Paul Gerard and Eric Mason each try to murder the lieutenant. Columbo anticipates and prepares for each move.

It's a new and tense variation on the traditional game. Indeed, "How to Dial a Murder" emphasizes the nature of the *Columbo* game.

"I'm sure you're very good at games, sir," Columbo tells Eric. Later, he says, "It's just that I enjoy the pleasure of the game."

CASE #45: THE CONSPIRATORS

(originally aired May 13, 1978)

Written by HOWARD BERK
  (based on an idea by Pat Robison)
Directed by LEO PENN
Produced by RICHARD ALAN SIMMONS
Director of photography: ISIDORE MANKOFSKY
Associate producer: ANTHONY KISER
Music: PATRICK WILLIAMS
Art director: HOWARD E. JOHNSON
Film editor: HOWARD S. DEANE
Set decorations: RICHARD B. GODDARD
Assistant director: PHIL BALL
Unit manager: JACK P. CUNNINGHAM
Casting by BILL KENNEY
Sound: JAMES PILCHER
Sound effects editor: WILLIAM WISTROM
Music editor: JAMES D. YOUNG
Costume designer: GEORGE R. WHITTAKER
Titles and optical effects by UNIVERSAL TITLE

CAST

LT. COLUMBO	PETER FALK
JOE DEVLIN	CLIVE REVILL
KATE O'CONNELL	JEANETTE NOLAN
GEORGE O'CONNELL	BERNARD BEHRENS
KERRY MALONE	MICHAEL HORTON
VINCENT PAULEY	ALBERT PAULSEN
CHUCK JENSEN	L.Q. JONES
ANGELA	DEBORAH WHITE
CAPTAIN	SEAN MCCLORY
MICHAEL MOORE	MICHAEL PRINCE
LEACH	DONN WHYTE
TOW TRUCK DRIVER	JOHNNY SILVER
CAROLE HEMMINGWAY	HERSELF
HARRY	TONY GIORGIO
BRANDON	JOHN MCCANN
BARMAID	DOREEN MURPHY
CUSTOMS OFFICER	KEDRIC WOLFE

* * *

Synopsis—While charming poet and author Joe Devlin talks about working for peace in his native Ireland, he is secretly helping O'Connell Industries send arms to the Irish Republican Army in Belfast. With one breath he renounces his youthful days as a terrorist, with another he purchases automatic weapons.

The genial Devlin is signing copies of his autobiography, *Up From Ignorance*, when a man hands him a book with the words "Ourselves Alone" printed on the first inside page. He is arms dealer Vincent Pauley and this is a signal. "Ourselves Alone" was the rallying cry of the Irish rebellion.

But during a meeting at Pauley's hotel, Joe learns that the arms dealer is demanding more money. The price of betrayal is death. Traitors must be executed. The poet shoots Pauley with one of his own pistols.

As Pauley falls to the floor, he knocks over a bottle of Joe's favorite whiskey, Full's Irish Dew. The slogan on the label reads, "Let Each Man Be Paid In Full." The mischievous Irishman can't resist making an ironic joke. He rolls the bottle near the body.

Lieutenant Columbo visits Joe the next day. The detective has found the copy of *Up From Ignorance* that was inscribed to Pauley. He also notices the "Ourselves Alone" message that the author signed over.

Still, Joe claims that he didn't know Pauley. He was just another face in the crowd.

The whiskey bottle causes Columbo to suspect Joe. It's the poet's favorite brand of liquor. Pauley was a diabetic who couldn't drink, so the murderer is someone who drinks Full's Irish Dew.

And the bottle was moved from the place where it spilled on the carpet. Why? It's the type of joke that fits Joe's personality.

Columbo soon learns that Pauley was an arms dealer. The only bit of paper found in his room had the number LAP 213. Mrs. Columbo is the one who figures out that it stands for Los Angeles Pier 213. That's where a vessel bound for Belfast is anchored.

Customs officers and the FBI search the ship, yet no arms are found. It looks as if Joe Devlin has outsmarted the authorities.

As the ship is pulling out of the harbor, though, Columbo spots something. The tugboat is flying the O'Connell Industries flag, and the O'Connells are Joe's very close friends. That's it. The guns aren't on the ship. They're on the tug. They'll be transferred to the ship just before it puts out to sea.

Columbo matches charm with Irish poet Joe Devlin (Clive Revill) in the last of NBC's forty-five Columbo *mysteries, "The Conspirators."*

Columbo also has figured out something else. The murderer has a habit of marking how much he'll drink by scratching the diamond in his ring across the Full's Irish Dew bottle. Each time he does this, the murderer says, "This far and no farther." Each diamond is unique and leaves a distinctive pattern. The scratch on the bottle near the dead man is identical to the scratches on Joe's bottles.

The poet accepts defeat by offering Columbo a drink. Well, maybe a little, the lieutenant says.

"This far and no farther."

Although Howard Berk's "By Dawn's Early Light" is hailed as one of the best *Columbo* episodes, the writer voices a preference for "The Conspirators," the last of the forty-five mysteries.

"Actually, I'm more fond of 'The Conspirators,'" Berk explained. "It's more grandiose in its perception. It has a pseudo-political theme that elevates it."

Except for the usual bloating that accompanies most of the two-hour episodes, "The Conspirators" is a splendid finale for the series. Grins masking their deadly serious game, Falk and Revill (the original Fagin in the stage version of *Oliver!*) try to out-charm each other. It is a whimsical duel between two leprechauns. The weapons are savvy and blarney.

One is reminded that Levinson and Link originally described Columbo as a leprechaun. The episode even provides Columbo with an appropriate exit line: "This far and no farther." It would prove all too true.

The End of the Trail

In early 1978, Peter Falk told a reporter that it was "a flip of the coin" as to whether there would be another season of *Columbo*. But the coin had been deemed too expensive by NBC, which no longer cared to pick up the budget overruns. There was no official cancellation notice. The series was just quietly discontinued.

"I wanted more time to do other things," Falk said, "but that was only part of the reason. *Columbo* just wasn't that important to the network anymore. When the *Mystery Movie* was around, I think it was important for the network to lock up Sunday nights for a season. When we were part of the wheel, *Columbo* helped nail down Sunday night. Five or six movies weren't as important to them. On its own, *Columbo* no longer was life and death to the network."

It's a brutally honest bit of appraisal. Whatever the reasons, *Columbo* had reached the end of its prime-time trail. After seven seasons and as many Emmys, the raincoat could be put away in Falk's closet.

The actor knew what he had lost. With seven years worth of distance from the last episode, Falk tried to sum up his feelings about *Columbo*.

"I don't expect to ever have it that good again," he said. "The hours were ferocious. There were no other regular characters, so I was going ten, eleven o'clock, midnight. I was bone-tired. I don't know if I ever had to work as hard as that. But I'm very proud of those shows and I love that character."

PART **IX**

AFTER *COLUMBO*

"You're a great detective."

—ALEX BENEDICT (JOHN CASSAVETES)
"Etude in Black" (1972)

Falk Talk

Peter Falk remains very proud of the fact that *Columbo* became an international hit. Distributed around the world, the sloppy lieutenant was a hero in several countries.

"It's a very good image for America around the world," the actor said. "It's a nonviolent show. There's no cheap sex in it. It has a main character who does not rely on force, fighting, shooting and car chases. You're not wiping out forty people a second, so death means nothing."

Columbo was described as "TV's cult hero" in Great Britain. He was a runaway hit in Italy. And the series became a national obsession in Japan.

Actor Yves Montand told Bill Link that *Columbo* was his favorite program. Film director Federico Fellini has left dinner parties to catch *Columbo* episodes.

The show's popularity abroad has inspired at least five of Falk's favorite stories. They are:

1) Rumania: "The Rumanian government called the American ambassador and they had a meeting. They've got a grievance problem in Rumania. What's the problem? They've got this show from America that's very popular. It's so popular that they play it on Friday and Saturday nights because the people who can't see it on Friday insist that they get to see it right away. Now, it is true that the Rumanian government has strict import restrictions. However, in this case, they've got every episode that has been made. But the people don't believe this. They think the restrictions are to blame for no more *Columbos*. Would it be possible to have this guy—Columbo—talk to the Rumanian people?

"Now they call the State Department and the State Department calls me to make a film. So I end up in a hotel room at one in the morning. They've got a camera set up and I'm speaking Rumanian phonetically. I say, 'Put down your guns. Be patient. Your government is not responsible. There'll be more *Columbos.*'"

2) The Netherlands: "In Holland, they have a parliamentary system, like they have in England. There's a big central issue. The ruling government is in danger of falling over this issue. There's going

to be a vote, and both the party in power and the opposition are given the chance to present their side on television. The government goes on and presents its side. Now the opposition is going on, but they're scheduled against *Columbo*. There's a new issue. The opposition claims that the government purposely scheduled *Columbo* against them so they would lose."

3) Iran: "Another time, I'm in Washington, D.C. I'm there to testify before some committee. Walter Mondale was investigating to see if some charity was on the up-and-up. There was trouble in the Middle East, and they had some security guys around. As I got out of the car, all of a sudden, two guys all in black are running at me. I didn't know what was going to happen. One of the security guards shoved me to the ground. Then they grabbed these guys in black. It turns out they were Iranian security guards. They saw Columbo and wanted autographs for their families back in Iran."

4) Japan: "When the Emperor of Japan visited this country, he requested that Columbo come to the White House so he could meet him. Unfortunately, I couldn't make it."

5) Ecuador: While working on the film *Vibes* (1988) in the small South American country, Falk was climbing a rocky path into an isolated village. "We were in the Andes Mountains, 18,000 feet above sea level, going up these steep cliffs," he said. "And there were Indians, descendants of the Incas, in hovels." When they spotted the actor, the cry went up—"Columbo! Columbo!"

"The purpose of these stories is to give you some idea of the impact *Columbo* has had around the world," Falk said. "How the hell can you know why four billion people like something. Why do these people respond to Columbo? It's very hard to answer. They like the man a lot. Columbo is a man who seems to know who he is. He's content with himself. He's good at his job. And he's not preoccupied with the shallow things in life. . . . I like the guy a lot."

A hit in Great Britain, Japan, Rumania, Iran, The Netherlands, Mexico, Italy, France and, of course, the United States. Passing cab drivers still yell at Falk, "Just one more question."

The Star, the Producers and the Story Editors After *Columbo* . . .

PETER FALK: starred in the movies *The Brink's Job* (1978), *The Cheap Detective* (1978), *The In-Laws* (1979) and . . . *All the Marbles* (1981). He also played the grandfather in director Rob Reiner's 1987 film version of William Goldman's novel *The Princess Bride.*

RICHARD LEVINSON and **WILLIAM LINK:** wrote and produced such TV movies as *The Execution of Private Slovik* (1974), *The Gun* (1974), *The Storyteller* (1977), *Murder by Natural Causes* (1979), *Crisis at Central High* (1981), *Rehearsal for Murder* (1982), *The Guardian* (1984), *Prototype* (1984), *Guilty Conscience* (1985) and *Vanishing Act* (1986). With Peter S. Fischer, they created the series *Murder, She Wrote* (CBS, 1984–present) and *Blacke's Magic* (NBC, 1986). The final Levinson and Link collaboration, the TV movie *Terrorist on Trial*, aired January 1988, ten months after Dick Levinson's death.

DEAN HARGROVE: teamed with Roland Kibbee to produce the series *The Family Holvak* (NBC, 1975) and the miniseries *Dear Detective* (CBS, 1979). In the eighties, he launched the new TV movie adventures of Raymond Burr's *Perry Mason* and a series titled *Matlock*, which starred Andy Griffith as an Atlanta lawyer. *Matlock* was a hit for NBC so, in 1987, Hargrove and partner Fred Silverman tried a mystery/action series for CBS: *Jake and the Fatman.*

STEVEN BOCHCO: became best known as the producer and co-creator of NBC's *Hill Street Blues* and *L.A. Law.* He also co-created one of the first "dramedies," ABC's *Hooperman.*

ROLAND KIBBEE: won an Emmy as co-executive producer of *Barney Miller.*

Peter Falk tries out a fancier raincoat as the title character in Neil Simon's
The Cheap Detective.

Peter Falk found immediate post-Columbo success starring with Alan Arkin in the hilarious film The In-Laws.

PETER S. FISCHER: produced *Richie Brockleman, Private Eye* (1978—a short-lived NBC series created by former *Columbo* writers Stephen J. Cannell and Steven Bochco), co-produced *Ellery Queen* (created by Levinson and Link) and created *The Eddie Capra Mysteries* (1978–79) His greatest success came as producer and co-creator of *Murder, She Wrote.*

Mrs. Columbo or Kate Loves a Mystery or Viewers Hate Kate

To most *Columbo* fans, the idea of doing a series about the never-seen Mrs. Columbo was sacrilege—nothing less. Still, Universal owned the rights to the character, so Richard Levinson and William Link were powerless to halt the heresy.

NBC reasoned that it could trade on the Columbo name without the high price of Falk. The network hoped to duplicate success at a much lower cost. The project was doomed to failure from the start.

In 1978, NBC entertainment president Fred Silverman (formerly top programmer at CBS and ABC) thought it would be a great idea to reverse the *Columbo* concept. The mother of a seven-year-old daughter and a reporter for the weekly *Valley Advocate* newspaper, the lieutenant's spouse also had remarkable sleuthing abilities. This time, though, you'd never see the policeman. Clever, huh? Huh? Huh?

Hoping to minimize the damage that would be done by shattering everyone's individual image of the unseen Mrs. Columbo, Levinson and Link made some urgent suggestions.

"Fred Silverman wanted the *Mrs. Columbo* series and he asked us and Peter Fischer to do it," Richard Levinson recalled. "We said no and he said, 'We'll do it without you.' So we suggested Maureen Stapleton. Silverman didn't want her. After testing a lot of actresses, we suggested Zohra Lampert. He didn't want her. He wanted somebody young and gorgeous. So we walked."

Mrs. Columbo went on the air in February 1979. Kate Mulgrew, a talented but totally miscast actress, had the title role. The reviews and the ratings were not encouraging. To help boost interest, rumors were circulated that Falk might show up in a cameo appearance. Fat chance.

"It was a bad idea," Falk said. "I would have preferred that it was never done. It was disgraceful."

"The magic of Columbo's wife is that you never see her," Levinson

A Columbo *murderer*, Donald Pleasence, *turns up as the killer in the* "Murder is a Parlor Game" *episode of NBC's ill-advised and ill-fated* Mrs. Columbo, *which starred Kate Mulgrew.*

commented. "We saw Maureen Stapleton, but that was a reluctant choice."

Struggling from the very start, *Mrs. Columbo* went through a major overhaul and three title changes in a year. They tried giving her a divorce (an offensive idea to viewers who loved the idea of Columbo and his devoted missus). They tried giving her a new name and dropping all association with *Columbo* (too little too late). *Mrs. Columbo* became *Kate Columbo*, then *Kate the Detective*, then *Kate Loves a Mystery*. It was mercifully canceled in December 1979. Nobody complained.

Yet Levinson and Link had their revenge planned.

"If there was ever another *Columbo*," Levinson said, " we were going to have him say, 'There's a woman running around pretending to be my wife. She's charging things. She's a young girl. I wish my wife was like that. She's an imposter.'"

Late Night *Columbo*

In the late seventies, reruns of *Columbo* showed up on the CBS *Late Movie* schedule. They performed well, so CBS kept repeating them for about five years.

While keeping *Columbo* before the public, these broadcasts infuriated purists. In order to cram two features in one *Late Movie* presentation, the network had to cut several scenes from each *Columbo* episode.

The butchering process didn't hurt a *McCloud* or *McMillan* nearly so much as it did the carefully constructed *Columbo* mysteries. Vital clues and bits of dialogue would be missing. The ninety-minute shows were particularly hard hit.

The clumsy editing infuriated Falk, Levinson and Link.

"That turned me off to watching them," Falk said. "I'd look forward to a certain scene and it would be edited out."

Levinson got even angrier: "I watch an episode and then I don't watch them anymore. Literally twenty minutes might be missing from a ninety-minute episode. I can't even follow them. Bill and I were attending a seminar at the Museum of Broadcasting and a woman came up to us and said, 'I want to introduce myself, but you're probably going to hate me. I'm the editor who takes twenty minutes out of each episode for the *Late Night Movie*.' She said, 'I'm only doing my job.' I said, 'Yeah, so was Eichmann.' My daughter would see them on the *Late Movie* and be terribly confused."

Fortunately for *Columbo* fans, MCA Television started syndicating the *Mystery Movie* episodes from market to market, and many stations were allowing the full running time, restoring favorite scenes that hadn't been seen for years.

At the same time that *Columbo* was airing on the CBS *Late Movie*, more than one viewer noticed the similarities between our lieutenant and McGruff, the animated crime dog who appears in the "Take a Bite Out of Crime" spots. It would seem that Columbo had an influence.

More *Columbos*

Almost since the day "The Conspirators" aired in 1978, there was speculation about the possibility of more *Columbo* mysteries. In May 1988, after ten years and several failed attempts, ABC Entertainment president Brandon Stoddard announced that, yes, Peter Falk had agreed to revive the character as one of three revolving elements in a *Saturday Mystery Movie* wheel. Richard Alan Simmons would be the producer for the return of *Columbo*. William Link would be executive producer for the new wheel, overseeing *Columbo* and the two other detective series. It had been a complex road to revival. The mid eighties success of Raymond Burr's *Perry Mason* TV movies had helped fuel interest in new *Columbo* mysteries.

Like Perry Mason, Columbo is a somewhat timeless character—timeless and ageless. Remember, Thomas Mitchell was quite elderly when he played the lieutenant on stage. Still, the Peter Falk of 1989 looks little different from the Peter Falk of 1978. He could effortlessly slip into the raincoat again.

Most television revivals and reunions are sad or strained because viewers are too busy looking at how old everyone has gotten. It becomes an exercise in nostalgia. That doesn't have to be with either *Perry Mason* or *Columbo*. Everything revolves around one intriguing character, and the concept can be as fresh today as it was twenty years ago. If you do a reunion movie for, say, *The Andy Griffith Show*, you have to blend old themes with new old ideas. That's not so with *Columbo*. You can pick up right where you left off. The format stays the same.

When rumors about a *Columbo* return became annual column items, the people closest to the series voiced different ideas about a possible revival. The late Richard Levinson thought they shouldn't go home again.

"I don't want more," he said. "I'd rather people remember it with affection. I don't think it could be any better than it was."

Peter S. Fischer took the opposite view: "I think you could do four TV movies a year. It could be wonderful. There's no reason it couldn't work."

William Link agreed with Fischer: "The format is so solid. You can't change it. Universal owns the character and Universal would like to see it again. I'd like to see it again. Now, you can't do it as a weekly series. It's still too rich a mixture to swallow every week. But you could do it as part of another wheel or a series of TV movies. The character doesn't age physically, so if anything can be brought back, it's *Columbo*."

And what did Falk think?

"Maybe it could happen," he said in 1985. "I'm ready to play the character again."

There were talks. In 1979, NBC and Universal had tentative negotiations about bringing the series back. The studio wanted the network to again pick up budget overruns. Falk wanted no time or budget limitations. The deal fell through.

In 1984, with *Columbo* reruns doing well on its *Late Movie* schedule, CBS approached Falk about a revival. A couple of years later, CBS considered a new mystery wheel with *Columbo* and *Kojak* as the key elements. That also fell through.

It seemed that conditions would never be just right for star, studio and network. Still, Falk continued to say that "it could happen."

Conditions seemed to be coming together in 1988. William Link and Universal had interested ABC in a new *Mystery Movie* anthology. But the key to the package was getting Falk to agree. The actor does not make decisions quickly, and his hesitancy put the future of the project in doubt. By late March, Link felt confident enough to announce to a Los Angeles County Museum of Art audience that ABC and Universal were planning a new *Mystery Movie* wheel, which would include six episodes of *Columbo*.

The money terms were generous, but Falk's main concern was for completed scripts. Before committing to the revival, he wanted to see at least four strong treatments. Then the Writers Guild went on strike and all work on scripts stopped. In May 1988, mere days before ABC had to announce its fall schedule, Falk agreed to sign.

"I wanted to do *Columbo* ever since it went off the air," Falk said. "It was a tricky thing to work out."

ABC was elated because *Columbo* and the *Mystery Movie* could help the network make gains on its very weak Saturday night. Link had lined up two big names to alternate with Falk. Burt Reynolds would play B.L. Stryker, a retired New York police detective who moves to Florida and becomes a private investigator crossing paths with the rich and powerful of Palm Beach. Oscar winner Louis Gossett, Jr. (*An Officer and a Gentleman*) would have the title role in *Gideon Oliver*, a series about a globe-trotting anthropology professor with a talent for solving baffling mysteries. As the writers' strike stretched from weeks

*Yes, Columbo will come
back to ask "one more
thing."*

to months, however, it became obvious that the ABC *Mystery Movie*
wouldn't make a fall premiere.

The strike was settled in August, and the networks asked producers
to push their series onto the air as quickly as possible. The trouble was
that *Columbo* needs more preparation than most series and you can't
make Falk settle for less than a quality script. "We'll give it our best
shot," said Link, who was aiming at a January 1989 premiere for

Columbo. When the strike ended, all Link and Simmons had were a few ideas and the fragment of the script Falk had started during the 1971–72 season.

In December, ABC decided to move the new *Mystery Movie* anthology from Saturdays to 9–11 P.M. Mondays, filling the time slot left open when *Monday Night Football* ended its season. "What we've seen of *The ABC Mystery Movie* has exceeded our expectations in terms of quality and potential audience appeal," Stoddard said, "and we've decided to debut the series on Monday, when viewing levels are higher than on Saturday and where the program can have a greater impact on our schedule." And the *Mystery Movie* premiere was postponed from January to February 6. The Simmons team got three additions: Philip Saltzman as supervising producer; Peter Ware as co-producer; and Abby Singer as coordinating producer. Anthony Andrews (*Brideshead Revisited*) and Fisher Stevens were signed to play the first two guest murderers. The plan was to finish as many as five or six episodes by the end of the season.

Yet Falk's enthusiasm remained undiminished. With Columbo poised to return for "one more thing," the actor wasn't at all worried about being forever recognized for just one character: "It never bothered me about the identification. I think anybody who's troubled by that has got to be crazy. The whole world knows it and loves it."

Will Columbo have changed?

"He will have gotten a little older," Falk remarked with a grin. "And he'll be using reading glasses."

And how about that raincoat?

"I honestly don't know whether or not this one can make it through another season," the actor said. "I would like it to, but it's getting weary. It's really very, very thin."

Simmons had his own reasons for resuming the daunting tasks of being the producer of *Columbo:* "There ain't nothing wrong with *Columbo.* The values are all correct."

PART **X**

VIVA COLUMBO!

"Oh, there's just one more thing."

—LIEUTENANT COLUMBO

COLUMBO AT THE EMMYS

1971–72:

Peter Falk—Outstanding Continued Performance by an Actor in a Leading Role in a Dramatic Series

Richard Levinson and William Link ("Death Lends a Hand")—Outstanding Writing Achievement in Drama (Series)

Edward Abroms— Outstanding Achievement in Editing

1973–74:

Columbo—Outstanding Limited Series (Dean Hargrove and Roland Kibbee, executive producers; Douglas Benton, Robert F. O'Neill and Edward K. Dobbs, producers)

1974–75:

Peter Falk—Outstanding Lead Actor in a Limited Series

Patrick McGoohan ("By Dawn's Early Light")—Outstanding Single Performance by a Supporting Actor in a Comedy or Drama Series

1975–76:

Peter Falk—Outstanding Lead Actor in a Drama Series

COLUMBO IN PRINT

No, Lieutenant Columbo's career was not confined to the stage and television screen. In 1972, MCA Publishing started issuing a series of *Columbo* paperback books. It was not the first such tie-in arrangement (books inspired by a TV show or movie). There had been novels based on *Star Trek*, *The Avengers* and *The Man From U.N.C.L.E.*

But the success of the *Columbo* books in America, Great Britain and other countries sparked interest in similar paperbacks about *Kojak*, *McCloud*, *Cannon*, *The Rockford Files* and *Hawaii Five-O*. Printed by the Popular Library (now controlled by Warner Books), the six *Columbo* titles are:

1) *Columbo* (1972) by Alfred Lawrence. An original novel (titled *A Christmas Killing* when published by Star Books in Great Britain), this case finds Lieutenant Columbo trying to solve the murder of department store executive Shirley Bell.

2) *The Dean's Death* (1975) by Alfred Lawrence. Described as an original novel in American editions, the English version says it is adapted from Howard Berk's "By Dawn's Early Light," an episode aired during the fourth season. The stories have little in common, though. This novel is about a college president who kills a dean who knows about his affair with a beautiful coed.

3) *Any Old Port in a Storm* (1975) by Henry Clement. A faithful novel version of the outstanding third season episode (teleplay by Stanley Ralph Ross, story by Larry Cohen).

4) *By Dawn's Early Light* (1975) by Henry Clement. The true adaptation of Howard Burke's fourth season episode.

5) *Murder by the Book* (1976) by Lee Hays. The fifth book in the Popular Library series goes all the way back to the first *Mystery Movie* (written by story editor Steven Bochco).

6) *A Deadly State of Mind* (1976) by Lee Hays. A lively translation of Peter S. Fischer's finale for the fourth season.

Although the Popular Library series ended with *A Deadly State of Mind*, a seventh *Columbo* novel was published by Walter J. Black in 1980. *Columbo and the Samurai Sword* was written by Bill Magee and Craig Schenck. This one has some very un-*Columbo*-like touches, including a high-speed chase through Hollywood, graphic details of a murder victim and a long scene in which the killer advances on our hero with a sword. But Magee and Schenck also include some nuances that demonstrate familiarity with the *Columbo* formula. Columbo arrives at the murder scene in need of coffee, and, after looking at the shoes on a corpse, he wonders how much they cost.

A COLUMBO CHARACTER SKETCH

Richard Levinson and William Link believed that the less we knew about Columbo, the more interesting he would be. That formula worked, yet tantalizing bits of information were dropped during the forty-five mysteries.

Of course, one can't always go by what Columbo says. He is apt to make something up just to throw off the murderer.

"I always figured that Columbo was full of it in the best sense of the term," said writer Steven Bochco. "Nothing came out of his mouth by accident. It always was carefully calculated. He didn't even cough by accident."

Peter Falk confirms that interpretation. Ask him about specifics and he responds, "Oh, I'm not going to talk about that. That's the beauty of it. Everyone can think about what the wife should look like. Did he have children? Did he have one? Did he have ten? That's up to them to decide. You never know when Columbo is genuine. I tried to play it so you could never tell whether the politeness was part of his nature or part of his act. Let the viewers decide. You always have that ambiguity. Almost everything he does can be taken two ways. A lot of what he says he might be making up while he's sitting having chili somewhere."

With that warning in mind, let's look at what we know about Columbo. After all, often we hear him talking to his wife when there is no need for an act. Sometimes he reveals something about himself when there is no reason for lying.

Lieutenant Columbo was born and raised in New York City. Located near Chinatown, the Columbo household included the future policeman's Italian grandfather, parents, five brothers and sister. His father wore glasses and did the cooking when his mother was in the hospital having another baby. His grandfather let him stomp the grapes when they made wine in the cellar. He is Italian on both sides.

Columbo's father, who never made more than $5,000 a year, taught him how to play pool, an obsession that stuck with the future detective. Hardly a model child, Columbo broke street lamps, played pinball and ran with a crowd of boys that enjoyed a good prank. His boyhood hero was Joe DiMaggio, although he liked gangster pictures.

During high school, he dropped chemistry and took wood shop. While he dated a girl named Theresa in high school, he also met his future wife at this time. After serving in the Army during the Korean

War, Columbo joined the New York police force and was assigned to the 12th Precinct. He trained under Sergeant Gilhooley, a genial Irishman who tried to teach him the noble game of darts. He moved to Los Angeles in 1958 (better substantiate that one: in "Requiem for a Falling Star," shot in 1972, Columbo says that he has been in Los Angeles for fourteen years).

Columbo drives an ancient Peugeot (license plate 044 APD). He doesn't carry a gun. He's a poor shot. He's easily winded.

Columbo doesn't like great heights, flying, needles, elevators, the sight of blood, guns. He is prone to air sickness and seasickness. He has allergies. He needs eight hours of sleep.

He is frugal (a family trait) and compulsive about little details. He is not good with numbers. He likes pool, cooking, limericks, bowling, Westerns, Italian opera, Strauss waltzes, golf, classical music and football on television.

It is normal for his blood pressure to be a little low. Little things keep him awake at night and he likes to bounce ideas off his wife. He goes bowling when depressed. Mysteries relax him, but he can't figure them out. He can't hold on to a pencil. His favorite song is "This Old Man." In 1972, he made $11,000 a year. His parents and his grandfather, who wore dentures, are dead.

His very favorite food is chili (with crackers), which he eats for lunch between games of pool at a greasy spoon called Burt's. Columbo also loves coffee and drinks it black. His breakfast usually consists of coffee and a hard-boiled egg.

Other favorite foods and beverages include hot dogs (charred), seafood ("anything that comes out of the sea"), root beer, hamburgers, raisins, candy bars, malts, ginger ale and cream soda.

He likes beer. He's been known to drink both scotch and bourbon whiskey. He prefers red wine to white.

Cooking is a hobby. He speaks Italian and a little Spanish (he took it in high school). He can't swim.

The Columbos have children but the exact number is not certain (really better substantiate this one: he mentions children in "The Most Crucial Game," "Any Old Port in a Storm" and "Mind Over Mayhem"). They also have a basset hound named Dog.

Columbo outlines the closest thing he has to a code in "The Bye-Bye Sky High I.Q. Murder Case": "You know, sir, it's a funny thing. All my life I kept running into smart people. In school, there were lots of smarter kids. And when I first joined the force, sir, they had some very clever people there. And I could tell right away that it wasn't going to be easy making detective as long as they were around.

Physical exertion never was one of the lieutenant's strong suits.

But I figured that if I worked harder than they did—put in more time, read the books, kept my eyes open—maybe I could make it happen. And I did. And I really love my work, sir."

Less reliable than all of this is the chronicle of Columbo relatives. If he is to be believed, the lieutenant has a sister who likes modern furniture, a nearly perfect cousin Ralph, a nephew who wears contact lenses, a brother-in-law named George, a niece named Marilyn (his wife's sister's girl, who got divorced and remarried a cop with six kids), a father-in-law who loves Western movies, a brother-in-law who's a lawyer, a brother-in-law who loves photography, a brother-in-law in the National Guard, a brother-in-law who's a waiter, an uncle who played bagpipes with the Shriners, a cousin in Albany who wears thick glasses and plays chess, a nephew majoring in dermatology at UCLA, a brother who's thirty-eight and still has his high school sneakers, an uncle who drove a bus until he made a killing in real estate, a cousin and a brother-in-law who run an auto body shop in the Valley, nieces who like rock music, a sister-in-law who drinks, a nephew who is a champion weightlifter and needlepointer, a nephew who wants to be an accountant, a teenage nephew who wants to be a director and a mother-in-law in Fresno.

THE REAL MRS. COLUMBO

Using the information provided in the forty-five episodes, we can put together a brief sketch of Mrs. Columbo.

The Columbos were high school sweethearts. "Never exactly thin," Mrs. Columbo is something of an athlete. She's an expert bowler and belongs to a league.

Although not a good cook, she has many other abilities. She handles the finances and does the taxes. She takes accounting courses and other night classes. She's a good dancer and singer.

Mrs. Columbo reads constantly. She loves crossword puzzles, Ann Landers, African violets, opera, classical, country and rock music. She loves having a good time and can get very loud when carried away.

She gives her husband a pencil every morning. She has a proverb for every occasion. She would prefer her husband take up a pipe, but he can't get used to it.

MULTIPLE APPEARANCES ON *COLUMBO*

Although Peter Falk was the only true regular in the *Columbo* series, that doesn't mean familiar faces didn't show up from time to time. These are the actors and actresses who appeared in more than one episode:

Dog (8) "Etude in Black," "The Most Dangerous Match," "Mind Over Mayhem," "Playback," "Forgotten Lady," "Now You See Him," "Try and Catch Me" and "Make Me a Perfect Murder."

Bruce Kirby (6) "Lovely but Lethal," "By Dawn's Early Light," "A Deadly State of Mind," "Identity Crisis," "Last Salute to the Commodore" and "Make Me a Perfect Murder."

John Finnegan (6) "Blueprint for Murder," "The Most Dangerous Match," "Lovely but Lethal," "A Friend in Deed," "Last Salute to the Commodore" and "Fade in to Murder."

Vito Scotti (5) "Any Old Port in a Storm," "Candidate for Crime," "Swan Song," "Negative Reaction" and "Identity Crisis."

Val Avery (4) "Dead Weight," "The Most Crucial Game," "A Friend in Deed" and "Identity Crisis."

Fred Draper (4) "Lovely but Lethal," "A Deadly State of Mind," "Last Salute to the Commodore" and "Fade in to Murder."

Jack Cassidy (3) "Murder by the Book," "Publish or Perish" and "Now You See Him."

Robert Culp (3) "Death Lends a Hand," "The Most Crucial Game" and "Double Exposure."

Charles Macaulay (3) *Ransom for a Dead Man*, "Etude in Black" and "Mind Over Mayhem."

Timothy Carey (3) *Ransom for a Dead Man*, "Dead Weight" and "Fade in to Murder."

Arlene Martell (3) "The Greenhouse Jungle," "Double Exposure" and "A Friend in Deed."

Manuel DePina (3) "The Most Dangerous Match," "Double Exposure" and "An Exercise in Fatality."

Cliff Carnell (3) "The Most Crucial Game," "Blueprint for Murder" and "Identity Crisis."

Jimmy Joyce (3) "Blueprint for Murder," "Last Salute to the Commodore" and "Fade in to Murder."

Richard Stahl (3) "The Most Crucial Game," "Lovely but Lethal" and "Double Exposure."

Dennis Robertson (3) "Double Exposure," "Mind Over Mayhem" and "An Exercise in Fatality."

Harvey Gold (3) "Negative Reaction," "Forgotten Lady" and "A Case of Immunity."

Jerome Guardino (3) "Forgotten Lady," "Try and Catch Me" and "Make Me a Perfect Murder."

Victor Izay (3) "An Exercise in Fatality," "Now You See Him" and "Fade in to Murder."

William Windom (2) *Prescription: Murder* and "Short Fuse."

Robert Vaughn (2) "Troubled Waters" and "Last Salute to the Commodore."

Ray Milland (2) "Death Lends a Hand" and "The Greenhouse Jungle."

Patrick O'Neal (2) "Blueprint for Murder" and "Make Me a Perfect Murder."

Patrick McGoohan (2) "By Dawn's Early Light" and "Identity Crisis" (also directed "Identity Crisis" and "Last Salute to the Commodore").

Ida Lupino (2) "Short Fuse" and "Swan Song."

James Gregory (2) "Short Fuse" and "The Most Crucial Game."

Leslie Nielsen (2) "Lady in Waiting" and "Identity Crisis."

Mariette Hartley (2) "Publish or Perish" and "Try and Catch Me."

Bob Dishy (2) "The Greenhouse Jungle" and "Now You See Him."

Wilfred Hyde-White (2) "Dagger of the Mind" and "Last Salute to the Commodore."

John Dehner (2) "Swan Song" and "Last Salute to the Commodore."

Bernard Fox (2) "Dagger of the Mind" and "Troubled Waters."

Michael Fox (2) "Etude in Black" and "The Most Dangerous Match."

Tim O'Connor (2) "Double Shock" and "Old Fashioned Murder."

Dean Stockwell (2) "The Most Crucial Game" and "Troubled Waters."

Joyce Van Patten (2) "Negative Reaction" and "Old Fashioned Murder."

Anne Francis (2) "Short Fuse" and "A Stitch in Crime."

Jeanette Nolan (2) "Double Shock" and "The Conspirators."

Clete Roberts (2) "Dead Weight" and "Candidate for Crime."

George Gaynes (2) "Etude in Black" and "Any Old Port in a Storm."

Shera Danese (2) "Fade in to Murder" and "Murder Under Glass."

Sorrell Booke (2) "Swan Song" and "The Bye-Bye Sky High I.Q. Murder Case."

Don Keefer (2) "Death Lends a Hand" and "The Most Crucial Game."

Regis Cordic (2) "Any Old Port in a Storm" and "Candidate for Crime."

John McCann (2) "Any Old Port in a Storm" and "The Conspirators."

Bill Zuckert (2) "Negative Reaction" and "A Case of Immunity."

Danny Wells (2) "A Deadly State of Mind" and "Forgotten Lady."

Jay Varela (2) "Candidate for Crime" and "A Case of Immunity."

Stuart Nisbet (2) "Short Fuse" and "The Most Dangerous Match."

James McEachin (2) "Etude in Black" and "Make Me a Perfect Murder."

Darrell Zwerling (2) "Mind Over Mayhem" and "An Exercise in Fatality."

Jefferson Kibbee (2) "Mind Over Mayhem" and "Swan Song."

Larry Burrell (2) "Candidate for Crime" and "Swan Song."

Bernie Kuby (2) "Murder by the Book" and "A Friend in Deed."

Bart Burns (2) "Requiem for a Falling Star" and "Playback."

Mike Lally (2) "Swan Song" and "A Friend in Deed."

Lew Brown (2) "Short Fuse" and "Candidate for Crime."

Robert Karnes (2) "The Greenhouse Jungle" and "Candidate for Crime."

Todd Martin (2) "The Bye-Bye Sky High I.Q. Murder Case" and "Murder Under Glass ."

George Sperdakos (2) "Now You See Him" and "The Bye-Bye Sky High I.Q. Murder Case."

CLASSIC COLUMBO LINES

Culled from the forty-five mysteries, this is a compendium of the Columbo wit and wisdom. If some of it sounds repetitive, well . . .

"Gee, you don't have a pencil, do you? Thanks. You know, my wife, she gives me one every morning and I just can't seem to hold on to it."
—*Prescription: Murder* (1968)

"Oh, one more thing . . ."
—*Prescription: Murder* (1968)

"There's one detail that bothers me . . ."
—*Prescription: Murder* (1968)

"I seem to be making a pest of myself."
—*Prescription: Murder* (1968)

"You've got some beautiful place here."
—*Ransom for a Dead Man* (1971)

"Do you have a pen?"
—*Ransom for a Dead Man* (1971)

"I worry. I mean, little things bother me. I'm a worrier. I mean, little insignificant details—I lose my appetite. I can't eat. My wife, she says to me, 'You know, you can really be a pain.'"
—*Ransom for a Dead Man* (1971)

"There's just one thing I'm not clear about."
—"Murder by the Book" (1971)

"I'm sorry, I didn't mean to bother you. . . . I'm making a pest of myself. . . . It's because I keep asking these questions, but, I tell you, I can't help myself."
—"Murder by the Book" (1971)

"Do you have a match?"
—"Murder by the Book" (1971)

"Gotta match?"
—"Death Lends a Hand" (1971)

"After a while, the old nose just tells you when someone's not giving you the truth."
—"Death Lends a Hand" (1971)

"That bothered me."
—"Death Lends a Hand" (1971)

"Sorry I bothered ya'."

—"Death Lends a Hand" (1971)

"Say, you got a beautiful place here."

—"Dead Weight" (1971)

"Gotta match?"

—"Dead Weight" (1971)

"Oh, one thing I almost forgot . . ."

—"Dead Weight" (1971)

"There are a couple of loose ends I'd like to tie up. Nothing important, you understand."

—"Dead Weight" (1971)

"Gotta match?"

—"Dead Weight" (1971)

"I'll tell ya' what's botherin' me."

—"Suitable for Framing" (1971)

"Oh, listen, one more thing . . ."

—"Suitable for Framing" (1971)

"I get bugged by those little things."

—"Suitable for Framing" (1971)

"There were a couple of points that were bothering me."

—"Lady in Waiting" (1971)

"I have this bug about tying up loose ends."

—"Lady in Waiting" (1971)

"Just one more thing."

—"Lady in Waiting" (1971)

"I didn't mean to interrupt like this and barge in."

—"Blueprint for Murder" (1972)

"There are other things."

—"Blueprint for Murder" (1972)

"Do you have a lighter?"

—"Blueprint for Murder" (1972)

"That's me. I'm paranoic. Every time I see a dead body, I think it's been murdered."

—"Etude in Black" (1972)

"Terrific place."

—"Etude in Black" (1972)

"Do you have a match?"

—"Etude in Black" (1972)

"Beautiful place you have here."

—"Etude in Black" (1972)

"I hate to keep bothering you people."

—"Etude in Black" (1972)

"Oh, listen, just one more thing."

—"Etude in Black" (1972)

"Oh, there's one little thing."

—"The Greenhouse Jungle" (1972)

"You don't have a match, do you?"

—"A Stitch in Crime" (1973)

"I'm in lousy shape."

—"The Most Dangerous Match" (1973)

"That bothered me. As a matter of fact, I couldn't sleep last night."

—"The Most Dangerous Match" (1973)

"Well, there are a couple of things that bother me."

—"Double Shock" (1973)

"I'm sorry about being untidy. I'm just like that. I just can't correct that. I'm just very untidy. It's just my nature."

—"Double Shock" (1973)

"I have never met a cop with flat feet."

—"Double Shock" (1973)

"I'm sorry, forgive me. I didn't mean to intrude."

—"Lovely but Lethal" (1973)

"Oh, listen, there's one other thing I wanted to ask you about."

—"Lovely but Lethal" (1973)

"You don't have a pencil, do you?"

—"Any Old Port in a Storm" (1973)

"Just point me in the right direction. I'll find him. I'm good at that."

—"Any Old Port in a Storm" (1973)

"I'm probably the only Italian in the world who can't sing."
—"Any Old Port in a Storm"
(1973)

"My handwriting is so bad sometimes I think I should have been a doctor."
—"Any Old Port in a Storm"
(1973)

"Do you have a pencil I could borrow?"
—"Any Old Port in a Storm"
(1973)

"I'm sorry to bother you, ma'am. I just wanted to ask you one more question."
—"Any Old Port in a Storm"
(1973)

"Pencil?"
—"Candidate for Crime" (1973)

"You don't have a match, do you?"
—"Candidate for Crime" (1973)

"Oh, there one thing I almost forgot. . . . It's just one other thing that bothers me."
—"Candidate for Crime" (1973)

"Every once in a while I think about getting a new coat, but there's no rush on that, sir. There's still a lot of wear left in this fella."
—"Candidate for Crime" (1973)

"Just one more thing."
—"Mind Over Mayhem" (1974)

"One more thing."
—"Mind Over Mayhem" (1974)

"Some people say I'm snoopy."
—"Mind Over Mayhem" (1974)

"Oh, one other thing."
—"Mind Over Mayhem" (1974)

"Do you have a pencil?"
—"Swan Song" (1974)

"There's just one other thing, sir."
—"Swan Song" (1974)

"One other thing."

—"A Friend in Deed" (1974)

"I hate to bother you like this."

—"A Friend in Deed" (1974)

"Oh, one more thing, sir."

—"An Exercise in Fatality" (1974)

"Oh, there is one other thing."

—"An Exercise in Fatality" (1974)

"Do you have a pencil?"

—"An Exercise in Fatality" (1974)

"Oh, one more thing."

—"An Exercise in Fatality" (1974)

"May I borrow a pencil?"

—"An Exercise in Fatality" (1974)

"Gotta match?"

—"An Exercise in Fatality" (1974)

"One other thing."

—"Negative Reaction" (1974)

"I'll tell you what bothers me about this."

—"Negative Reaction" (1974)

"There are a couple of things that bother me."

—"Negative Reaction" (1974)

"One more thing, sir."

—"Negative Reaction" (1974)

"I just want to ask one question."

—"By Dawn's Early Light" (1974)

"I'm sorry to bother ya'."

—"By Dawn's Early Light" (1974)

"There's one other thing."

—"By Dawn's Early Light" (1974)

"Do you have a match?"

—"By Dawn's Early Light" (1974)

"That bothered me."

—"By Dawn's Early Light" (1974)

"I'll keep on something until it is finished."
—"Troubled Waters" (1975)

"Just one more thing, sir."
—"Troubled Waters" (1975)

"May I borrow a match?"
—"Troubled Waters" (1975)

"Oh, this is quite a place."
—"Forgotten Lady" (1975)

"Oh, one more thing."
—"Forgotten Lady" (1975)

"Oh, just one more thing, sir."
—"A Case of Immunity" (1975)

"One more thing, sir."
—"Identity Crisis" (1975)

"That's what's been bothering me."
—"Now You See Him" (1976)

"Do you have a match, sir?"
—"Now You See Him" (1976)

"Gotta match?"
—"Last Salute to the Commodore"
(1976)

"Oh, just a couple of little things bother me."
—"Last Salute to the Commodore"
(1976)

"Oh, there's one more thing, sir."
—"Fade in to Murder" (1976)

"I'm really sorry to bother you like this, sir."
—"Fade in to Murder" (1976)

"Uh, one thing, sir."
—"The Bye-Bye Sky High I.Q.
Murder Case" (1977)

"I can't think of a time when I wasn't working."
—"The Bye-Bye Sky High I.Q.
Murder Case" (1977)

"I like my job a lot."
—"Try and Catch Me" (1977)

"The two—trouble and murder—they seem to go together. At least that's been my experience, sir."

—"Murder Under Glass" (1978)

"Oh, there's just one other thing."

—"Murder Under Glass" (1978)

"One more question."

—"How to Dial a Murder" (1978)

"It's just that I enjoy the pleasure of the game."

—"How to Dial a Murder" (1978)

"Just one more thing, sir."

—"The Conspirators" (1978)

HOW THE MURDERERS SEE COLUMBO

"You're the most persistent creature I ever met, but likable. The astonishing thing is is you're likable."

"You're a sly little elf."

"You never stop, do you?"

"You're an intelligent man, Columbo, but you hide it."
—DR. RAY FLEMING (GENE BARRY)
Prescription: Murder (1968)

"You know, Columbo, you're almost likable in a shabby sort of way. Maybe it's the way you come slouching in here with your shopworn bag of tricks. . . . The humility, the seeming absentmindedness. The homey anecdotes about the family, the wife. Yeah, Lieutenant Columbo, fumbling and bumbling along, but it's always the jugular he's after. And I imagine that more often than not, he's successful."

"You're very lucky, Lieutenant. No, congratulations, you're very smart."
—LESLIE WILLIAMS (LEE GRANT)
Ransom for a Dead Man (1971)

"I'm beginning to like you."
—KEN FRANKLIN (JACK CASSIDY)
"Murder by the Book" (1971)

"You are so transparent, Columbo . . . a compulsively suspicious bureaucrat. . . . Would you please do me a favor and stop pestering me."
—DALE KINGSTON (ROSS MARTIN)
"Suitable for Framing" (1971)

"Lieutenant, anybody ever tell you you're very much like an arachnid . . . a tick. They're quite common but excessively tenacious. They hang on. They let go only under extreme prodding."
—ELLIOT MARKHAM
(PATRICK O'NEAL)
"Blueprint for Murder" (1972)

"You're a great detective."
—ALEX BENEDICT
(JOHN CASSAVETES)
"Etude in Black" (1972)

"Columbo, you're marvelous—transparent but marvelous."
——JARVIS GOODLAND (RAY MILLAND)
"The Greenhouse Jungle"
(1972)

"You're priceless."
——NORA CHANDLER (ANNE BAXTER)
"Requiem for a Falling Star"
(1973)

"Believe me, if there's anybody who could do anything about it, it's going to be Lieutenant Columbo."

"Lieutenant Columbo, you're remarkable. You have intelligence. You have perception. You have tenacity. You've got everything but proof."
——DR. BARRY MAYFIELD
(LEONARD NIMOY)
"A Stitch in Crime" (1973)

"Lieutenant, you're a pleasant enough man. You work hard. And I respect your motivations. But, please, stop this pretense."
——EMMET CLAYTON
(LAURENCE HARVEY)
"The Most Dangerous Match"
(1973)

"You really are a very stubborn man."
——VIVECA SCOTT (VERA MILES)
"Lovely but Lethal" (1973)

"Lieutenant, you really are one of a kind."

"You've learned very well, Lieutenant."
——ADRIAN CARSINI
(DONALD PLEASENCE)
"Any Old Port in a Storm"
(1973)

"You're about as subtle as a train wreck."

"If I didn't find you an extraordinarily amusing fellow, I might even be offended."

"You are an incredibly stubborn man."
——DR. BART KEPPLE (ROBERT CULP)
"Double Exposure" (1973)

"You have a very transparent mind."
——DR. MARSHALL CAHILL (JOSE FERRER)
"Mind Over Mayhem" (1974)

"I really do admire your enthusiasm. The force could use a hundred like you."

—MARK HALPERIN (RICHARD KILEY)
"A Friend in Deed" (1974)

"You know something, Columbo? You're a devious man."

"I don't care what you think. I don't care what you suspect. I don't care what visions you see when you look at your cigar ashes."

—MILO JANUS (ROBERT CONRAD)
"An Exercise in Fatality" (1974)

"You're like a little, shaggy-haired terrier—he's got a grip on my trousers and he won't let go."

"Lieutenant, you're priceless. You're a gem. A little flawed and not too bright, but you're one of a kind."

—PAUL GALESKO (DICK VAN DYKE)
"Negative Reaction" (1974)

"I think you're working too hard, Lieutenant. Everything is not a murder, you know."

—COLONEL LYLE C. RUMFORD
(PATRICK MCGOOHAN)
"By Dawn's Early Light" (1974)

"You know, Lieutenant, you're a marvelously deceptive man. You know the way you get to the point without ever getting to the point?"

—DR. MARCUS COLLIER
(GEORGE HAMILTON)
"A Deadly State of Mind"
(1975)

"I'm not what I appear to be, and then again, neither are you."

—THE GREAT SANTINI
(JACK CASSIDY)
"Now You See Him" (1976)

"Really, Lieutenant, really well done."

—WARD FOWLER (WILLIAM SHATNER)
"Fade in to Murder" (1976)

"You say a thing when you're ready to say it and not before."

—RUTH LYTTON (JOYCE VAN PATTEN)
"Old Fashioned Murder" (1976)

"You're a very able man, Lieutenant. I respect that. But I really don't care for you very much."

—PAUL GERARD (LOUIS JOURDAN)
"Murder Under Glass" (1978)

"You're a very special man, Lieutenant."

—KAY FREESTONE
(TRISH VAN DEVERE)
"Make Me a Perfect Murder"
(1978)

"You're an acute observer, Lieutenant."

—DR. ERIC MASON
(NICOL WILLIAMSON)
"How to Dial a Murder" (1978)

COLUMBO TRIVIA

How high is your *Columbo* I.Q.? Try these mind-twisters:

1) How many people are murdered in the forty-five Columbo mysteries?
2) What was the favorite method of killing for the *Columbo* murderer?
3) Only two actors played a *Columbo* murderer three times. Who were they?
4) Only one *Columbo* episode is a classic whodunit. Which one?
5) What is Columbo's license plate number?
6) What is Columbo's favorite food?
7) What is Columbo's favorite movie?
8) Does Columbo speak any foreign languages?
9) Where does Columbo's mother-in-law live?
10) What Los Angeles Police Department record does Columbo hold?
11) In "Murder by the Book," the writing team of Franklin and Ferris had created a famous sleuthing heroine for their mystery novels. What was her name?
12) In how many episodes did Columbo forsake his raincoat for a tuxedo?
13) What were the first words spoken by Columbo on television?
14) What killer was ambidextrous?
15) Who was the oldest murderer Columbo caught?
16) What flavor ice cream does Dog prefer?
17) How did the Columbos get to go on a cruise in "Troubled Waters"?
18) Who was the only murderer to ask Columbo his first name?
19) Who were the two murderers Columbo genuinely got angry with?
20) How does Columbo take his coffee?

ANSWERS:

1) Fifty-nine murders in forty-five episodes.
2) Twenty-two of the fifty-nine victims were shot (bludgeoning ran a distant second with twelve).
3) Jack Cassidy and Robert Culp.
4) "Last Salute to the Commodore."

5) It's clearly visible in several episodes: California 044 APD.

6) Chili (with crackers).

7) Although never specifically stated, twice ("Any Old Port in a Storm" and "Forgotten Lady") he expresses appreciation for the 1942 version of Graham Greene's *This Gun for Hire*, which starred Alan Ladd.

8) He had a working grasp of Italian (see "Identity Crisis" and "Murder Under Glass"), and speaks a little Spanish.

9) Fresno (mentioned in two episodes).

10) He avoided mandatory pistol range tests for ten years.

11) Mrs. Melville.

12) Three: "Forgotten Lady," "A Case of Immunity" and "Murder Under Glass."

13) "Dr. Fleming?"

14) Brimmer (Robert Culp) in "Death Lends a Hand."

15) Abigail Mitchell (Ruth Gordon) in "Try and Catch Me."

16) Vanilla (in "Forgotten Lady").

17) Mrs. Columbo bought the winning ticket in the Holy Name Society raffle.

18) Colonel Lyle C. Rumford (Patrick McGoohan) in "By Dawn's Early Light."

19) Dr. Barry Mayfield (Leonard Nimoy) in "A Stitch in Crime" and Milo Janus (Robert Conrad) in "An Exercise in Fatality."

20) Black.

Bibliography

Although interviews were the primary source of information for this study, several books and magazine articles were of great value to the research.

Books

Brooks, Tim, and Earle Marsh. *The Complete Directory to Prime Time Network TV Shows: 1946–Present* (Third Edition). New York: Ballantine Books, 1985.

Buchwald, Art. *I Never Danced at the White House*. New York: G. P. Putnam's Sons, 1973.

Campbell, Robert. *The Golden Years of Broadcasting: A Celebration of the First 50 Years of Radio and TV on NBC*. New York: Charles Scribner's Sons, 1976.

Castleman, Harry, and Walter J. Podrazik. *Watching TV: Four Decades of American Television*. New York: McGraw-Hill Book Company, 1982.

Clement, Henry. *Columbo # 3: Any Old Port in a Storm*. New York: Popular Library, 1975.

Fireman, Judy (ed.). *TV Book: The Ultimate Television Book*. New York: Workman Publishing Company, 1977.

Gerrold, David. *The World of Star Trek*. New York: Ballantine Books, 1973.

Gertner, Richard (ed.). *1984 International Television Almanac*. New York: Quigley Publishing Company, Inc., 1984.

Goldstein, Fred, and Stan Goldstein. *Prime-Time Television: A Pictorial History from Milton Berle to "Falcon Crest"*. New York: Crown Publishers, Inc., 1983.

Halliwell, Leslie. *The Filmgoers Companion*. (Sixth Edition). New York: Avon Books, 1978.

Hays, Lee. *Columbo # 5: Murder by the Book*. New York: Popular Library, 1976.

Hays, Lee. *Columbo # 6: A Deadly State of Mind*. New York: Popular Library, 1976.

Javna, John. *Cult TV*. New York: St. Martin's Press, 1985.

Lawrence, Alfred. *Columbo # 1*: New York: Popular Library, 1972.

Lawrence, Alfred. *Columbo # 2: The Dean's Death*. New York: Popular Library, 1975.

Levinson, Richard, and William Link. *Stay Tuned: An Inside Look at the Making of Prime-Time Television*. New York: St. Martin's Press, 1981.

Magee, Bill, and Craig Schenck. *Columbo and the Samurai Sword*. New York: Walter J. Black, Inc., 1980.

Maltin, Leonard (ed.). *TV Movies and Video Guide* (1987 Edition). New York: New American Library, 1986.

McCarthy, John, and Brian Kelleher. *Alfred Hitchcock Presents: An Illustrated Guide to the Ten-Year Television Career of the Master of Suspense*. New York: St. Martin's Press, 1985.

McNeil, Alex. *Total Television: A Comprehensive Guide to Programming from 1948 to the Present*. New York: Penguin Books, 1984.

Meyers, Richard. *TV Detectives*. San Diego: A.S. Barnes & Company, Inc., 1981.

Newcomb, Horace, and Robert S. Alley. *The Producer's Medium: Conversations with Creators of American TV*. New York: Oxford University Press, 1984.

Scheuer, Steven H. (ed.). *The Television Annual: 1978–79*. New York: Collier Books, 1979.

Winn, Dilys. *Murder Ink: The Mystery Reader's Companion*. New York: Workman Publishing Company, 1977.

Zicree, Marc Scott. *The Twilight Zone Companion*. New York: Bantam Books, 1982.

Zimmerman, Paul D., and Burt Goldblatt. *The Marx Brothers at the Movies*. New York: Berkley Windhover Books, 1975.

Magazines and Newspapers

Burgess, Anthony. "TV Is Debasing Your Lives." *TV Guide* (September 18, 1982), pp. 12–13.

Chase, Chris. "Peter Picked a Pip." *The New York Times*. (November 28, 1971), II, p. 1.

Condon, Maurice. "In Ossining, Peter Falk Is a Legend." *TV Guide* (May 5, 1973), pp. 27–31.

"Cop (and a Raincoat) for All Seasons." *Time* (November 26, 1973), pp. 117–20.

Falke, Ben. "The Man Inside the Raincoat." *Milwaukee Journal* (December 8, 1974).

Greenfield, Jeff. "Columbo Knows the Butler Didn't Do It." *The New York Times* (April 1, 1973), p. 19.

Hobson, Dick. "America Discovers Columbo." *TV Guide* (March 25, 1972), pp. 28–32.

Meyers, Richard. "Murder, They Wrote: An Interview with Levinson and Link." *The Armchair Detective* (Spring, 1987), pp. 116–26.

"Mutt for All Seasons." *Time* (December 13, 1971), p. 64.

Whitney, Dwight. "He Can Turn a Raincoat Into a Deadly Weapon." *TV Guide* (August 14, 1976), pp. 16–20.

Index